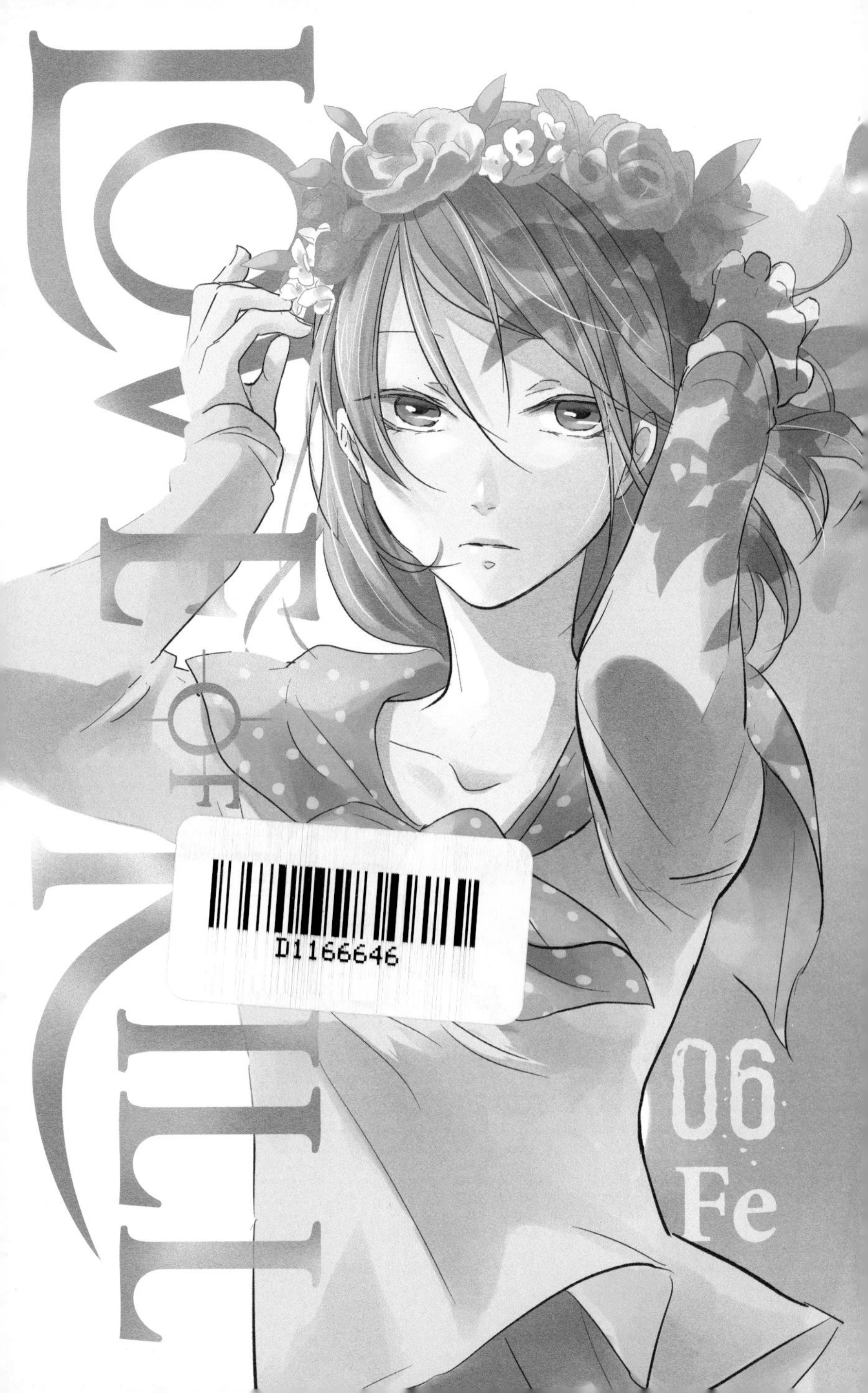
LOVE of KILL
06
Fe

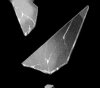

C
O
N
T
E
N
T
S

LOVE OF KILL

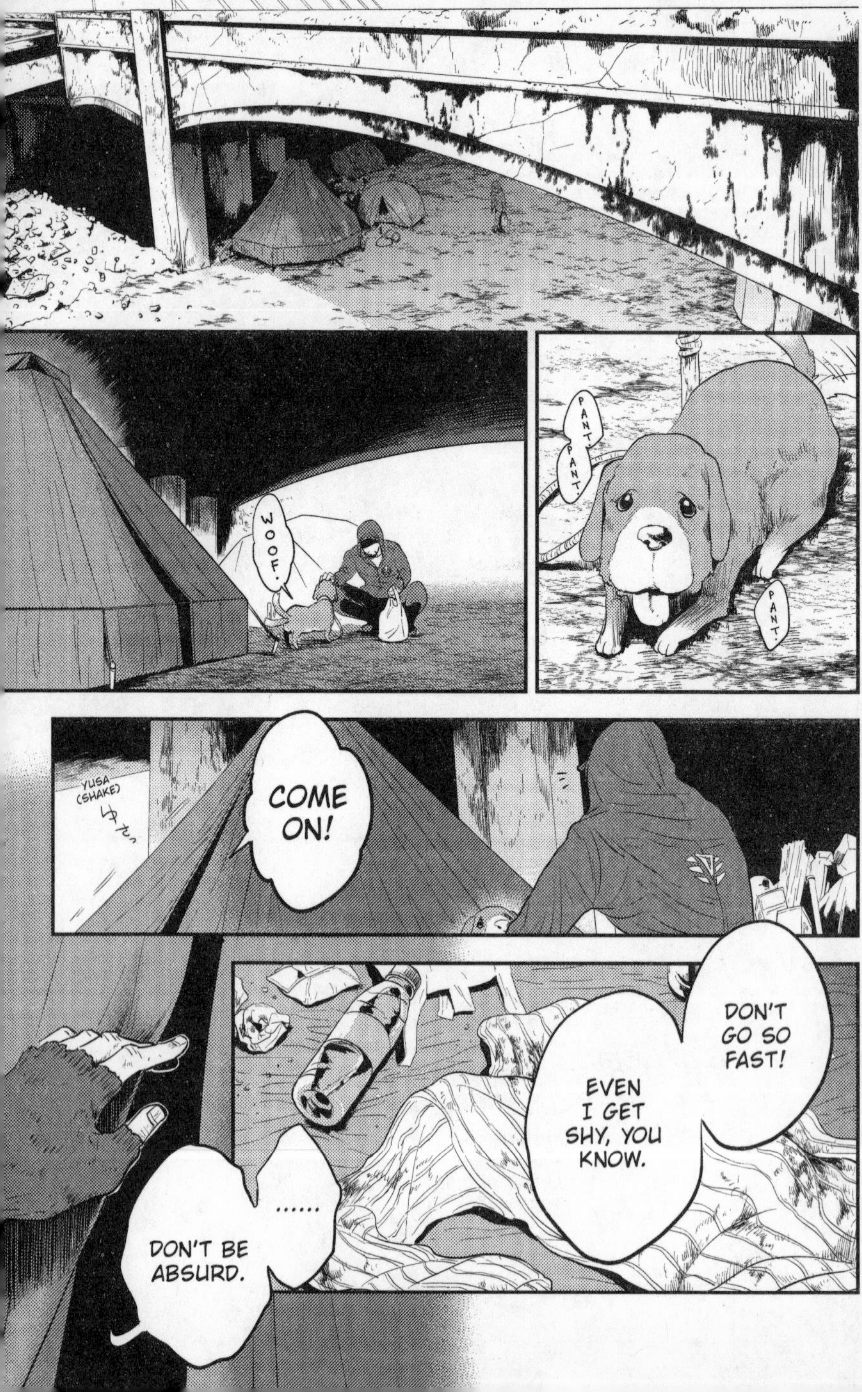
PANT PANT
PANT
WOOF.
COME ON!
YUSA (SHAKE)
ゆさっ
DON'T GO SO FAST!
EVEN I GET SHY, YOU KNOW.
......
DON'T BE ABSURD.

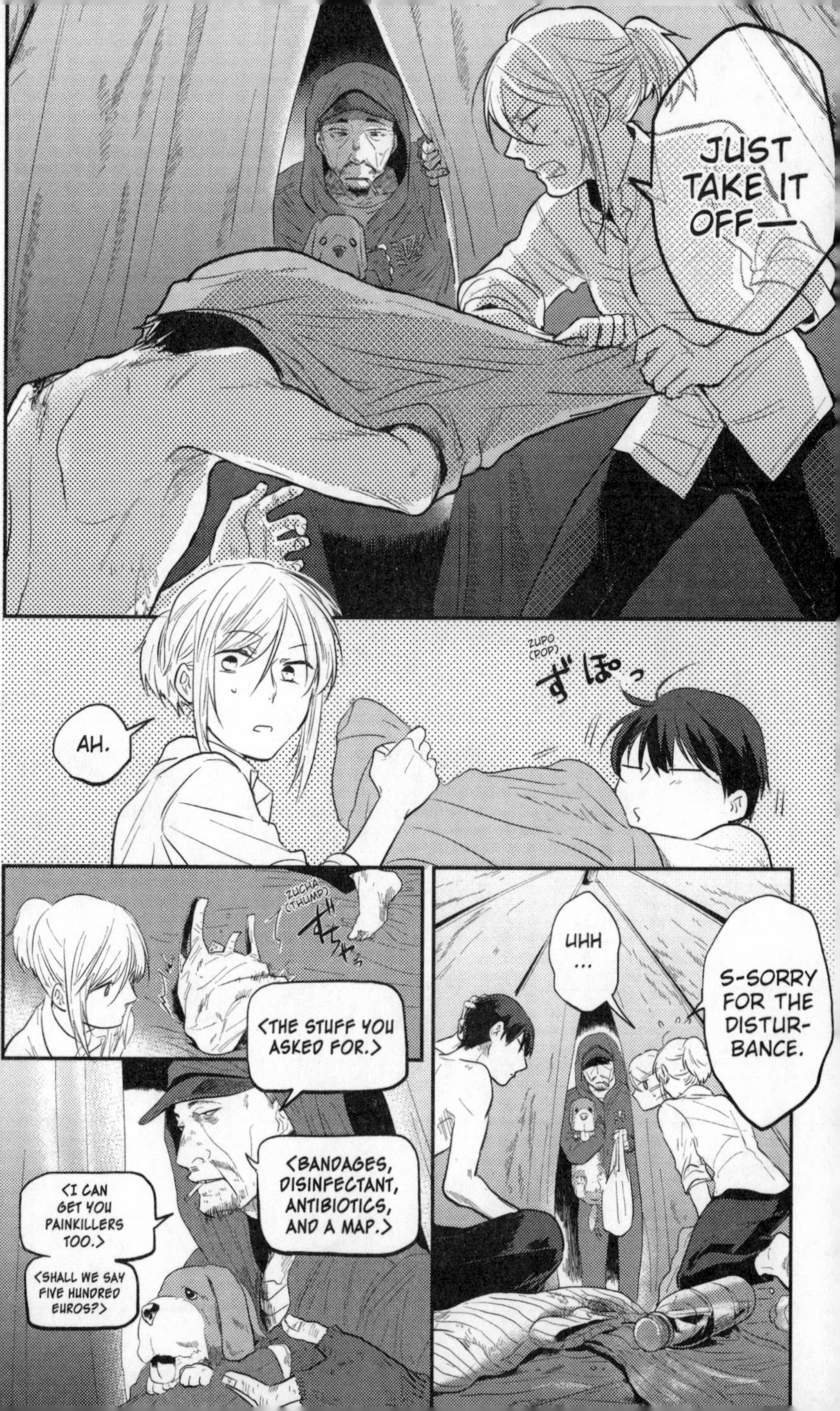
JUST TAKE IT OFF—
ZUPO (POP)
AH.
S-SORRY FOR THE DISTURBANCE.
UHH ...
ZUCHA (THUMP)
<THE STUFF YOU ASKED FOR.>
<BANDAGES, DISINFECTANT, ANTIBIOTICS, AND A MAP.>
<I CAN GET YOU PAINKILLERS TOO.>
<SHALL WE SAY FIVE HUNDRED EUROS?>

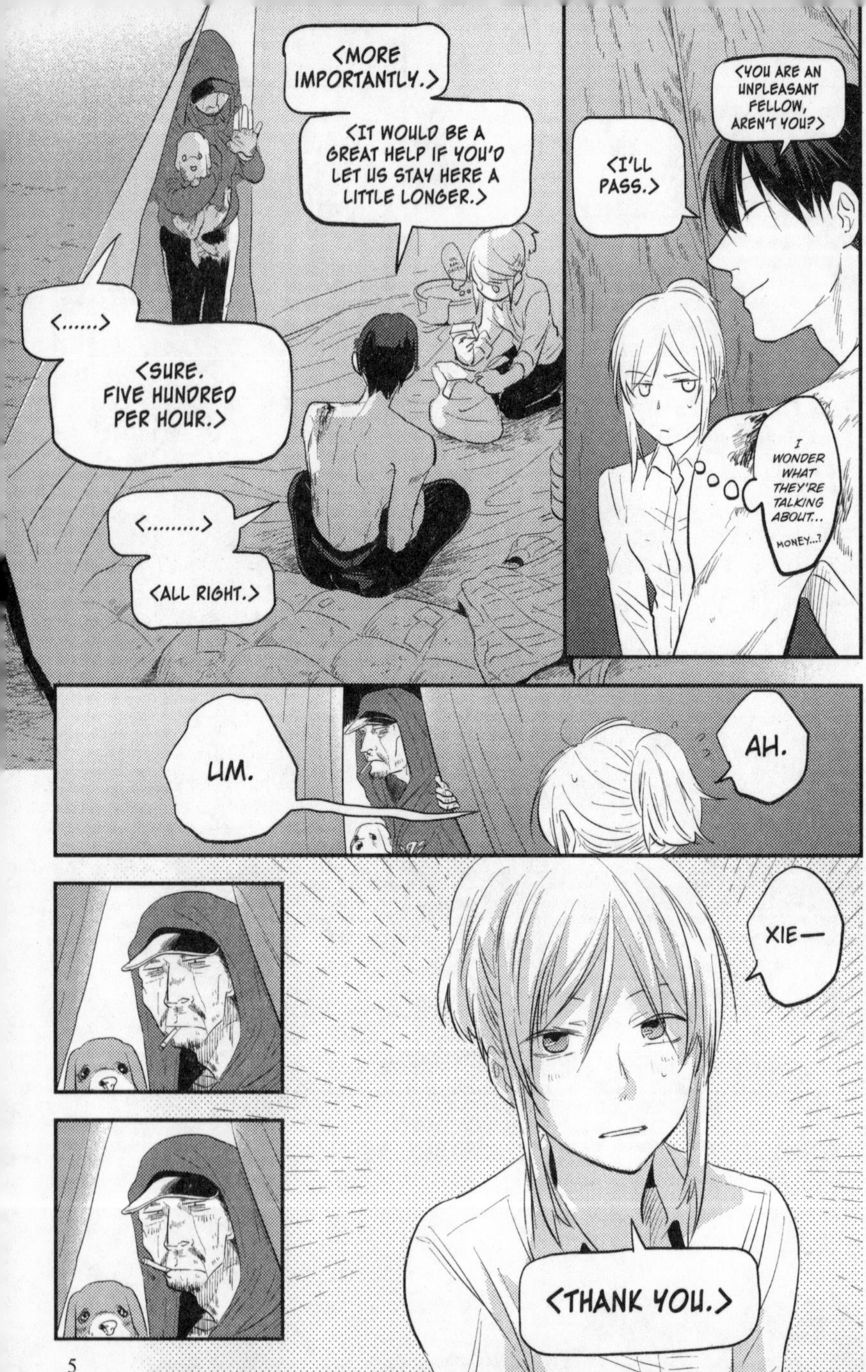
<YOU ARE AN UNPLEASANT FELLOW, AREN'T YOU?>
<I'LL PASS.>
I WONDER WHAT THEY'RE TALKING ABOUT... MONEY...?
<MORE IMPORTANTLY.>
<IT WOULD BE A GREAT HELP IF YOU'D LET US STAY HERE A LITTLE LONGER.>
<......>
<SURE. FIVE HUNDRED PER HOUR.>
<.........>
<ALL RIGHT.>
AH.
UM.
XIE—
<THANK YOU.>

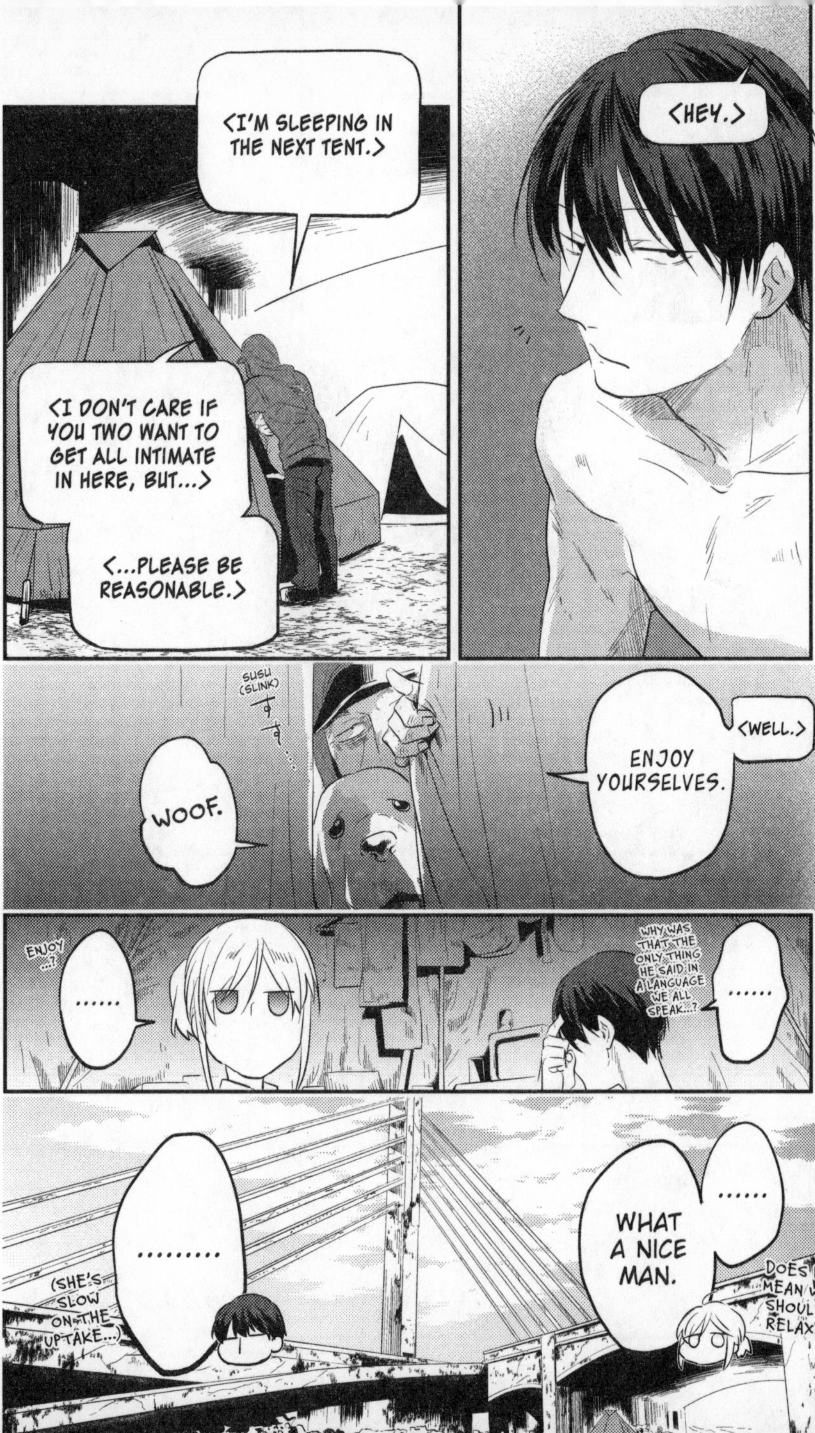

<HEY.>
<I'M SLEEPING IN THE NEXT TENT.>
<I DON'T CARE IF YOU TWO WANT TO GET ALL INTIMATE IN HERE, BUT...>
<...PLEASE BE REASONABLE.>
<WELL.>
ENJOY YOURSELVES.
SUSU (SLINK)
すす…
WOOF.
......
WHY WAS THAT THE ONLY THING HE SAID IN A LANGUAGE WE ALL SPEAK...?
ENJOY ...?
......
......
WHAT A NICE MAN.
DOES HE MEAN WE SHOULD RELAX?
.........
(SHE'S SLOW ON THE UPTAKE...)

# FILE 31 THANK YOU

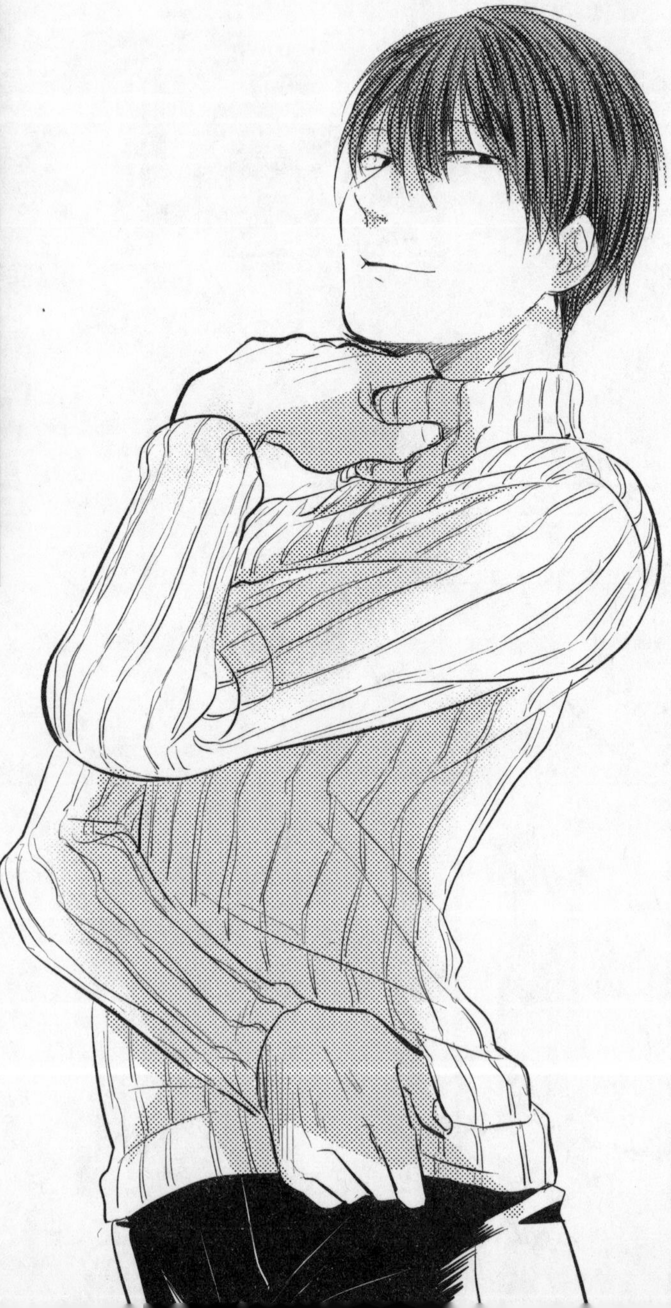

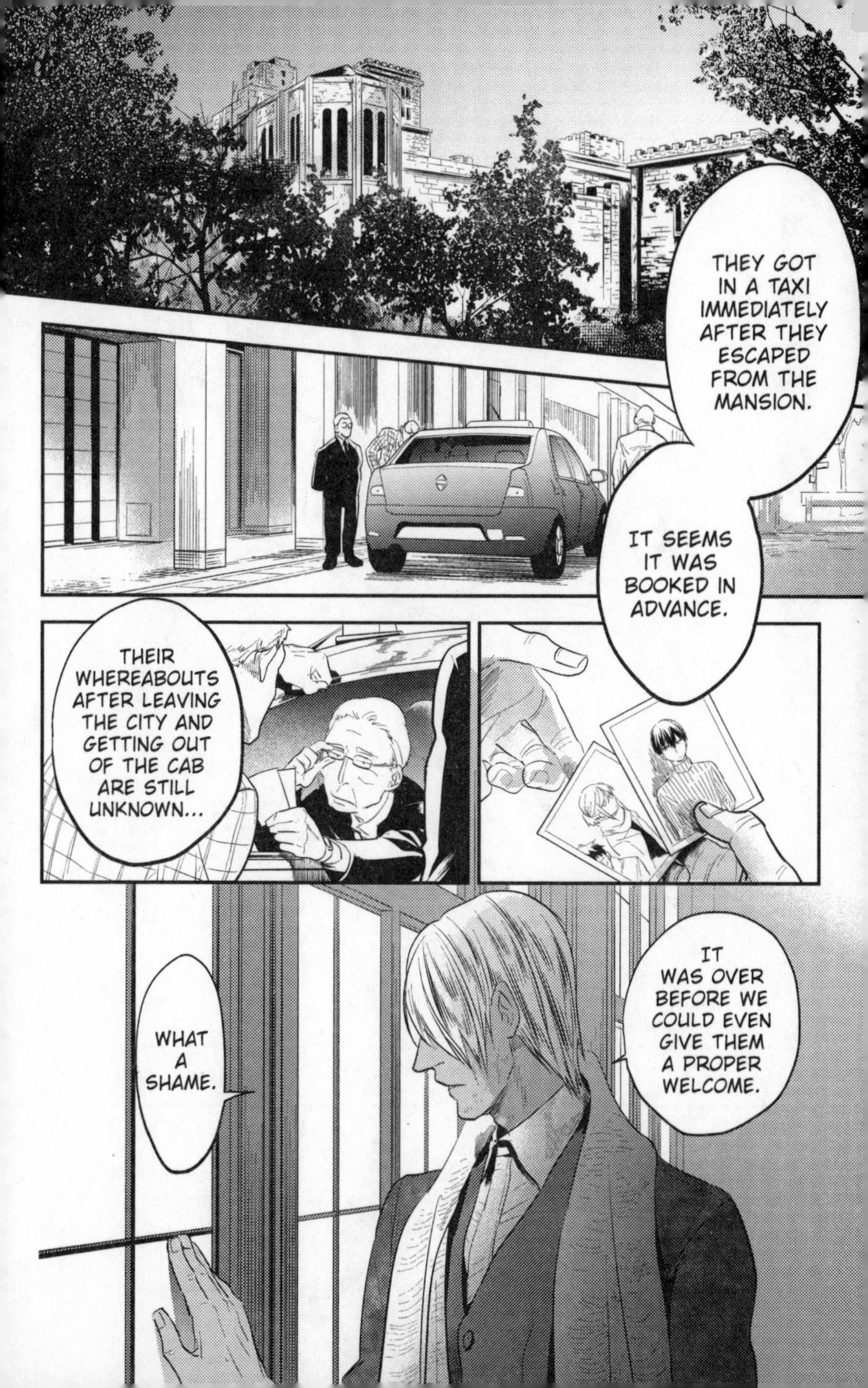
THEY GOT IN A TAXI IMMEDIATELY AFTER THEY ESCAPED FROM THE MANSION.
IT SEEMS IT WAS BOOKED IN ADVANCE.
THEIR WHEREABOUTS AFTER LEAVING THE CITY AND GETTING OUT OF THE CAB ARE STILL UNKNOWN...
IT WAS OVER BEFORE WE COULD EVEN GIVE THEM A PROPER WELCOME.
WHAT A SHAME.

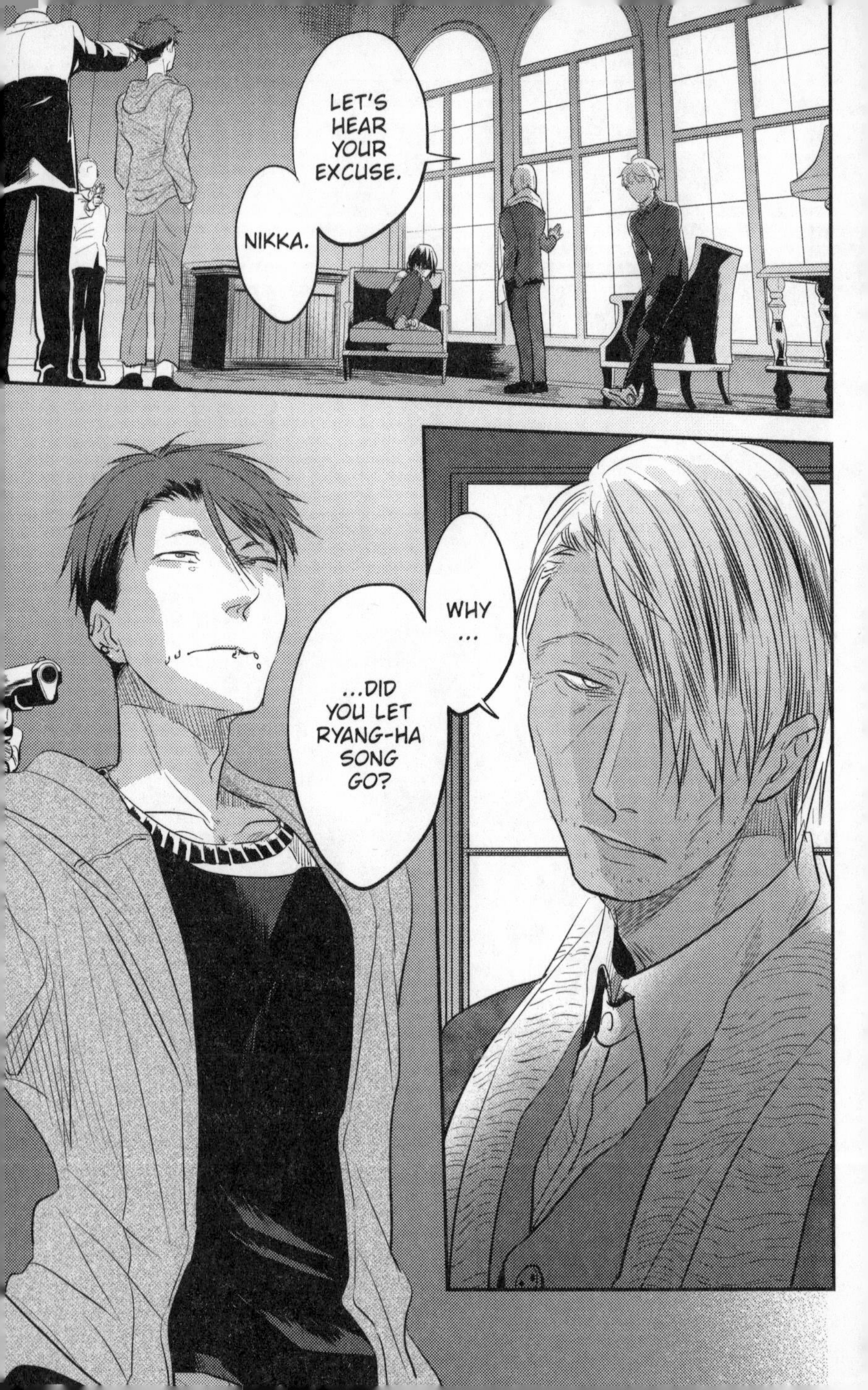
LET'S HEAR YOUR EXCUSE.
NIKKA.
WHY ...
...DID YOU LET RYANG-HA SONG GO?

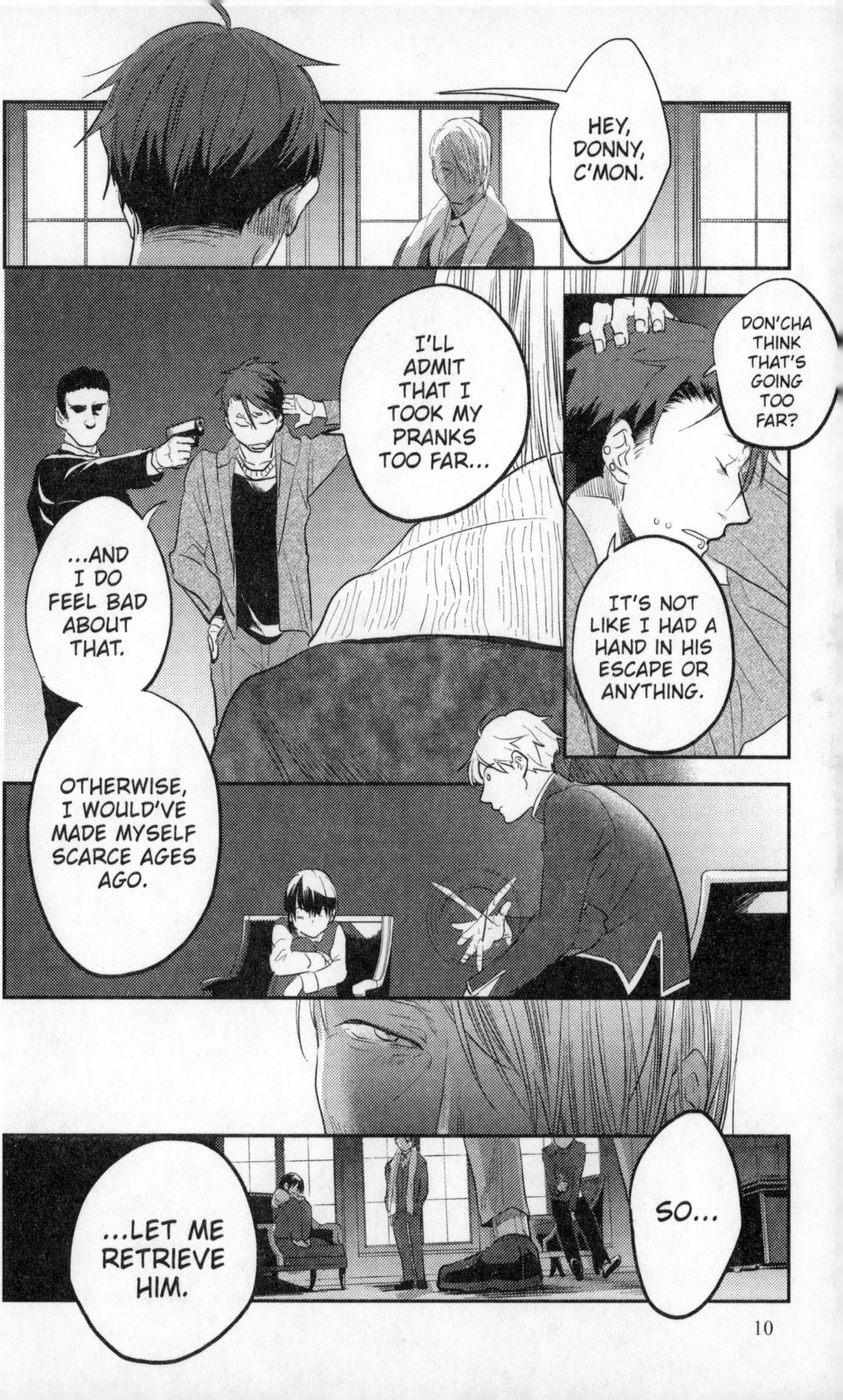
HEY, DONNY, C'MON.
DON'CHA THINK THAT'S GOING TOO FAR?
IT'S NOT LIKE I HAD A HAND IN HIS ESCAPE OR ANYTHING.
I'LL ADMIT THAT I TOOK MY PRANKS TOO FAR...
...AND I DO FEEL BAD ABOUT THAT.
OTHERWISE, I WOULD'VE MADE MYSELF SCARCE AGES AGO.
SO...
...LET ME RETRIEVE HIM.

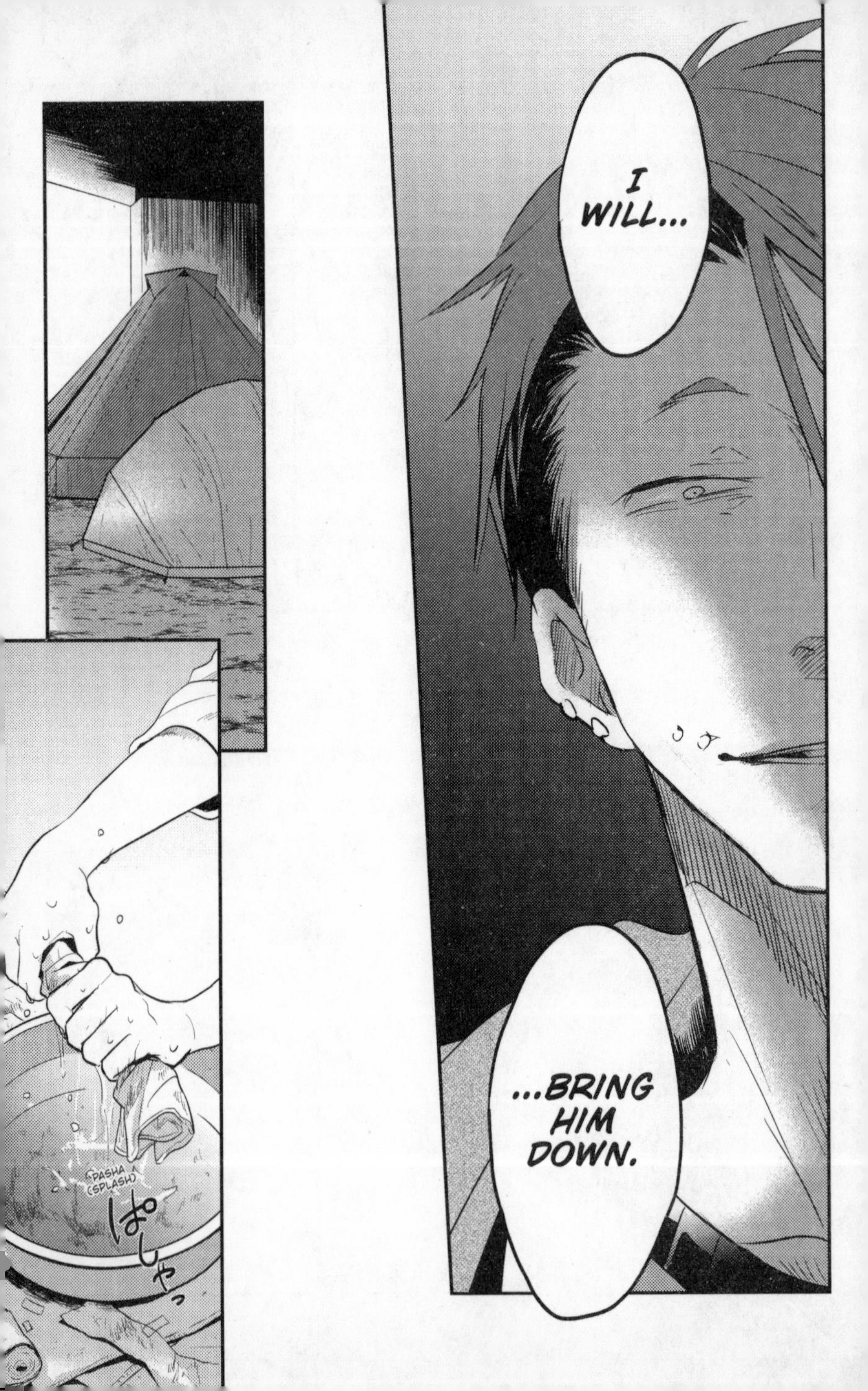
I WILL...
...BRING HIM DOWN.
PASHA (SPLASH)
ぱしゃっ

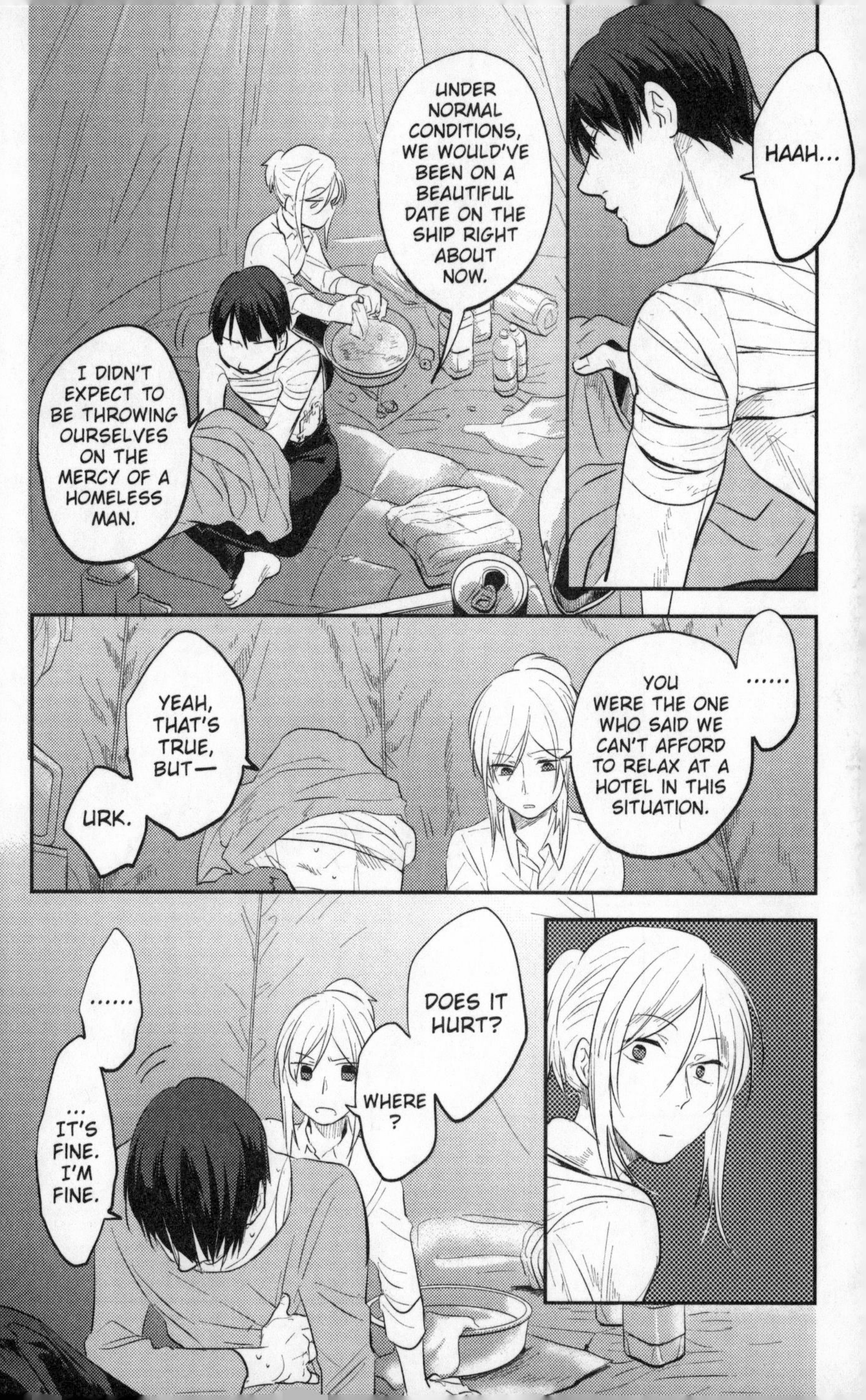
HAAH...
UNDER NORMAL CONDITIONS, WE WOULD'VE BEEN ON A BEAUTIFUL DATE ON THE SHIP RIGHT ABOUT NOW.
I DIDN'T EXPECT TO BE THROWING OURSELVES ON THE MERCY OF A HOMELESS MAN.
......
YOU WERE THE ONE WHO SAID WE CAN'T AFFORD TO RELAX AT A HOTEL IN THIS SITUATION.
YEAH, THAT'S TRUE, BUT—
URK.
DOES IT HURT?
WHERE?
......
... IT'S FINE. I'M FINE.

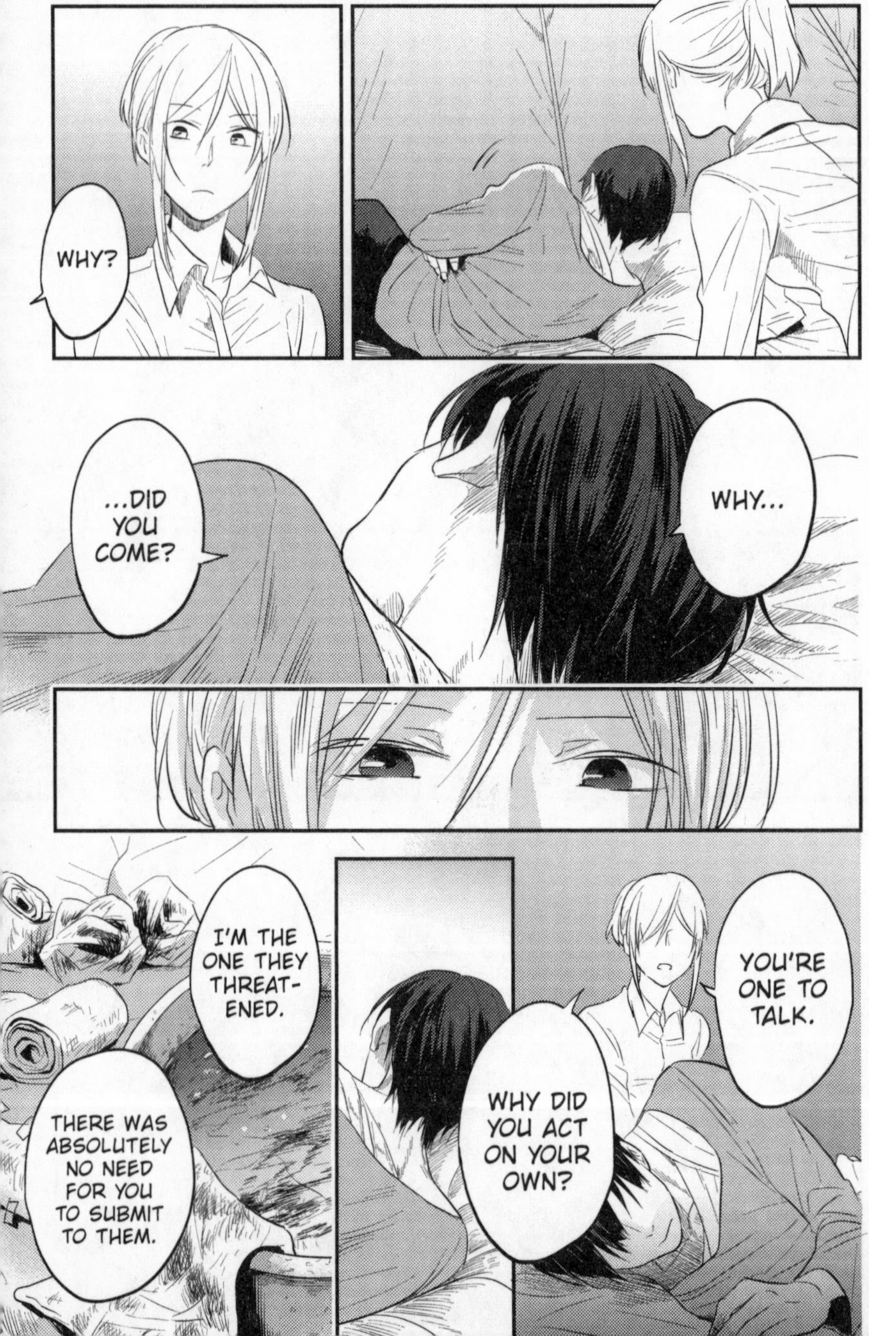
WHY?
WHY...
...DID YOU COME?
YOU'RE ONE TO TALK.
WHY DID YOU ACT ON YOUR OWN?
I'M THE ONE THEY THREAT-ENED.
THERE WAS ABSOLUTELY NO NEED FOR YOU TO SUBMIT TO THEM.

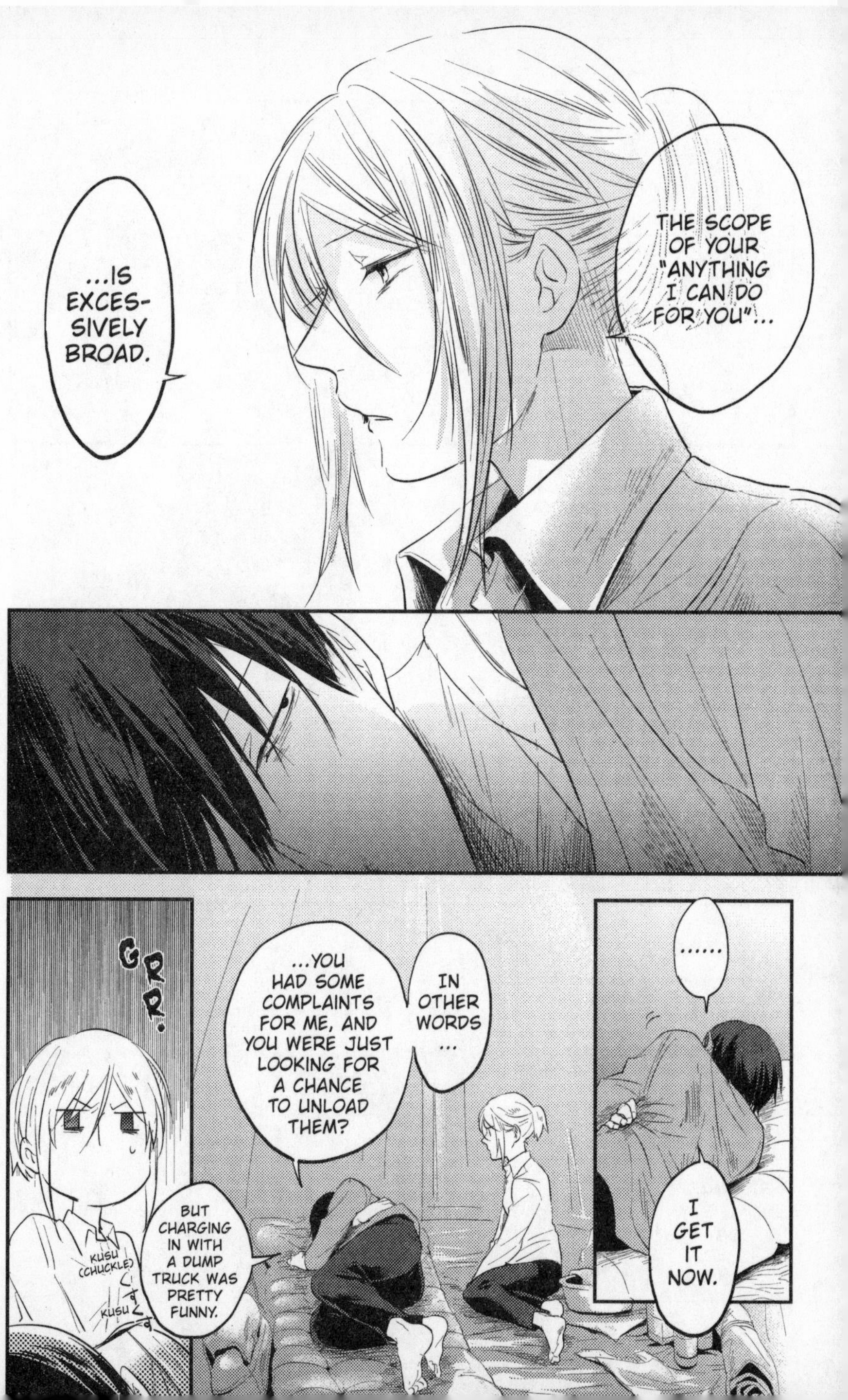
THE SCOPE OF YOUR "ANYTHING I CAN DO FOR YOU"...
...IS EXCES-SIVELY BROAD.
......
I GET IT NOW.
IN OTHER WORDS ...
...YOU HAD SOME COMPLAINTS FOR ME, AND YOU WERE JUST LOOKING FOR A CHANCE TO UNLOAD THEM?
BUT CHARGING IN WITH A DUMP TRUCK WAS PRETTY FUNNY.
KUSU (CHUCKLE) くす
KUSU くす
GRR

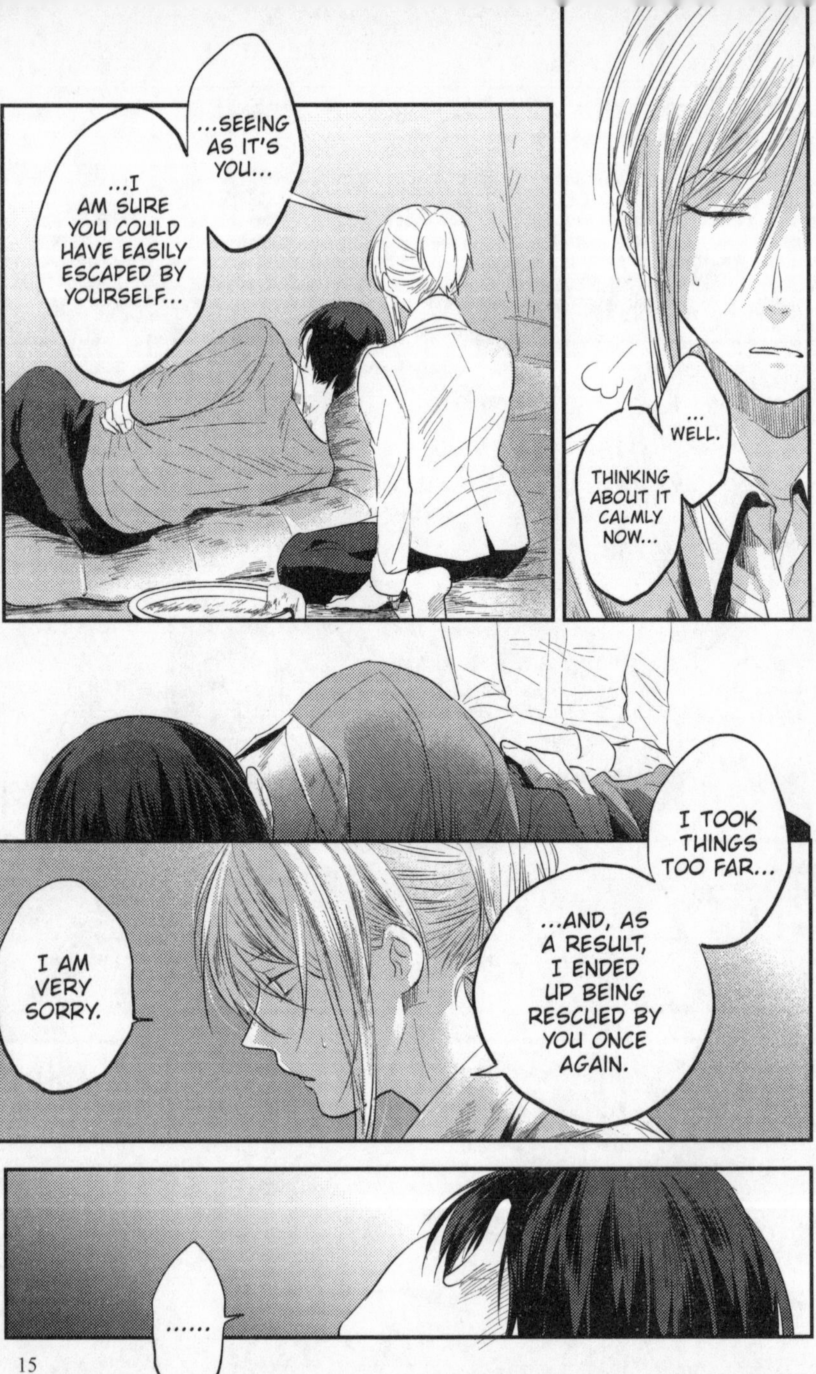
... WELL.
THINKING ABOUT IT CALMLY NOW...
...SEEING AS IT'S YOU...
...I AM SURE YOU COULD HAVE EASILY ESCAPED BY YOURSELF...
I TOOK THINGS TOO FAR...
...AND, AS A RESULT, I ENDED UP BEING RESCUED BY YOU ONCE AGAIN.
I AM VERY SORRY.
......

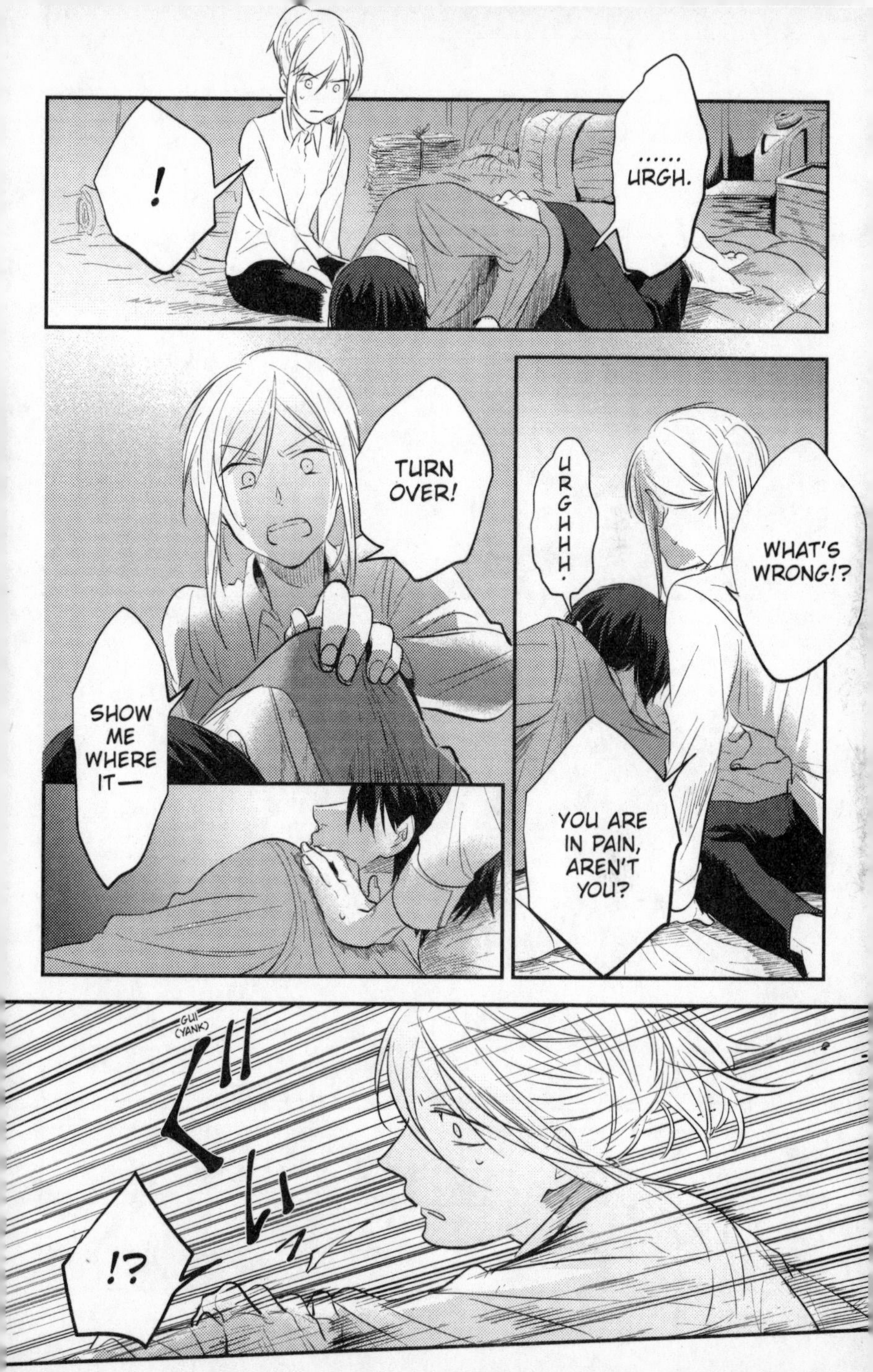
......
URGH.
!
WHAT'S WRONG!?
URGHHH.
YOU ARE IN PAIN, AREN'T YOU?
TURN OVER!
SHOW ME WHERE IT—
GUI (YANK)
!?

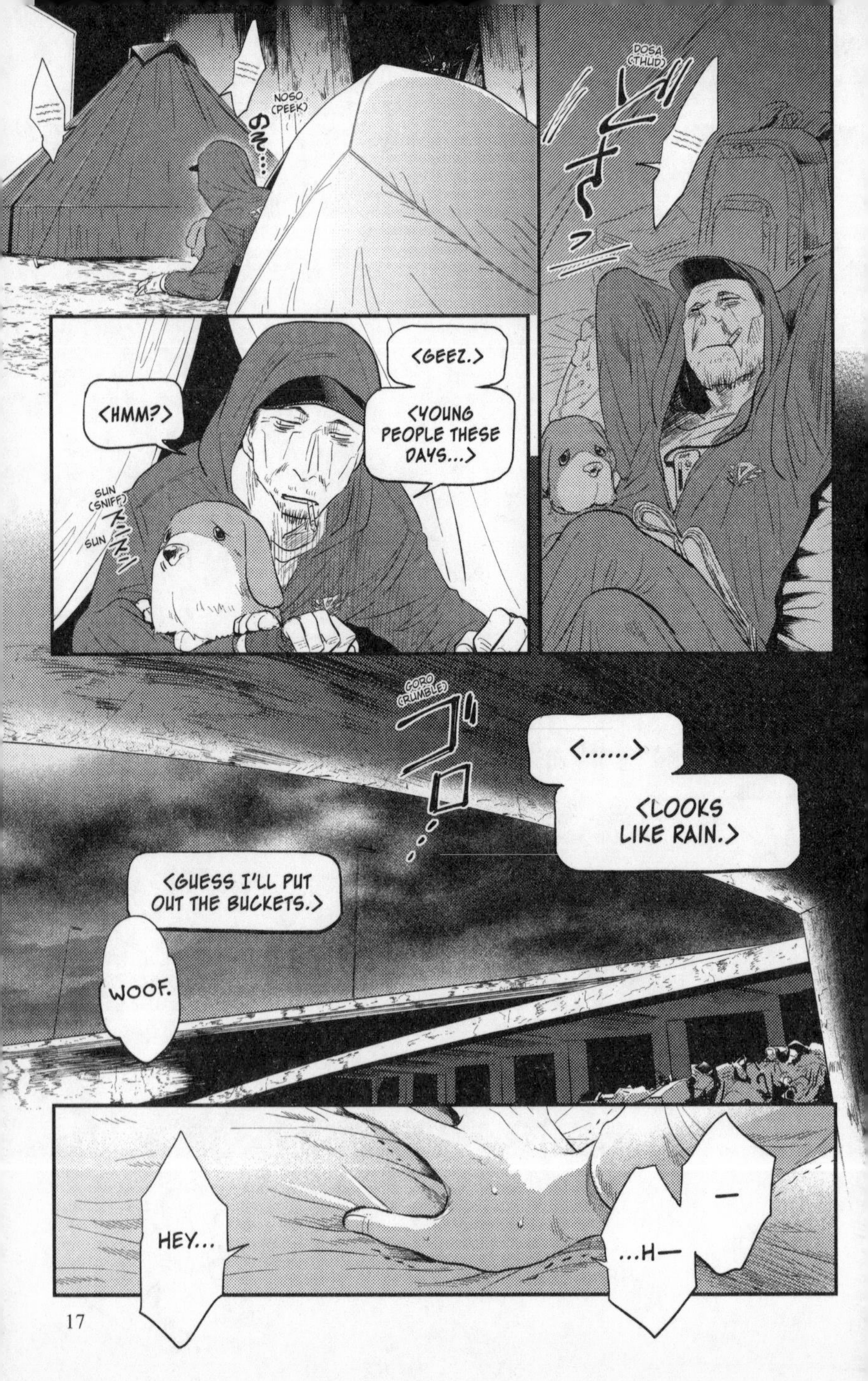
DOSA (THUD)
どさっ
NOSO (PEEK)
のそ…
<HMM?>
<GEEZ.>
<YOUNG PEOPLE THESE DAYS...>
SUN (SNIFF) SUN
GORO (RUMBLE)
ゴロ…
<......>
<LOOKS LIKE RAIN.>
<GUESS I'LL PUT OUT THE BUCKETS.>
WOOF.
—
...H—
HEY...

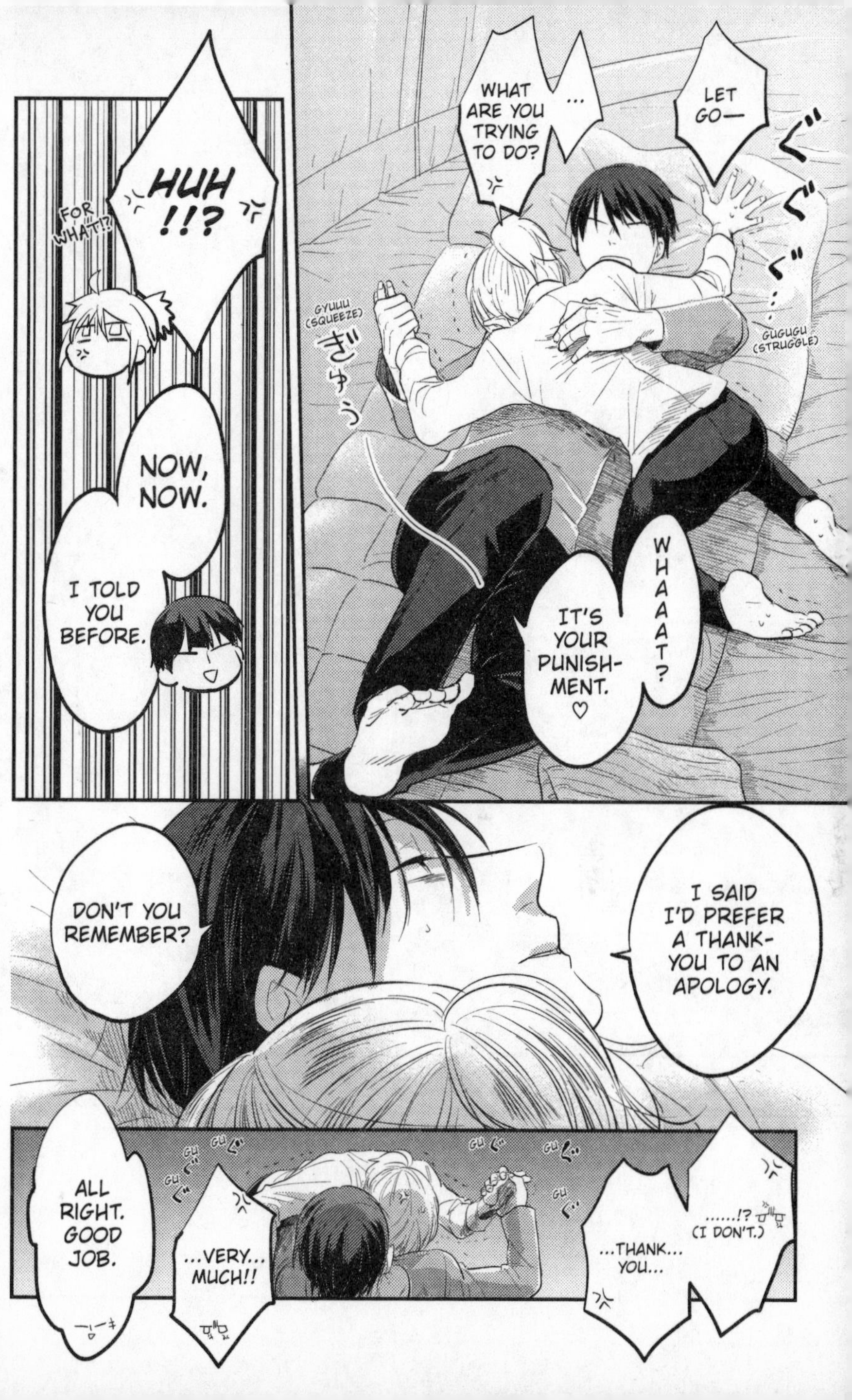
LET GO—
ぐぐぐ…
GUGUGU (STRUGGLE)
...
WHAT ARE YOU TRYING TO DO?
ぎゅう
GYUUU (SQUEEZE)
WHAAAT?
IT'S YOUR PUNISHMENT. ♡
HUH!!?
FOR WHAT!?
NOW, NOW.
I TOLD YOU BEFORE.
I SAID I'D PREFER A THANK-YOU TO AN APOLOGY.
DON'T YOU REMEMBER?
......!?
(I DON'T.)
...THANK... YOU...
GU GU GU GU GU GU
...VERY... MUCH!!
ALL RIGHT. GOOD JOB.

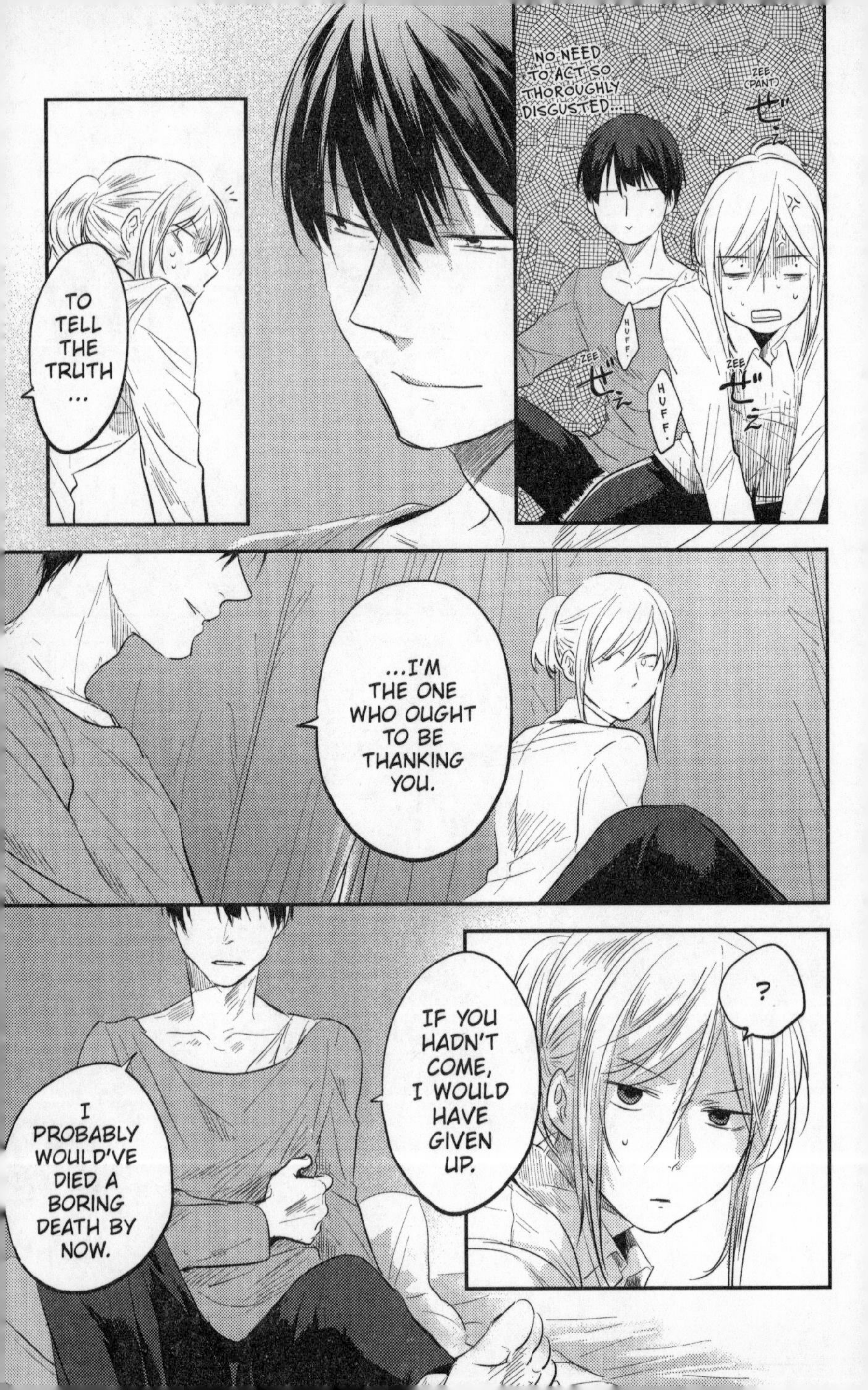
NO NEED TO ACT SO THOROUGHLY DISGUSTED...
ZEE (PANT)
HUFF.
ZEE
HUFF.
ZEE
TO TELL THE TRUTH...
...I'M THE ONE WHO OUGHT TO BE THANKING YOU.
?
IF YOU HADN'T COME, I WOULD HAVE GIVEN UP.
I PROBABLY WOULD'VE DIED A BORING DEATH BY NOW.

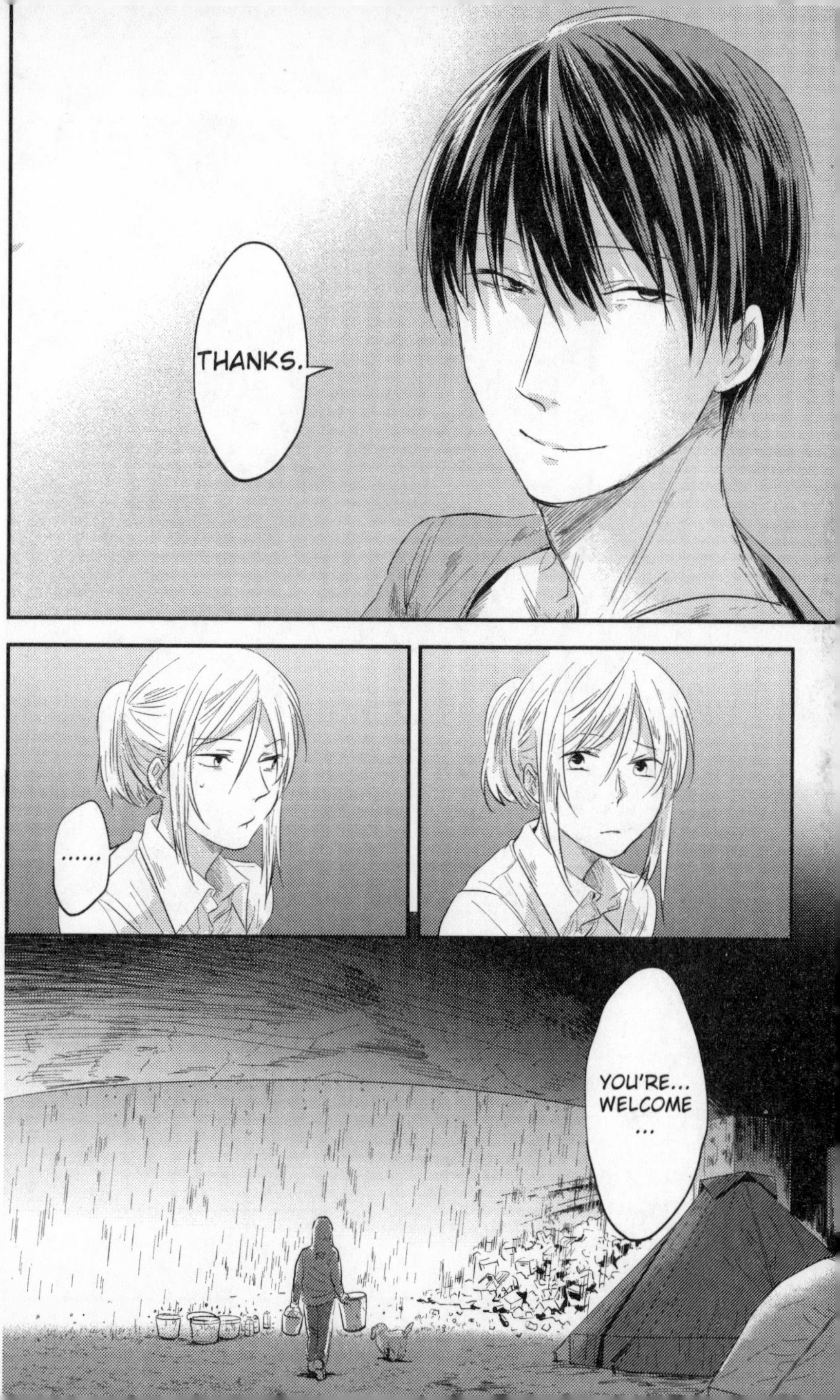
THANKS.
......
YOU'RE... WELCOME ...

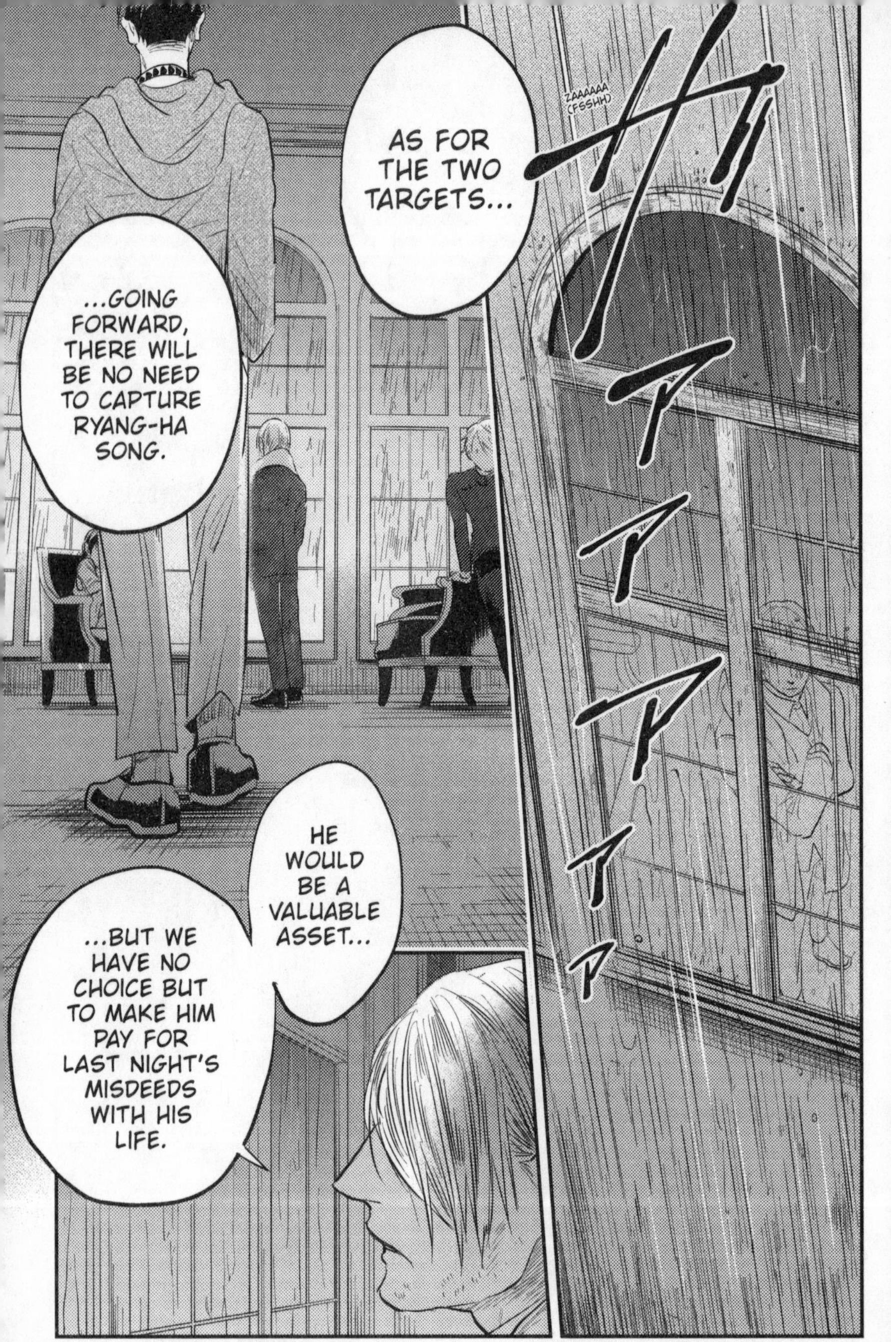
ZAAAAAA (FSSHH)
AS FOR THE TWO TARGETS...
...GOING FORWARD, THERE WILL BE NO NEED TO CAPTURE RYANG-HA SONG.
HE WOULD BE A VALUABLE ASSET...
...BUT WE HAVE NO CHOICE BUT TO MAKE HIM PAY FOR LAST NIGHT'S MISDEEDS WITH HIS LIFE.

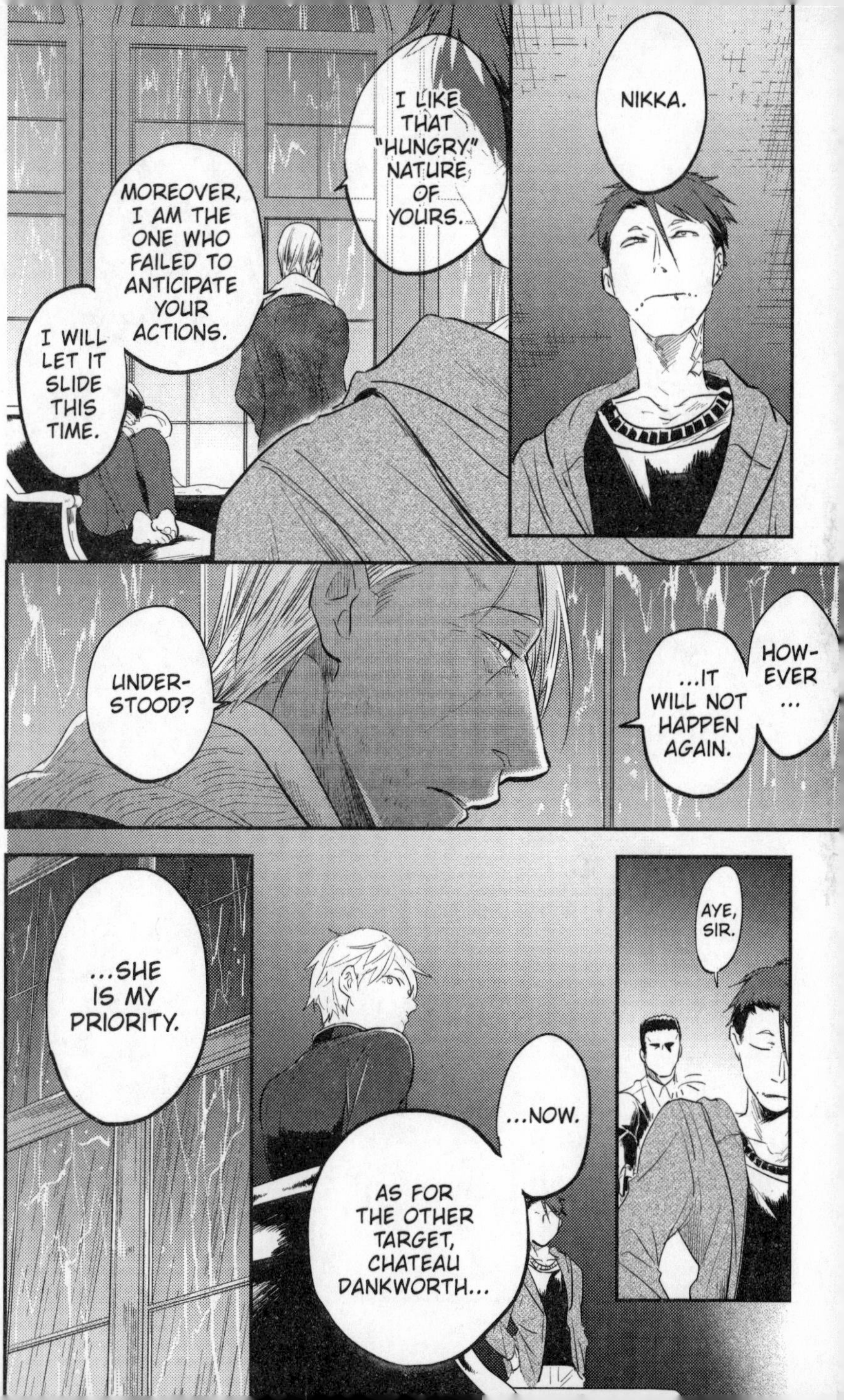
NIKKA.
I LIKE THAT "HUNGRY" NATURE OF YOURS.
MOREOVER, I AM THE ONE WHO FAILED TO ANTICIPATE YOUR ACTIONS.
I WILL LET IT SLIDE THIS TIME.
HOW-EVER...
...IT WILL NOT HAPPEN AGAIN.
UNDER-STOOD?
AYE, SIR.
...SHE IS MY PRIORITY.
...NOW.
AS FOR THE OTHER TARGET, CHATEAU DANKWORTH...

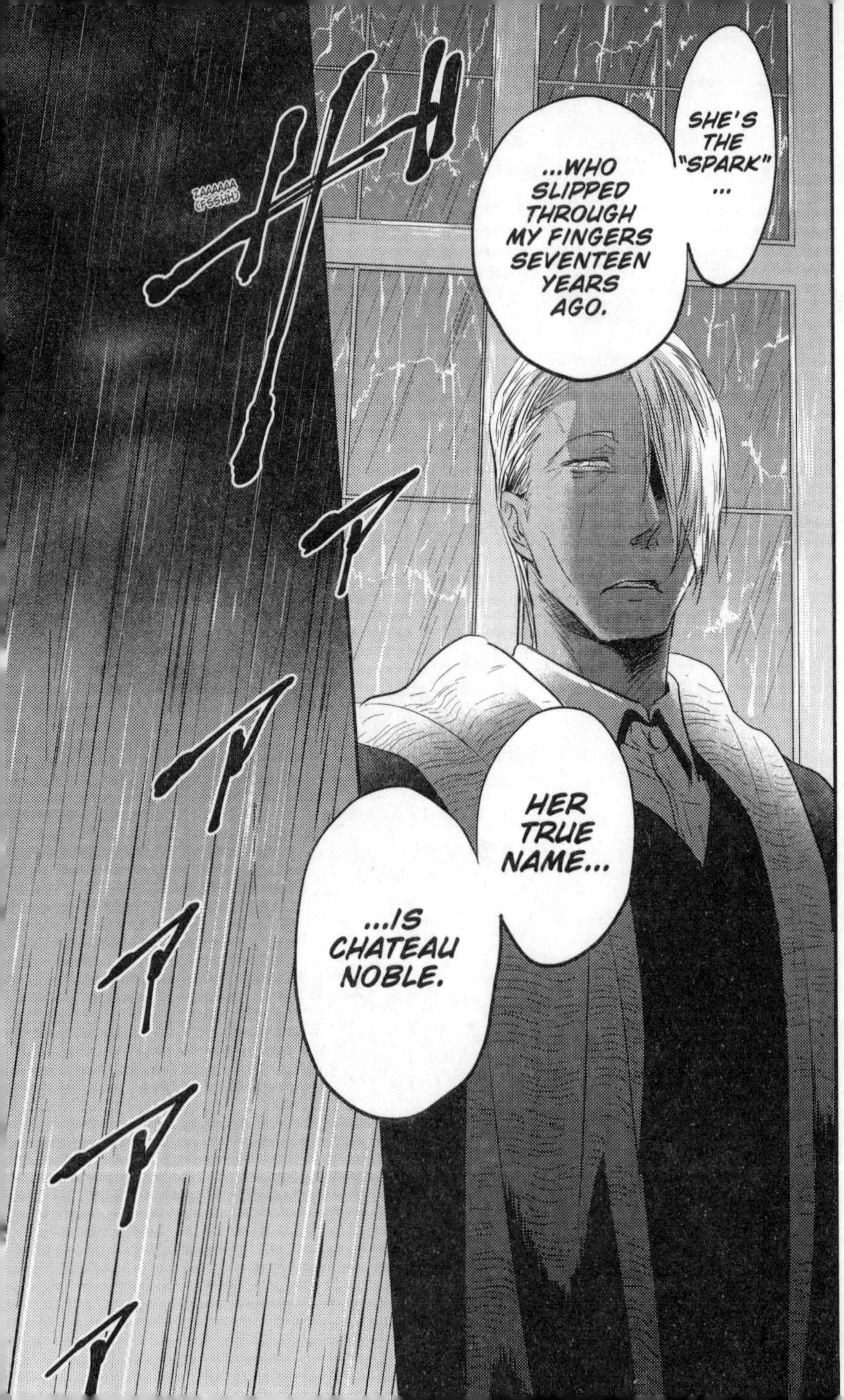
SHE'S THE "SPARK"...
...WHO SLIPPED THROUGH MY FINGERS SEVENTEEN YEARS AGO.
ZAAAAAA (FSSHH)
HER TRUE NAME...
...IS CHATEAU NOBLE.

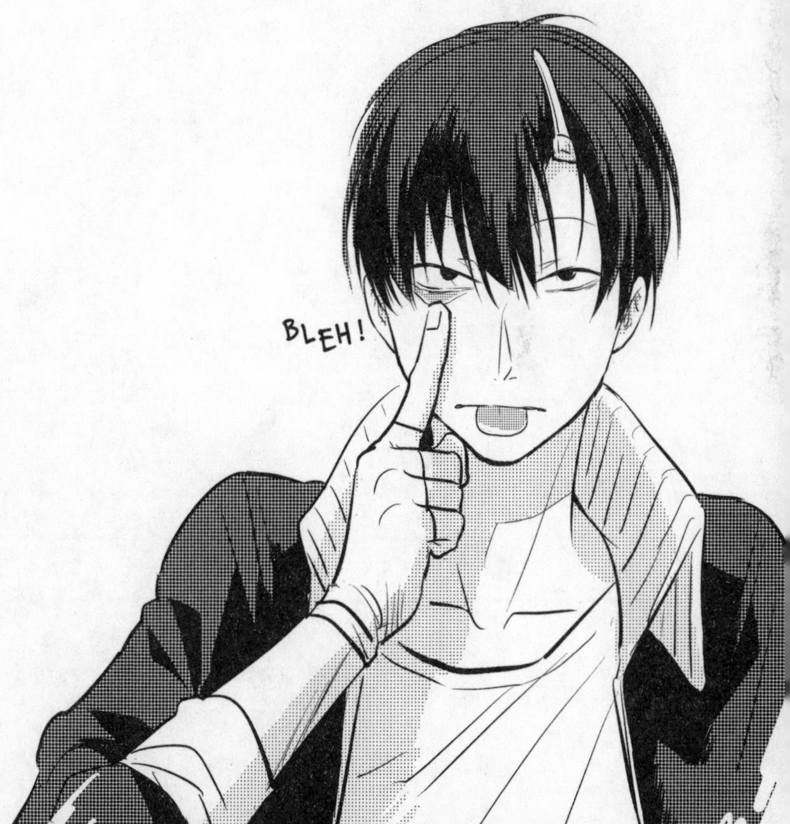
BLEH!

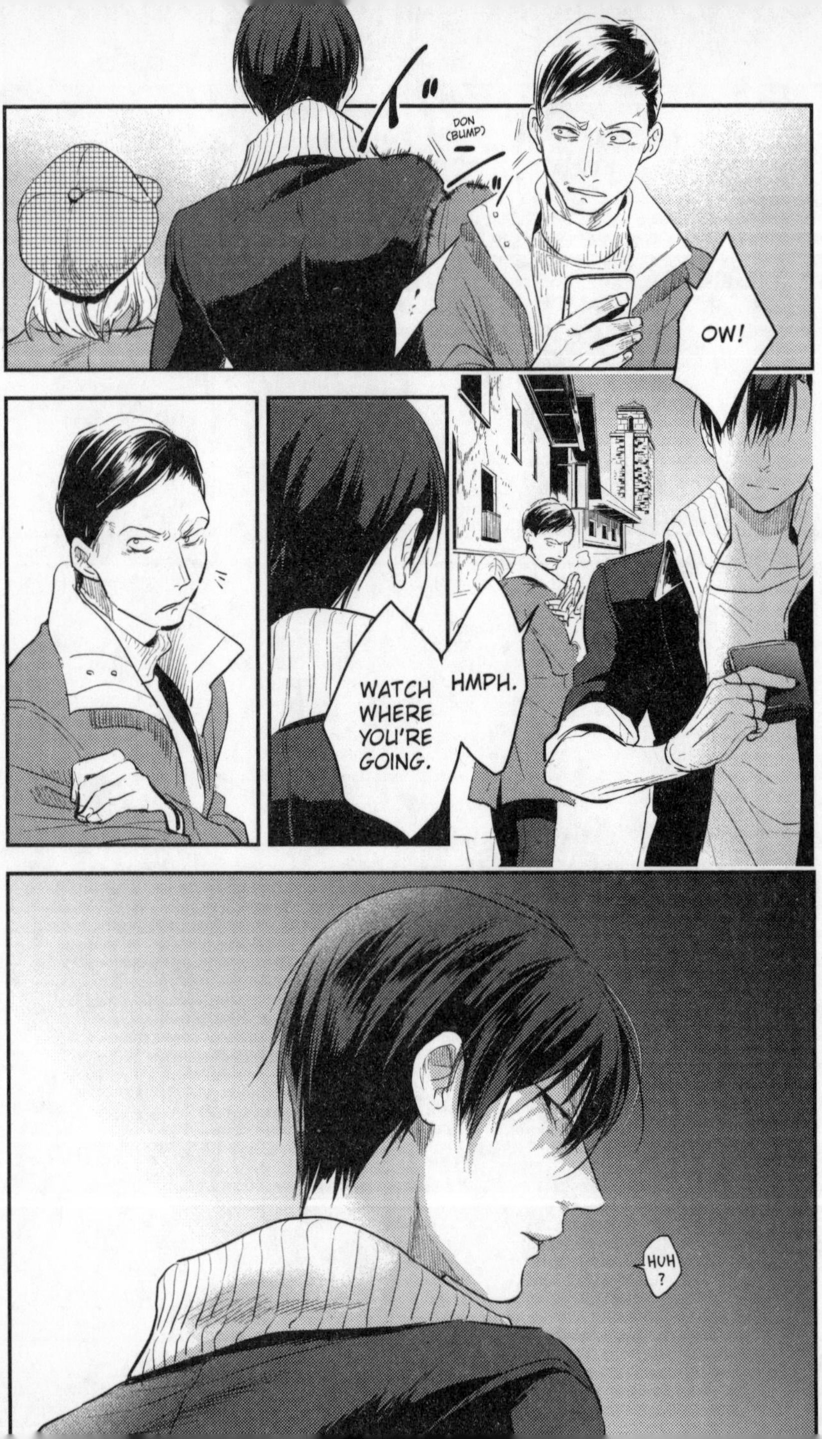
DON (BUMP)
OW!
HMPH.
WATCH WHERE YOU'RE GOING.
HUH?

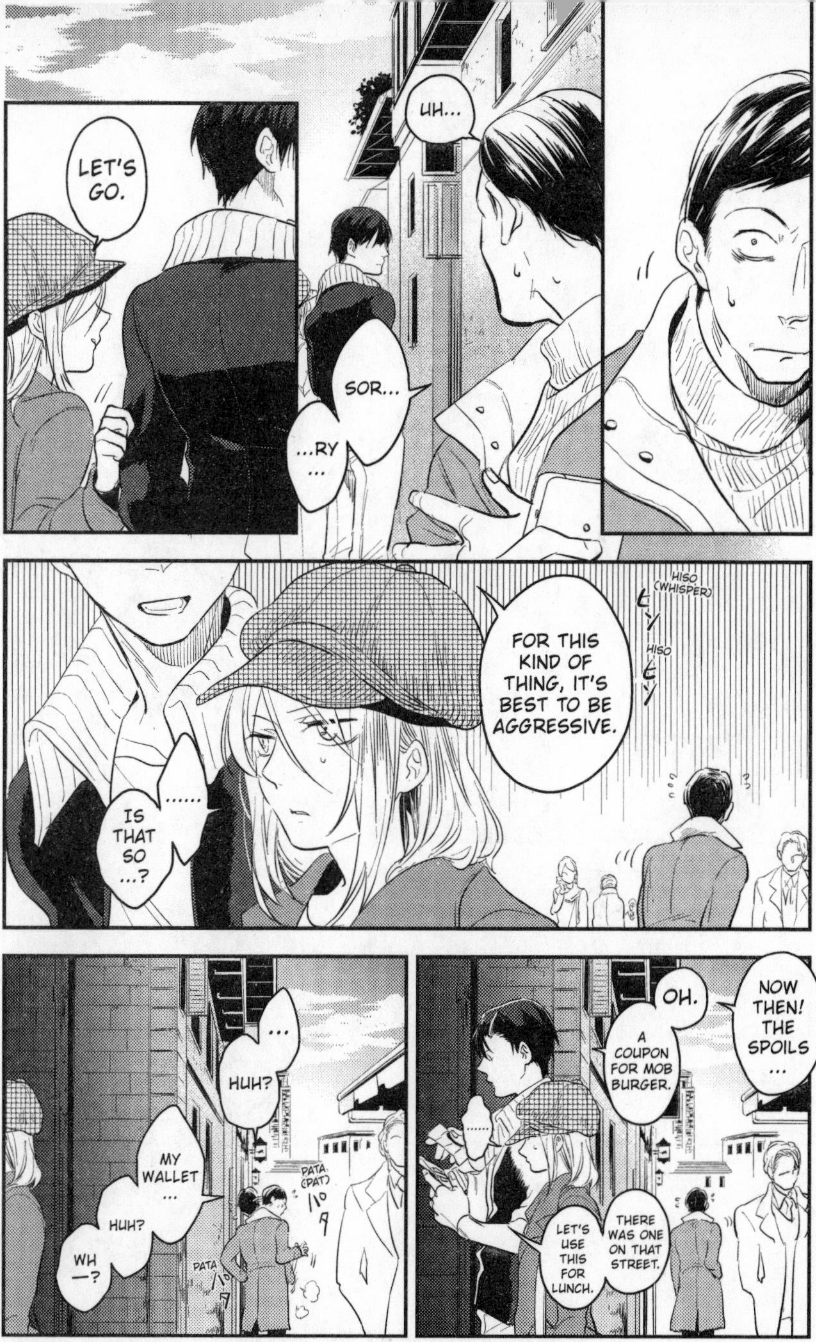
UH...
SOR...
...RY ...
LET'S GO.
HISO (WHISPER)
ヒソ
HISO
ヒソ
FOR THIS KIND OF THING, IT'S BEST TO BE AGGRESSIVE.
...... IS THAT SO ...?
NOW THEN! THE SPOILS ...
OH.
A COUPON FOR MOB BURGER.
......
THERE WAS ONE ON THAT STREET.
LET'S USE THIS FOR LUNCH.
... HUH?
PATA (PAT)
パタ
MY WALLET ...
HUH?
PATA
パタ
WH—?

# FILE 32 ALLY

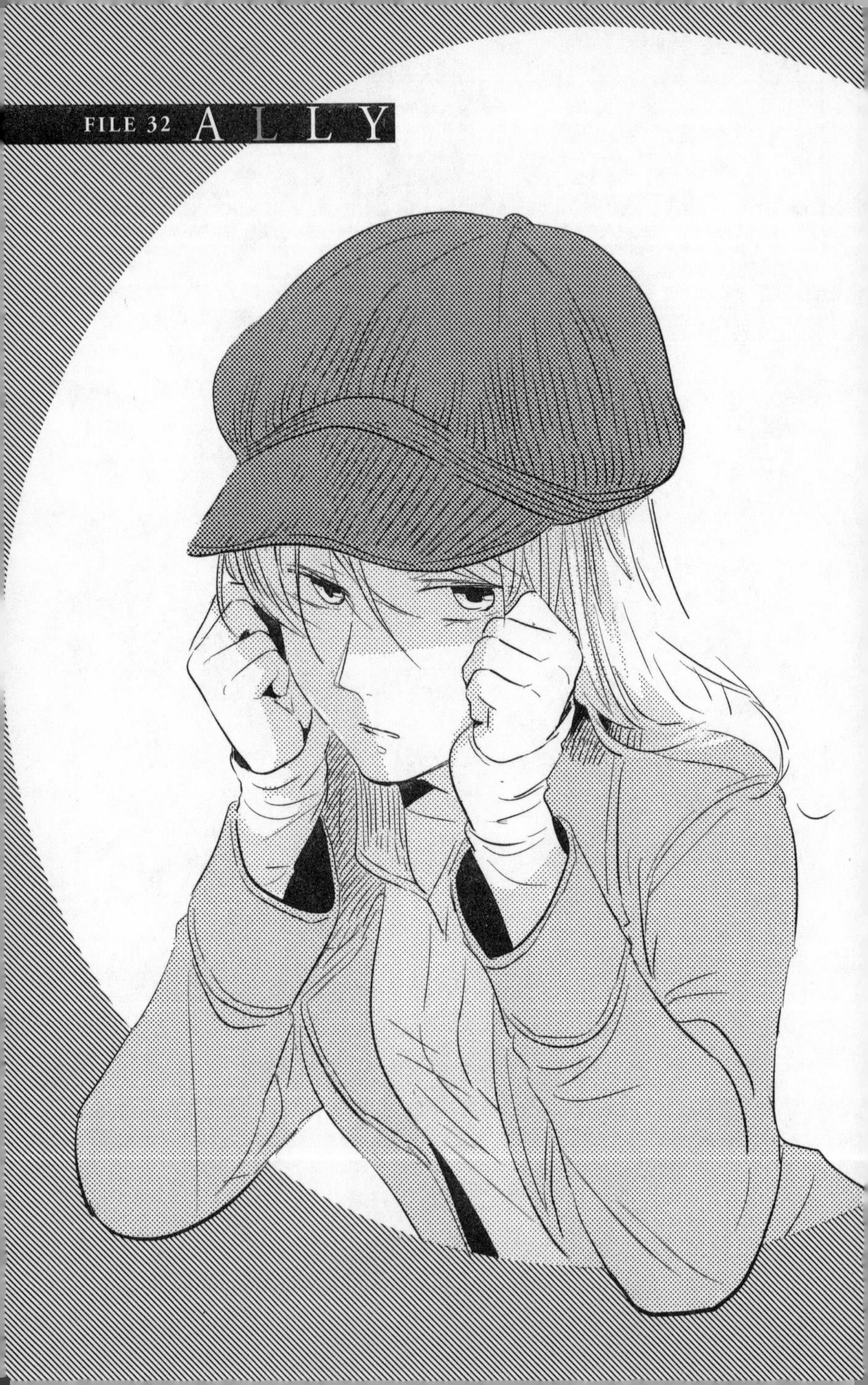

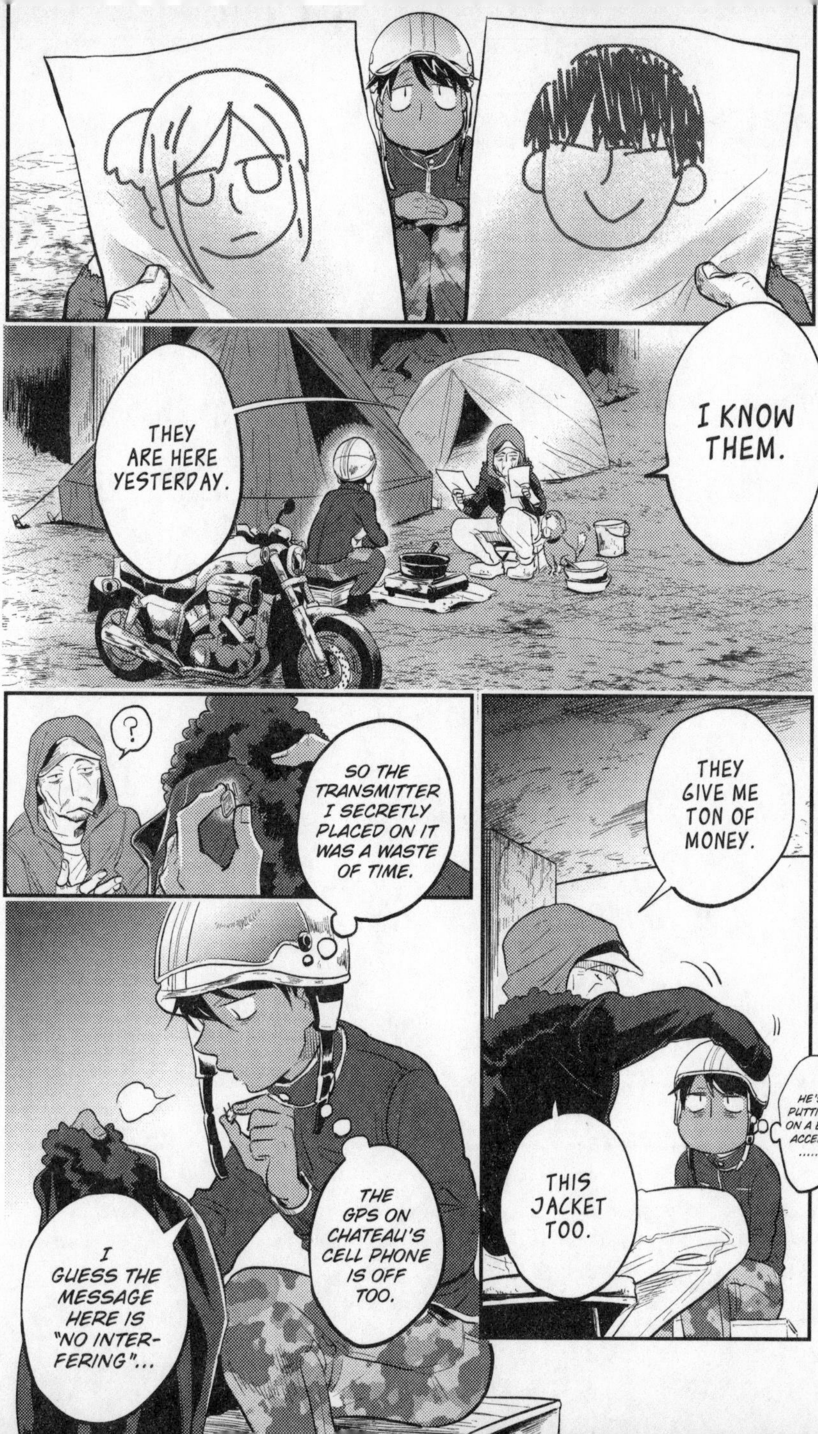
I KNOW THEM.
THEY ARE HERE YESTERDAY.
THEY GIVE ME TON OF MONEY.
HE'S PUTTING ON A BAD ACCENT ......
THIS JACKET TOO.
SO THE TRANSMITTER I SECRETLY PLACED ON IT WAS A WASTE OF TIME.
?
THE GPS ON CHATEAU'S CELL PHONE IS OFF TOO.
I GUESS THE MESSAGE HERE IS "NO INTER-FERING"...

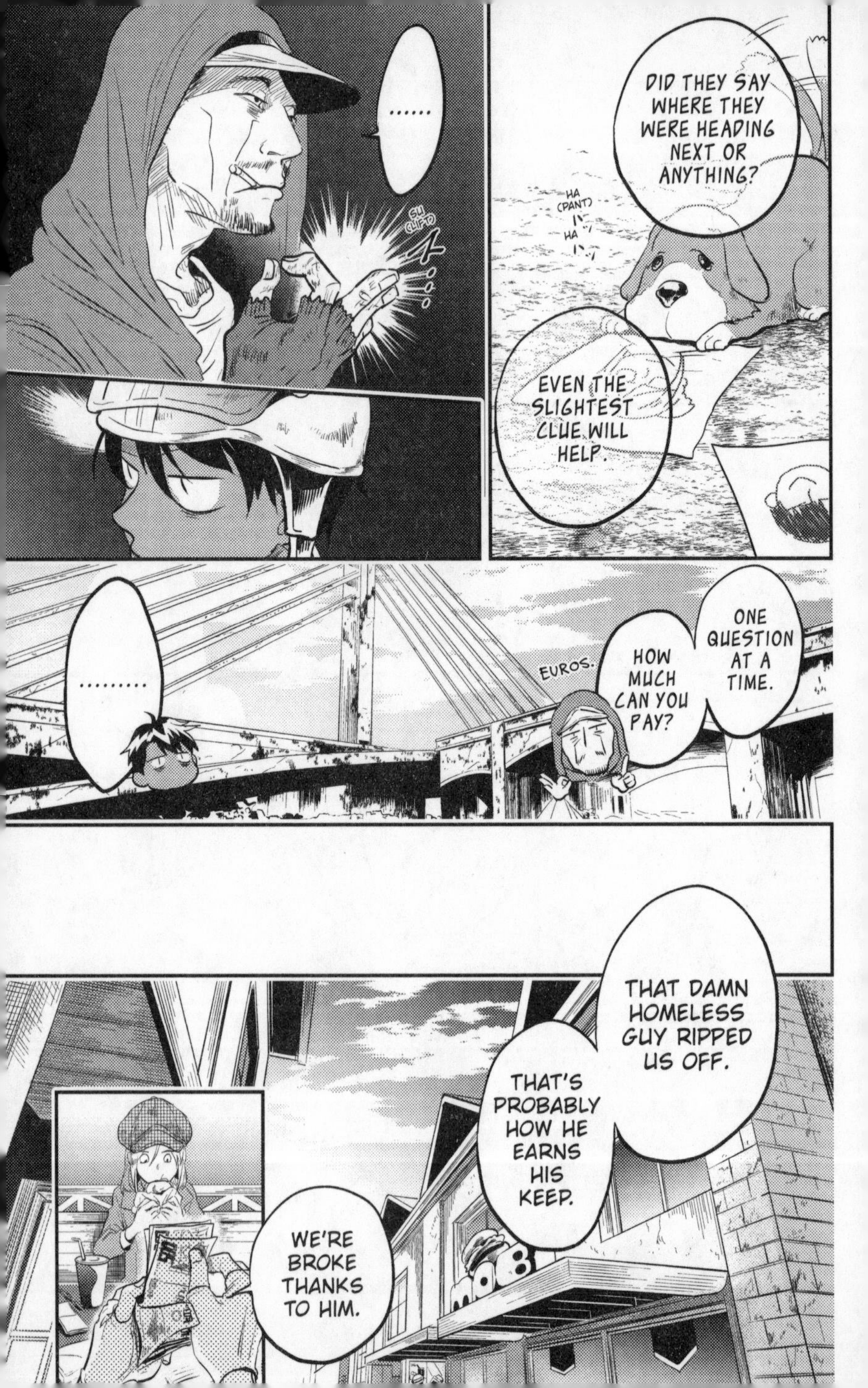
DID THEY SAY WHERE THEY WERE HEADING NEXT OR ANYTHING?
HA (PANT) HA
EVEN THE SLIGHTEST CLUE WILL HELP.
......
SU (LIFT)
ONE QUESTION AT A TIME.
HOW MUCH CAN YOU PAY?
EUROS.
.........
THAT DAMN HOMELESS GUY RIPPED US OFF.
THAT'S PROBABLY HOW HE EARNS HIS KEEP.
WE'RE BROKE THANKS TO HIM.

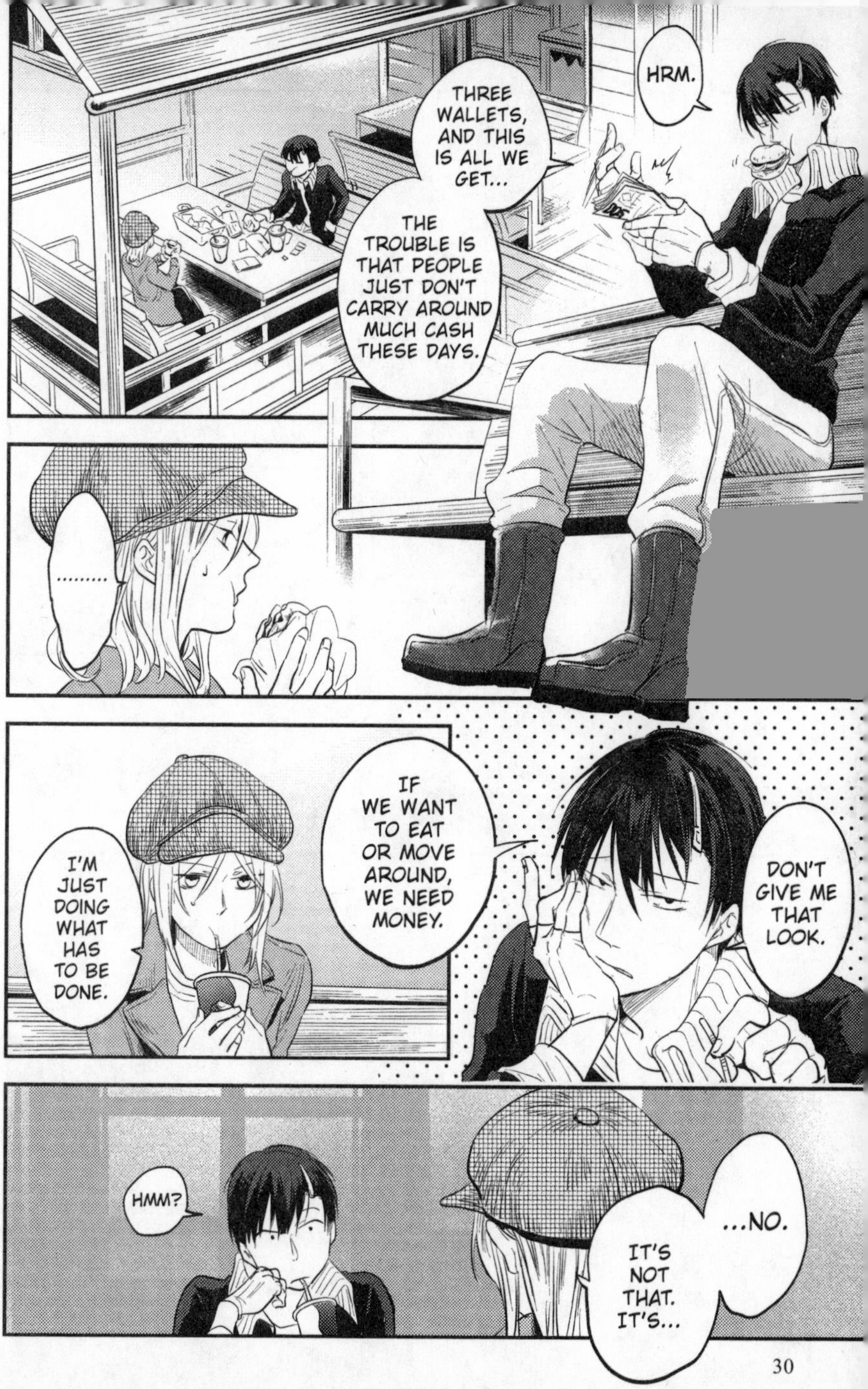
HRM.
THREE WALLETS, AND THIS IS ALL WE GET...
THE TROUBLE IS THAT PEOPLE JUST DON'T CARRY AROUND MUCH CASH THESE DAYS.
.........
IF WE WANT TO EAT OR MOVE AROUND, WE NEED MONEY.
DON'T GIVE ME THAT LOOK.
I'M JUST DOING WHAT HAS TO BE DONE.
...NO.
IT'S NOT THAT. IT'S...
HMM?

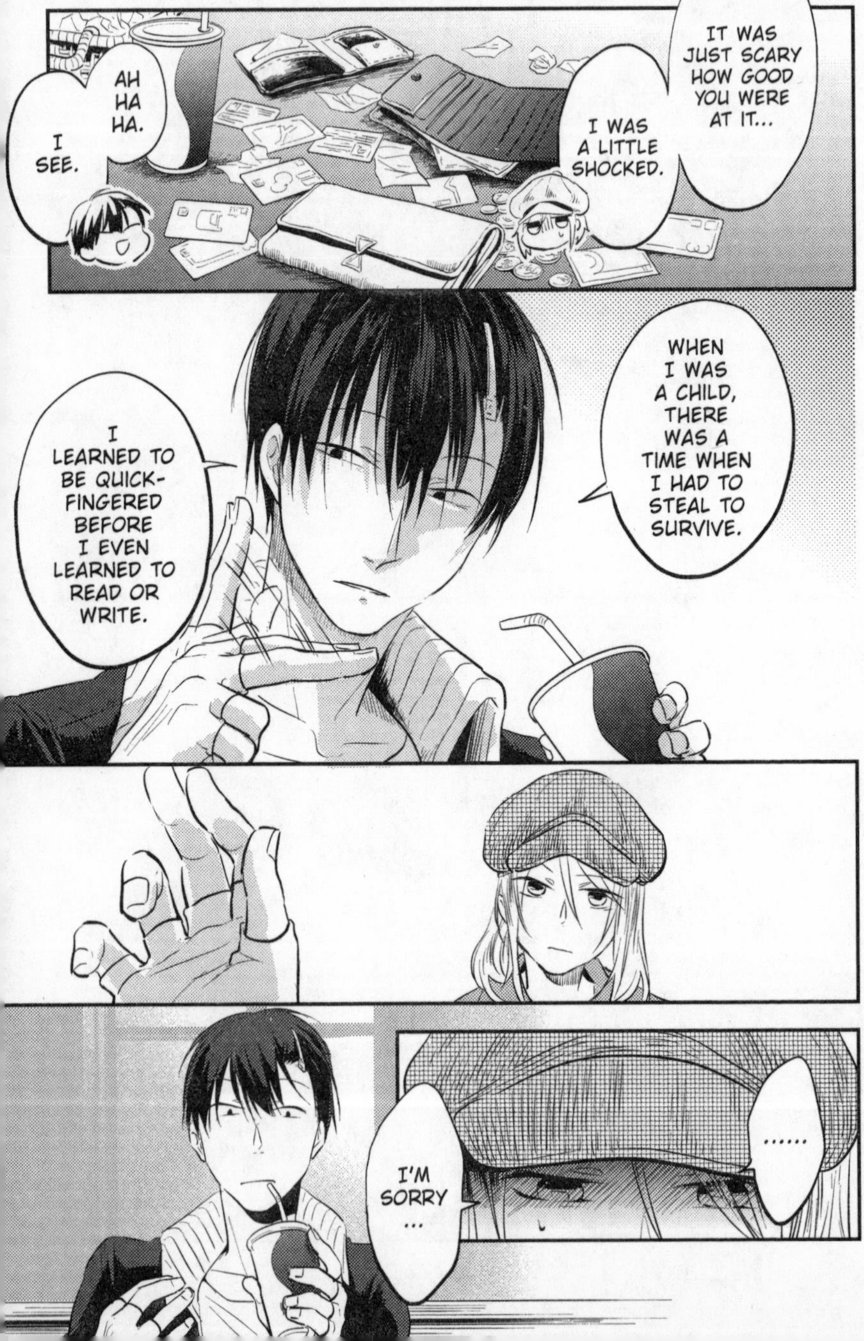
IT WAS JUST SCARY HOW GOOD YOU WERE AT IT...
I WAS A LITTLE SHOCKED.
AH HA HA. I SEE.
WHEN I WAS A CHILD, THERE WAS A TIME WHEN I HAD TO STEAL TO SURVIVE.
I LEARNED TO BE QUICK-FINGERED BEFORE I EVEN LEARNED TO READ OR WRITE.
......
I'M SORRY ...

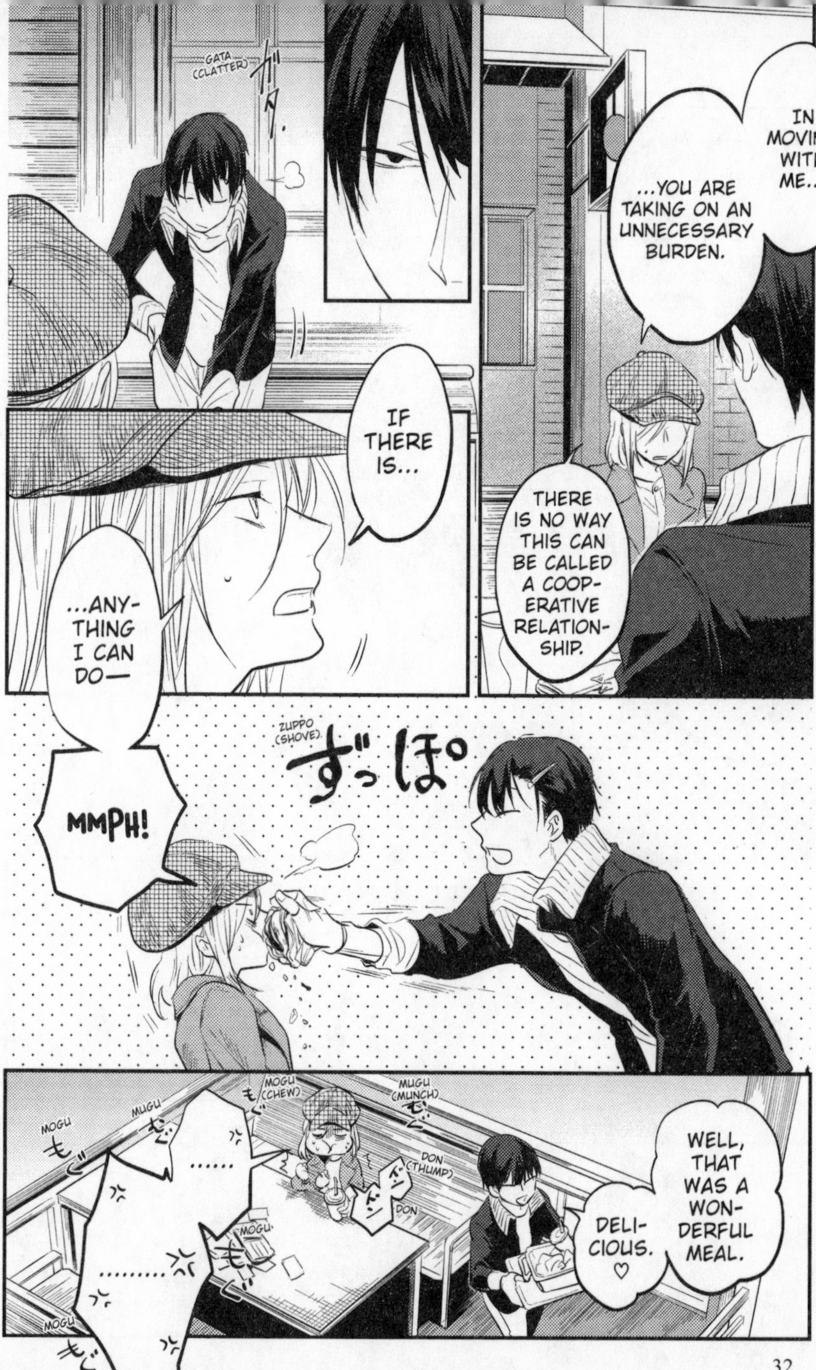
IN MOVING WITH ME...
...YOU ARE TAKING ON AN UNNECESSARY BURDEN.
THERE IS NO WAY THIS CAN BE CALLED A COOPERATIVE RELATIONSHIP.
GATA (CLATTER)
ガタ
IF THERE IS...
...ANYTHING I CAN DO—
ZUPPO (SHOVE)
ずっぽ
MMPH!
WELL, THAT WAS A WONDERFUL MEAL.
DELICIOUS. ♡
MUGU (MUNCH)
MOGU (CHEW)
DON (THUMP)
DON
......
MUGU
MOGU
MOGU
.........
MOGU

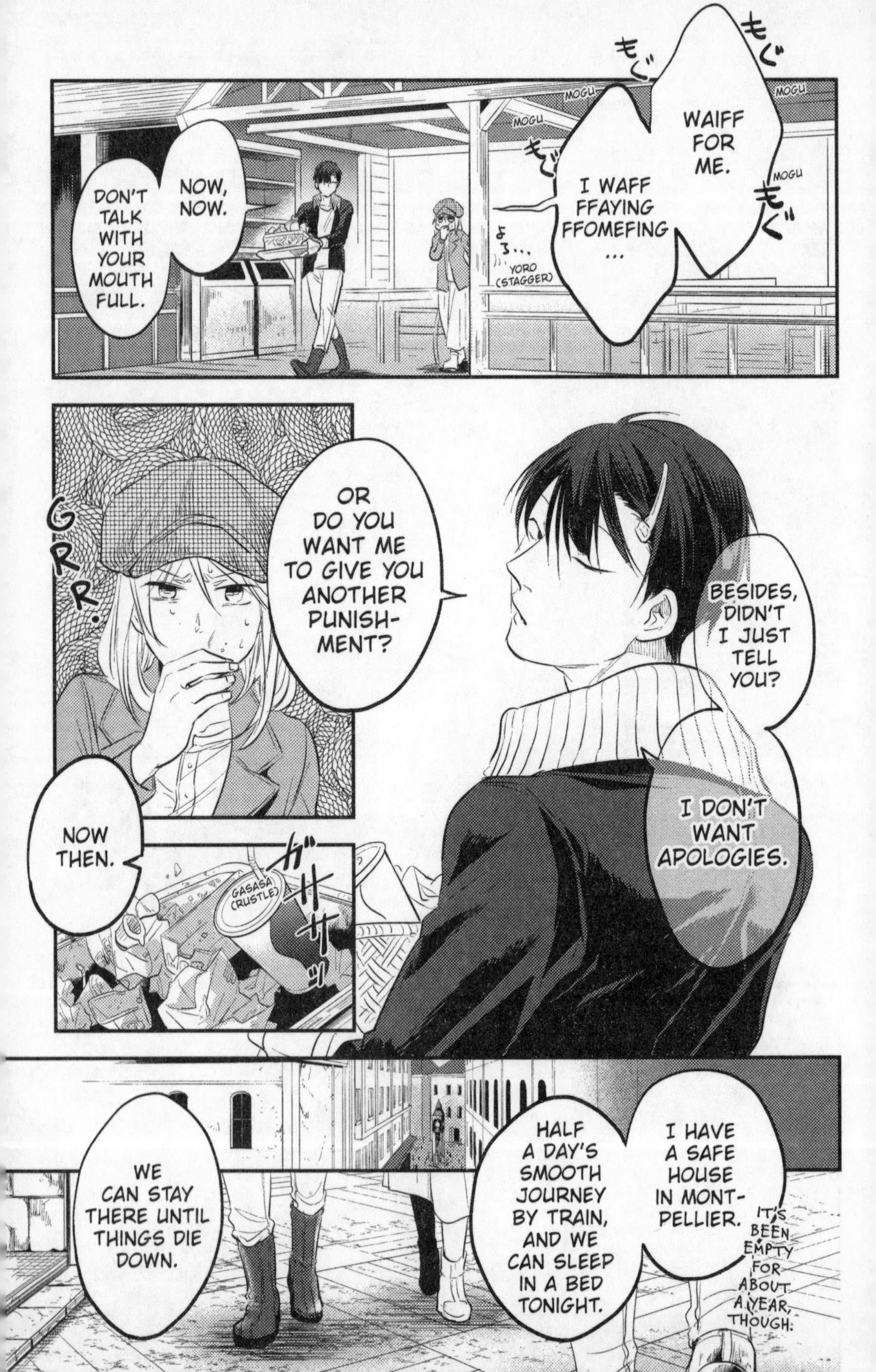
もぐ
MOGU
もぐ
MOGU
WAIFF FOR ME.
もぐ
MOGU
もぐ
MOGU
I WAFF FFAYING FFOMEFING ...
よろ...
YORO (STAGGER)
NOW, NOW.
DON'T TALK WITH YOUR MOUTH FULL.
BESIDES, DIDN'T I JUST TELL YOU?
I DON'T WANT APOLOGIES.
OR DO YOU WANT ME TO GIVE YOU ANOTHER PUNISH-MENT?
GRR.
NOW THEN.
ガサッ
GASASA (RUSTLE)
I HAVE A SAFE HOUSE IN MONT-PELLIER.
IT'S BEEN EMPTY FOR ABOUT A YEAR, THOUGH.
HALF A DAY'S SMOOTH JOURNEY BY TRAIN, AND WE CAN SLEEP IN A BED TONIGHT.
WE CAN STAY THERE UNTIL THINGS DIE DOWN.

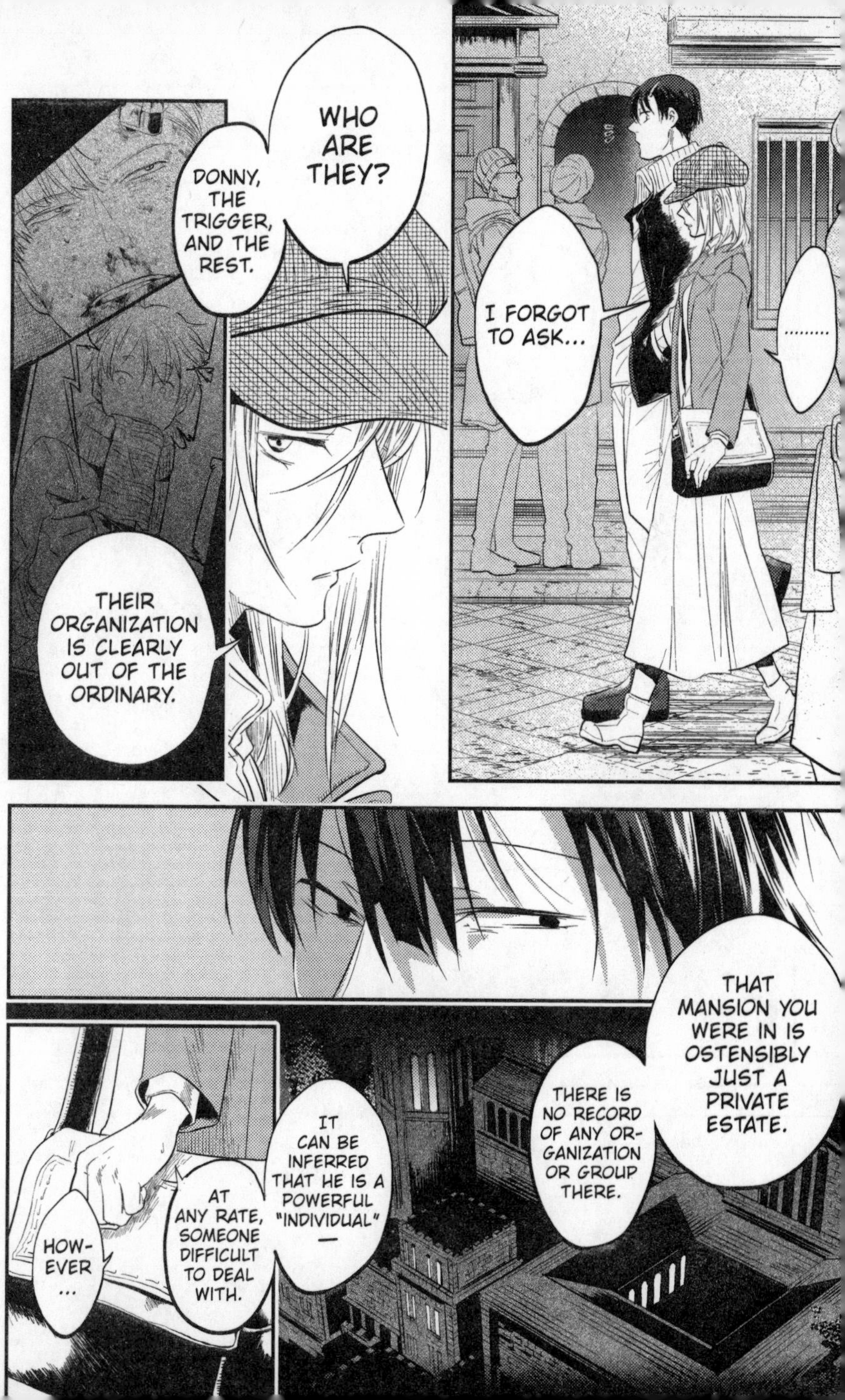
I FORGOT TO ASK...
........
WHO ARE THEY?
DONNY, THE TRIGGER, AND THE REST.
THEIR ORGANIZATION IS CLEARLY OUT OF THE ORDINARY.
THAT MANSION YOU WERE IN IS OSTENSIBLY JUST A PRIVATE ESTATE.
THERE IS NO RECORD OF ANY OR- GANIZATION OR GROUP THERE.
IT CAN BE INFERRED THAT HE IS A POWERFUL "INDIVIDUAL" —
AT ANY RATE, SOMEONE DIFFICULT TO DEAL WITH.
HOW- EVER ...

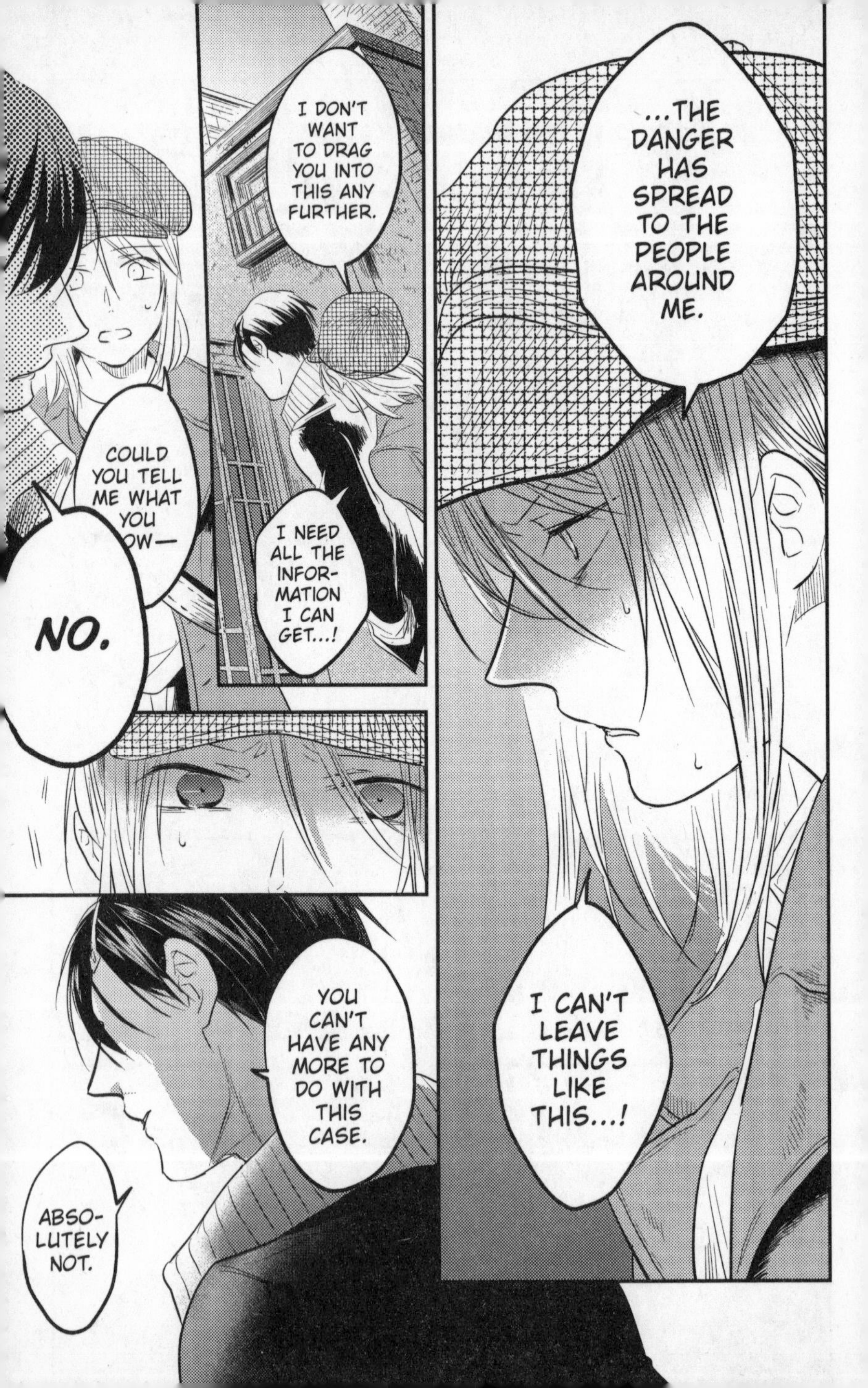
…THE DANGER HAS SPREAD TO THE PEOPLE AROUND ME.
I CAN'T LEAVE THINGS LIKE THIS…!
I DON'T WANT TO DRAG YOU INTO THIS ANY FURTHER.
I NEED ALL THE INFOR-MATION I CAN GET…!
COULD YOU TELL ME WHAT YOU OW—
NO.
YOU CAN'T HAVE ANY MORE TO DO WITH THIS CASE.
ABSO-LUTELY NOT.

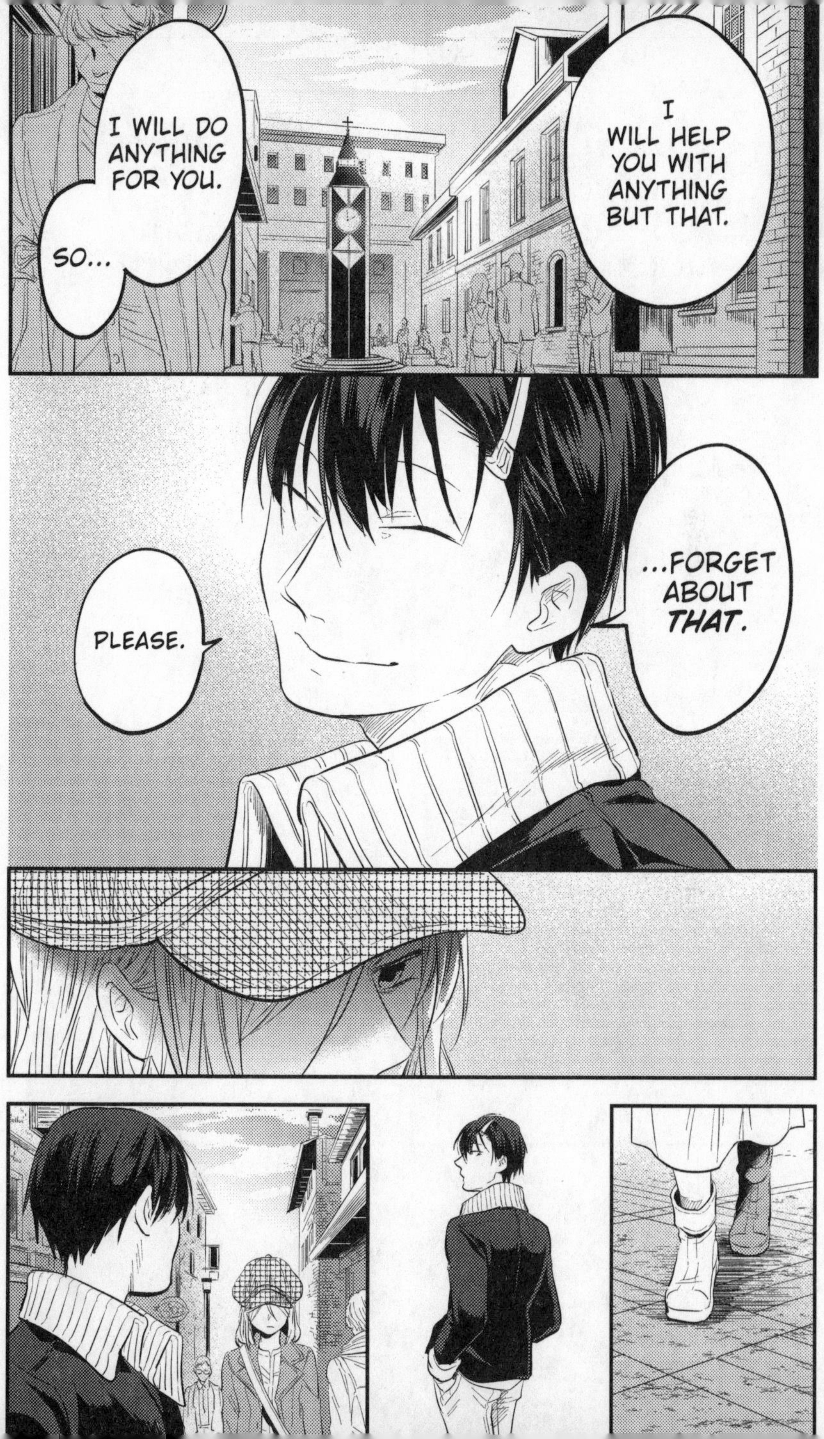
I WILL HELP YOU WITH ANYTHING BUT THAT.
I WILL DO ANYTHING FOR YOU.
SO...
...FORGET ABOUT *THAT*.
PLEASE.

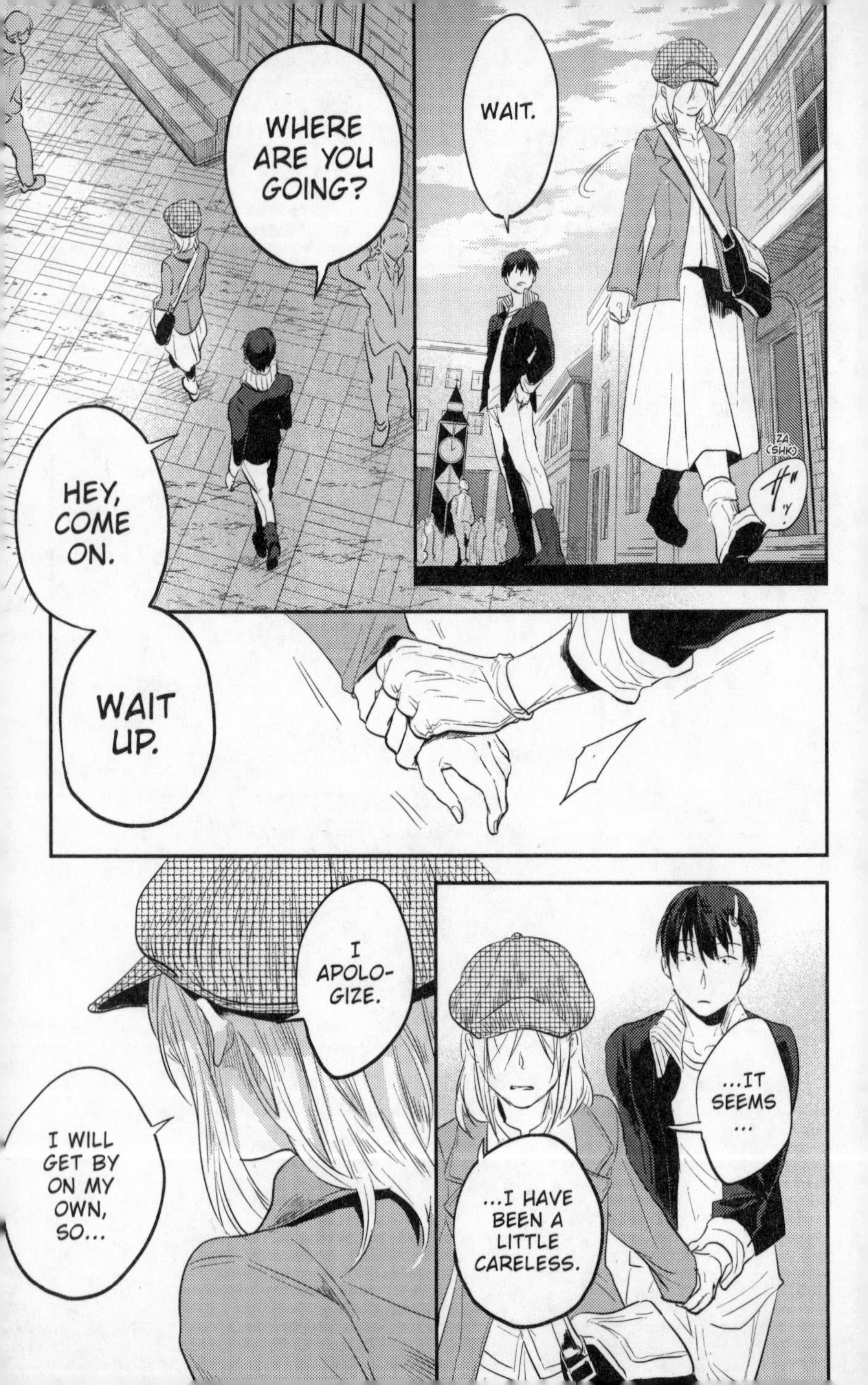
WAIT.
ZA (SHK)
WHERE ARE YOU GOING?
HEY, COME ON.
WAIT UP.
...IT SEEMS...
...I HAVE BEEN A LITTLE CARELESS.
I APOLOGIZE.
I WILL GET BY ON MY OWN, SO...

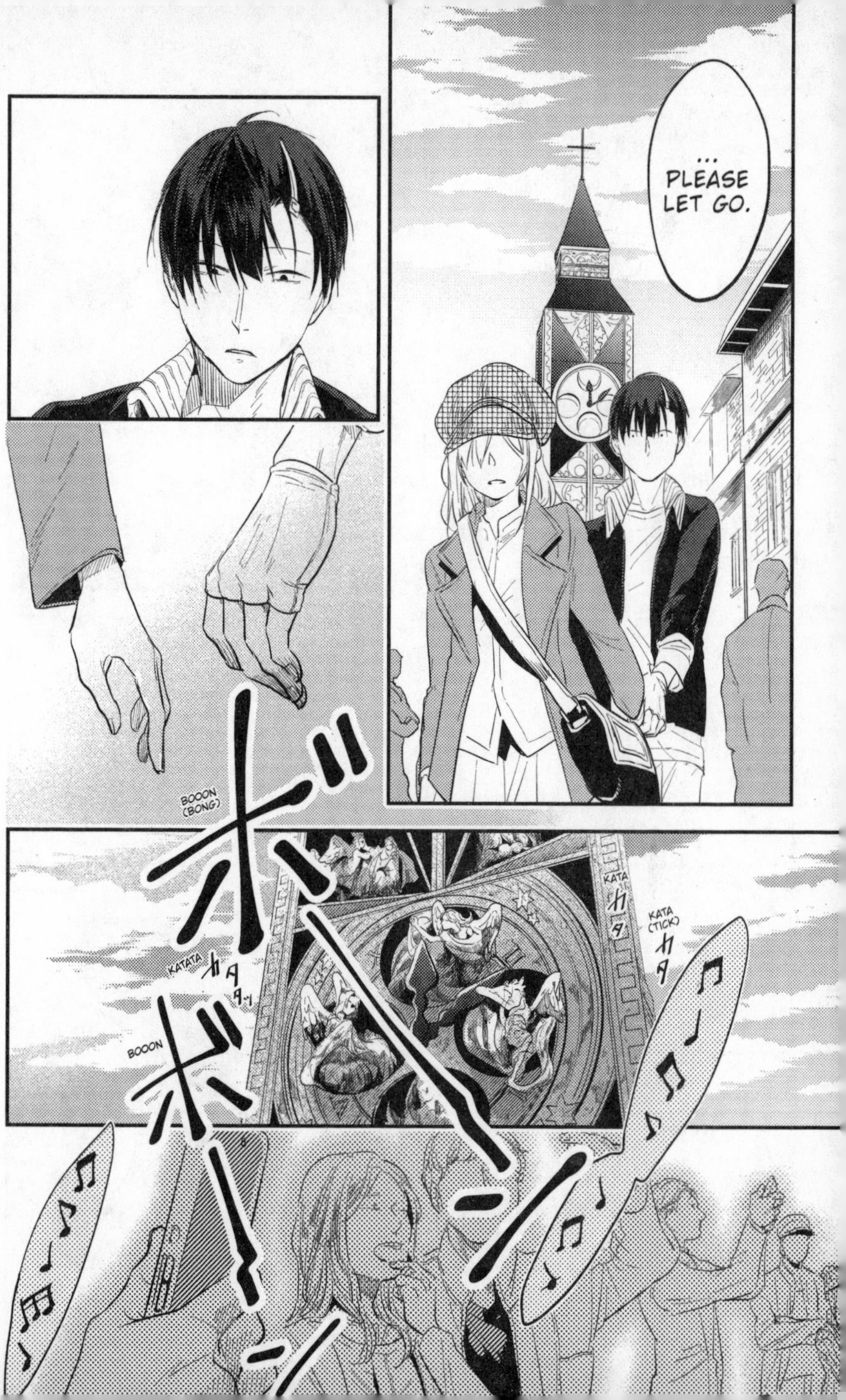
... PLEASE LET GO.
BOOON (BONG)
KATA
KATA (TICK)
KATATA
BOOON

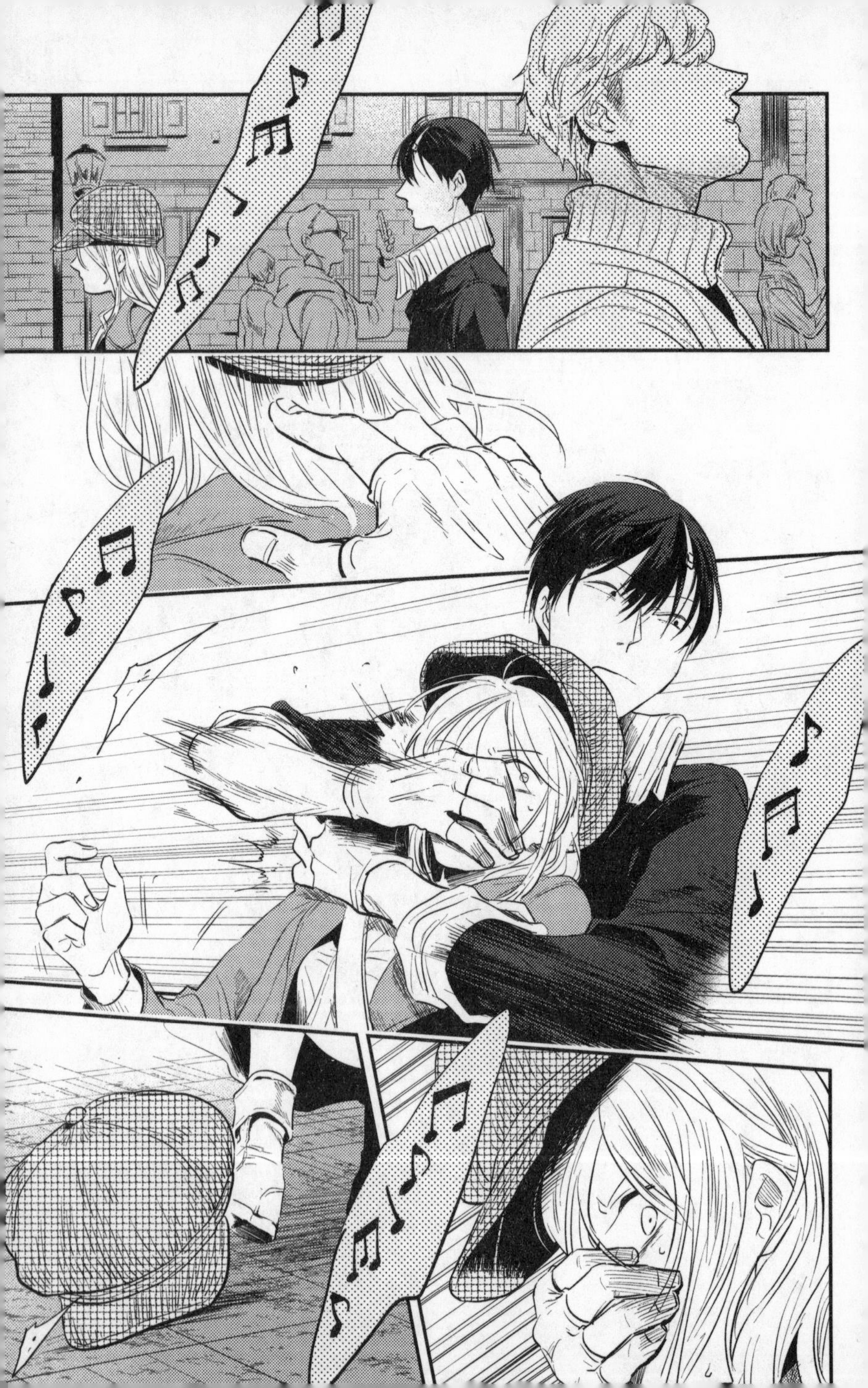

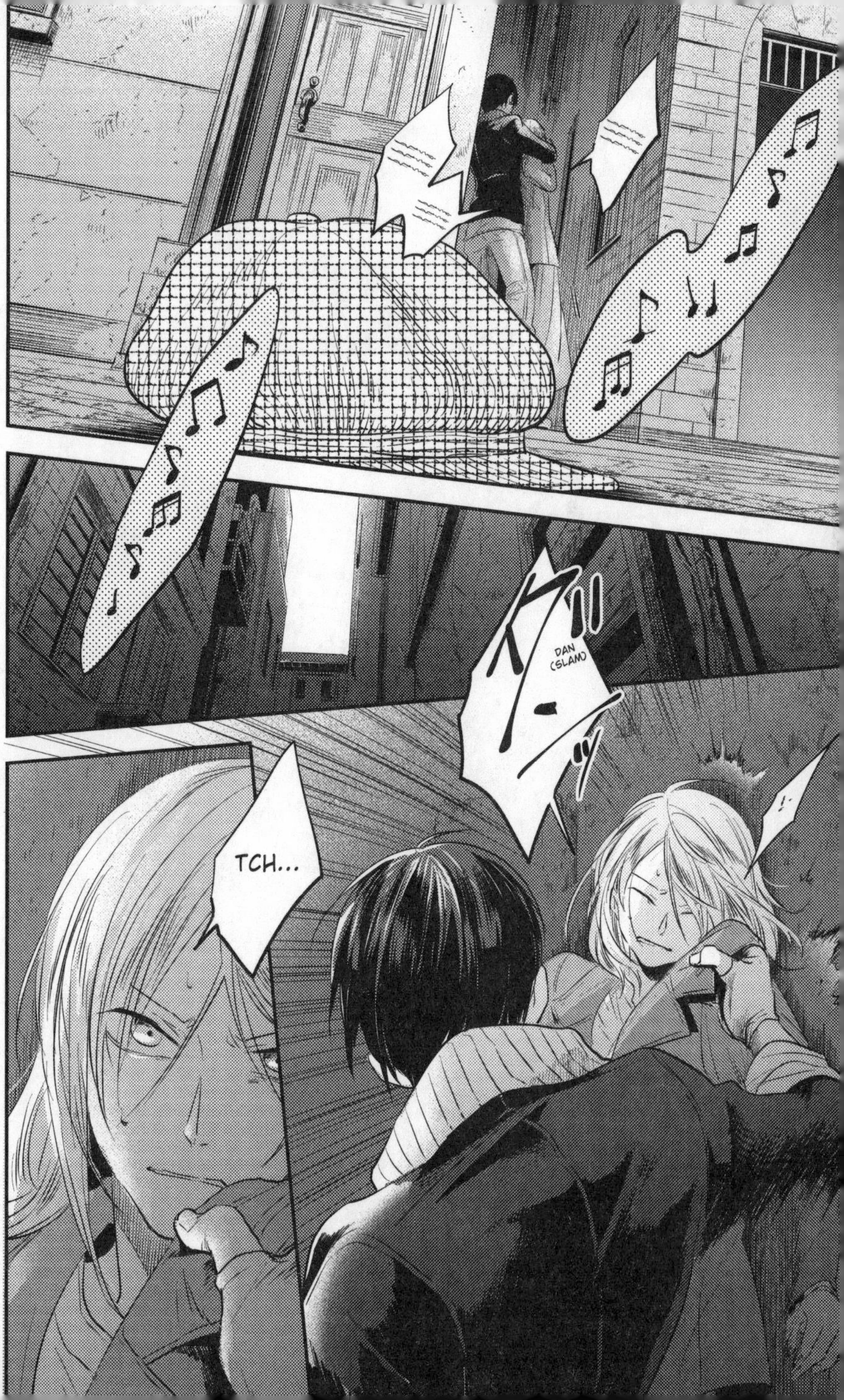
DAN (SLAM)
!
TCH...

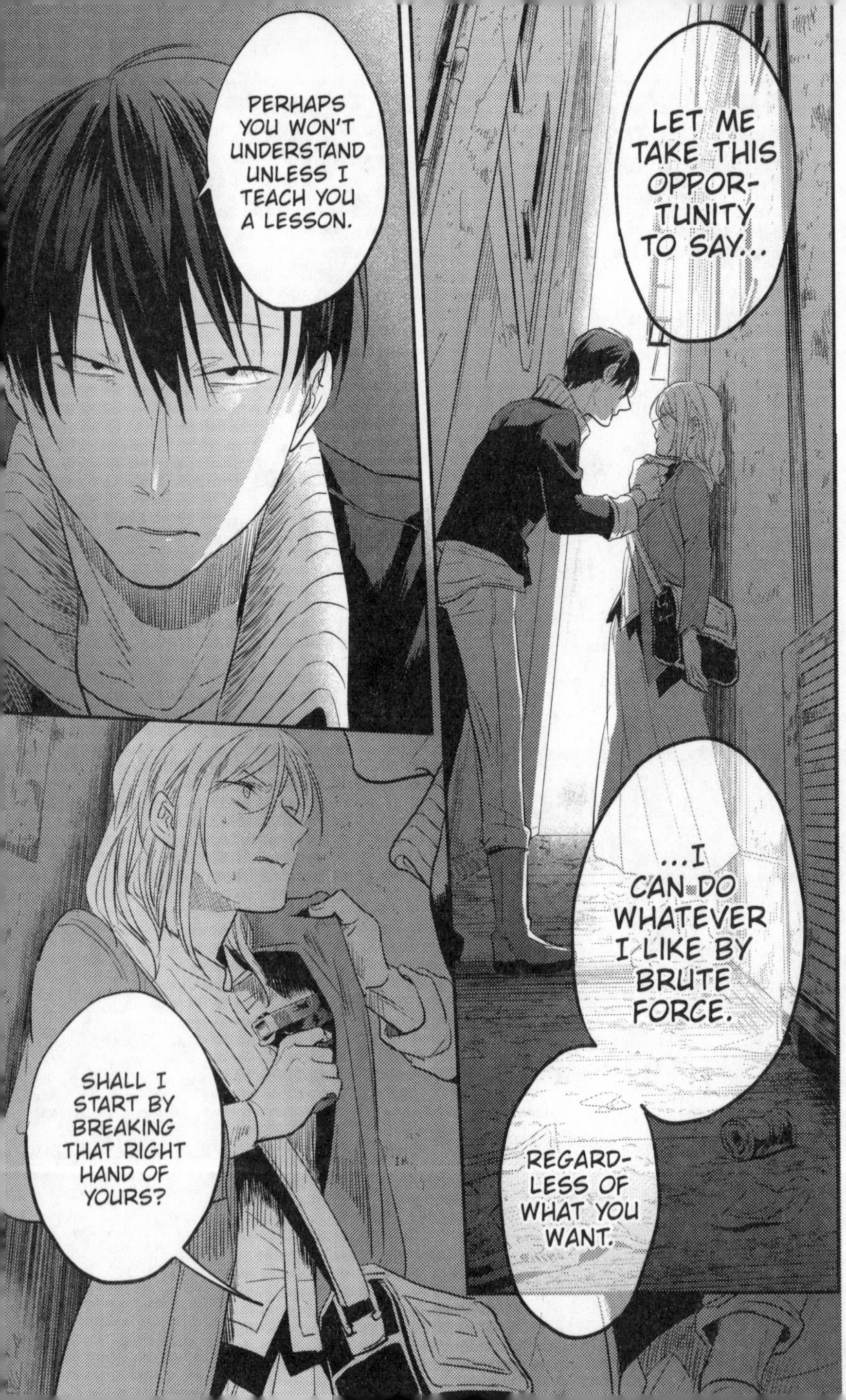
LET ME TAKE THIS OPPOR-TUNITY TO SAY...
...I CAN DO WHATEVER I LIKE BY BRUTE FORCE.
REGARD-LESS OF WHAT YOU WANT.
PERHAPS YOU WON'T UNDERSTAND UNLESS I TEACH YOU A LESSON.
SHALL I START BY BREAKING THAT RIGHT HAND OF YOURS?

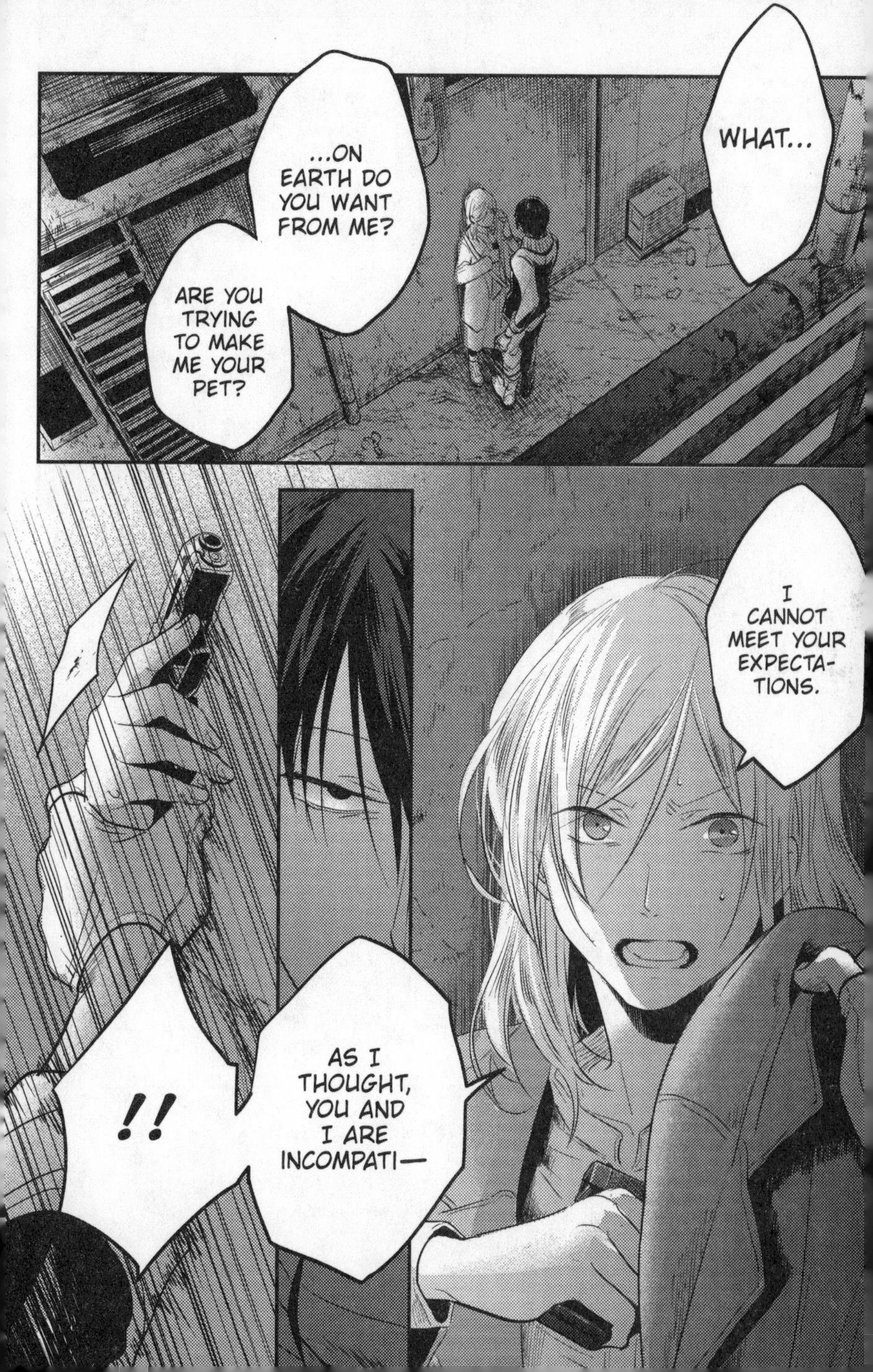
WHAT...
...ON EARTH DO YOU WANT FROM ME?
ARE YOU TRYING TO MAKE ME YOUR PET?
I CANNOT MEET YOUR EXPECTATIONS.
AS I THOUGHT, YOU AND I ARE INCOMPATI—
!!

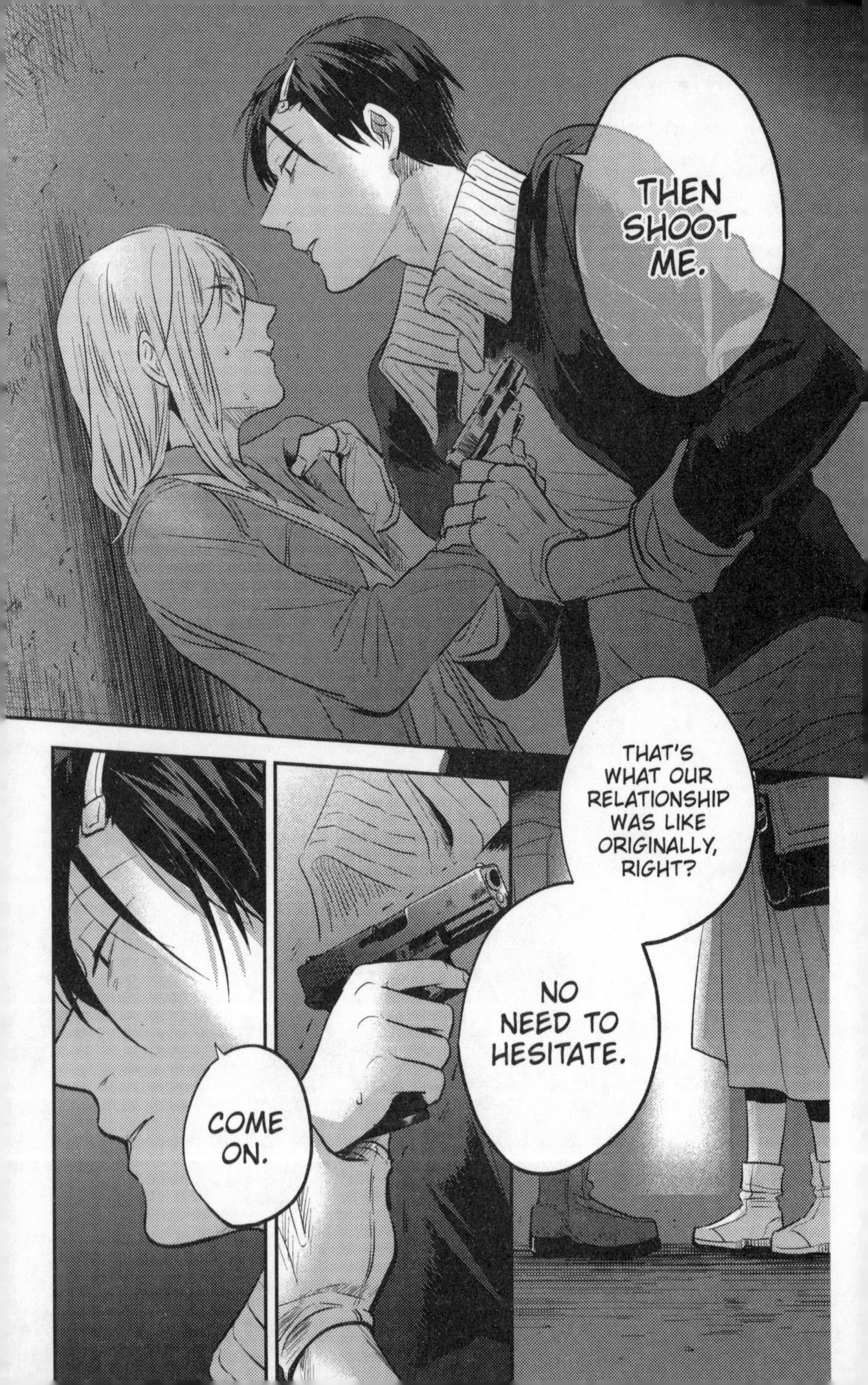
THEN SHOOT ME.
THAT'S WHAT OUR RELATIONSHIP WAS LIKE ORIGINALLY, RIGHT?
NO NEED TO HESITATE.
COME ON.

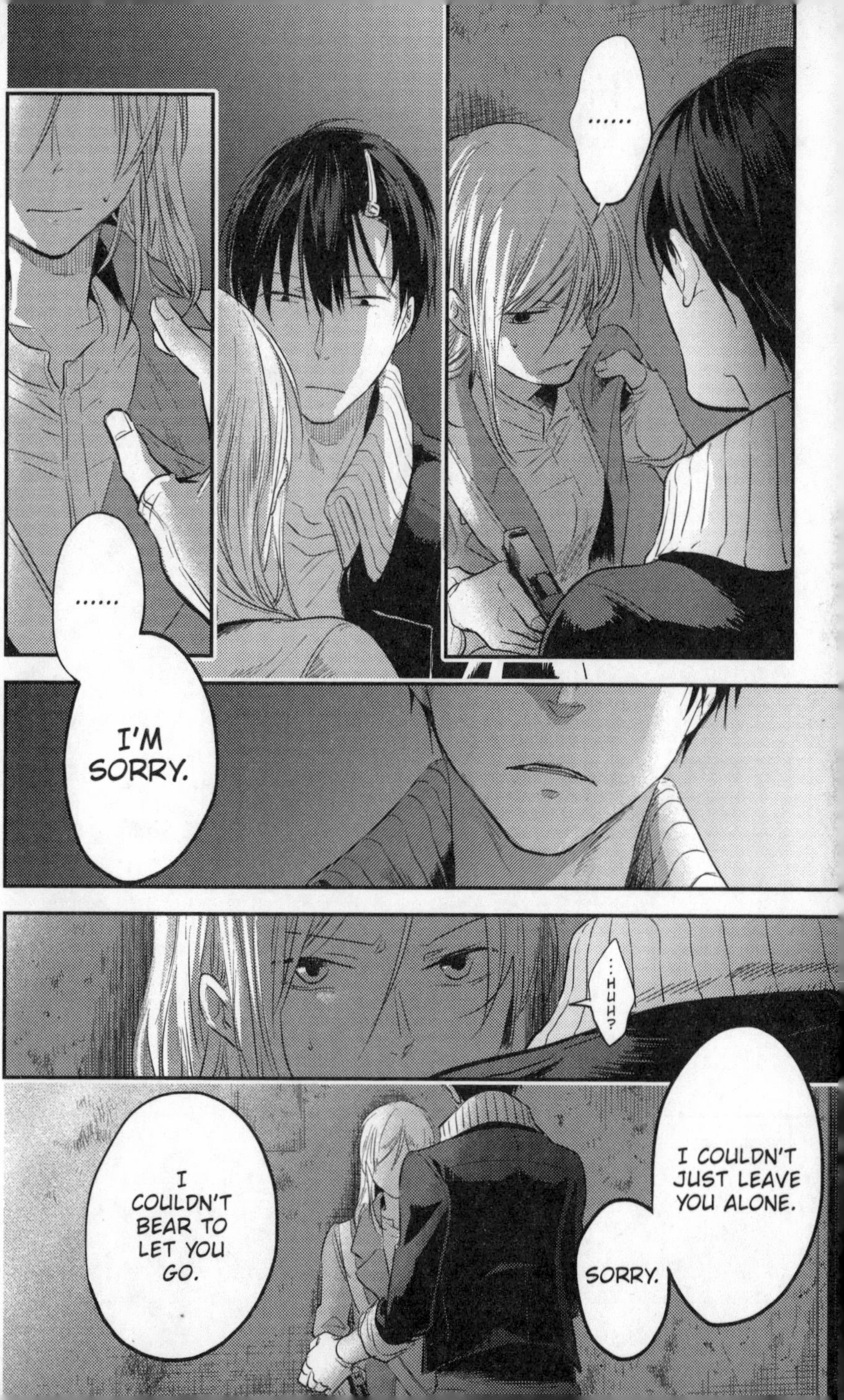
......
......
I'M SORRY.
...HUH?
I COULDN'T JUST LEAVE YOU ALONE.
SORRY.
I COULDN'T BEAR TO LET YOU GO.

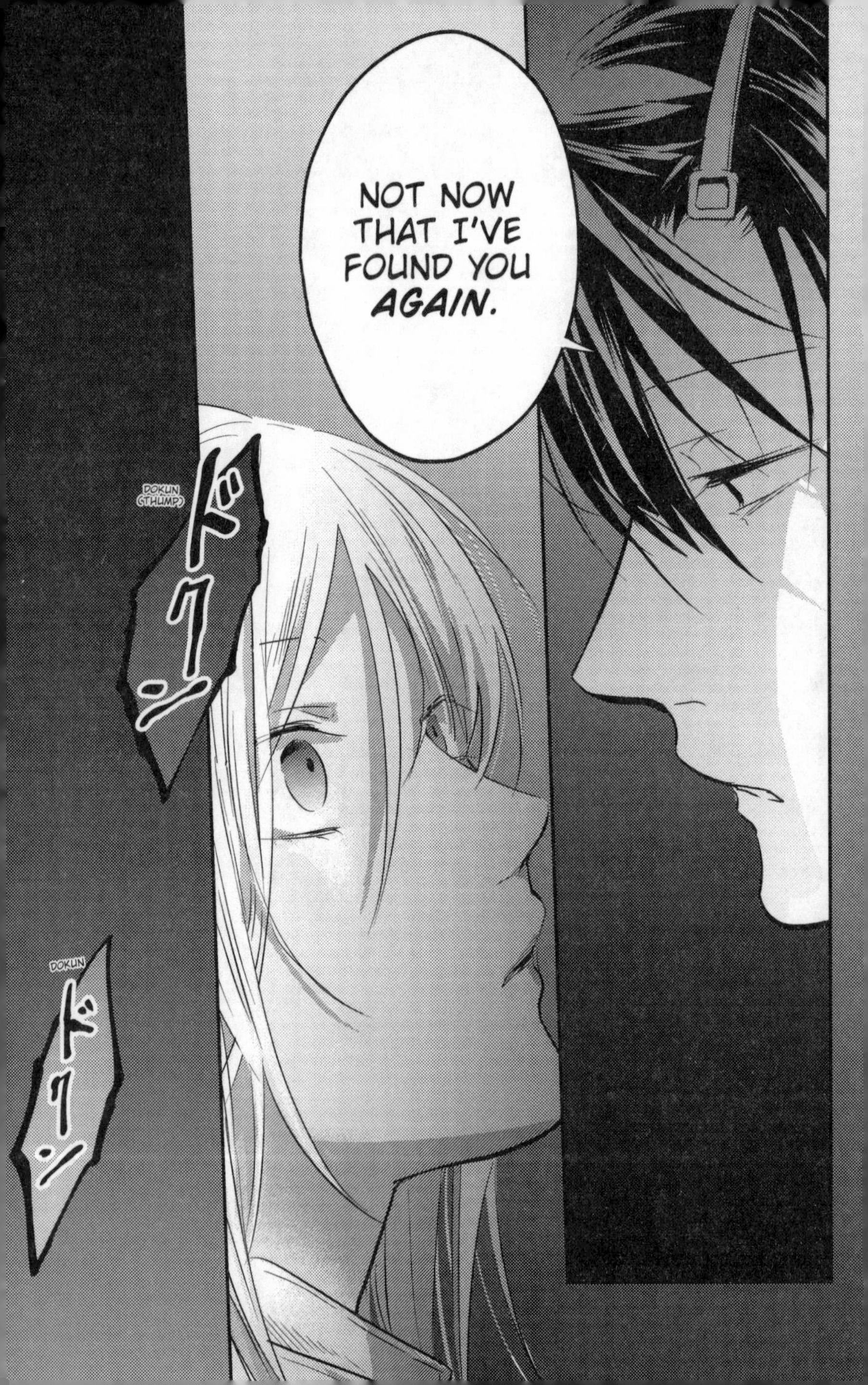
NOT NOW THAT I'VE FOUND YOU AGAIN.
DOKUN (THUMP)
ドクン
DOKUN
ドクン

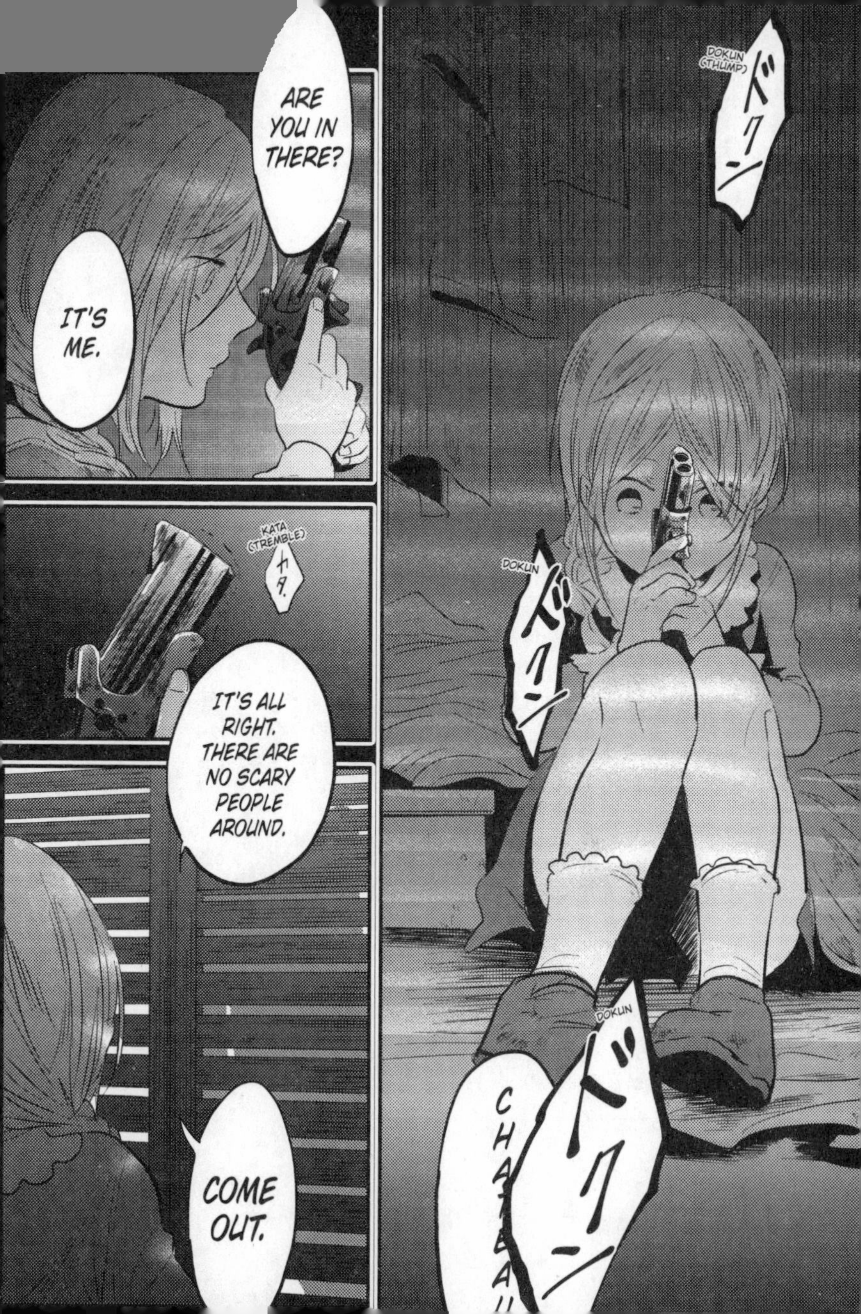
DOKUN (THUMP)
ドクン
DOKUN
ドクン
DOKUN
ドクン
ARE YOU IN THERE?
IT'S ME.
KATA (TREMBLE)
カタ
IT'S ALL RIGHT. THERE ARE NO SCARY PEOPLE AROUND.
COME OUT.

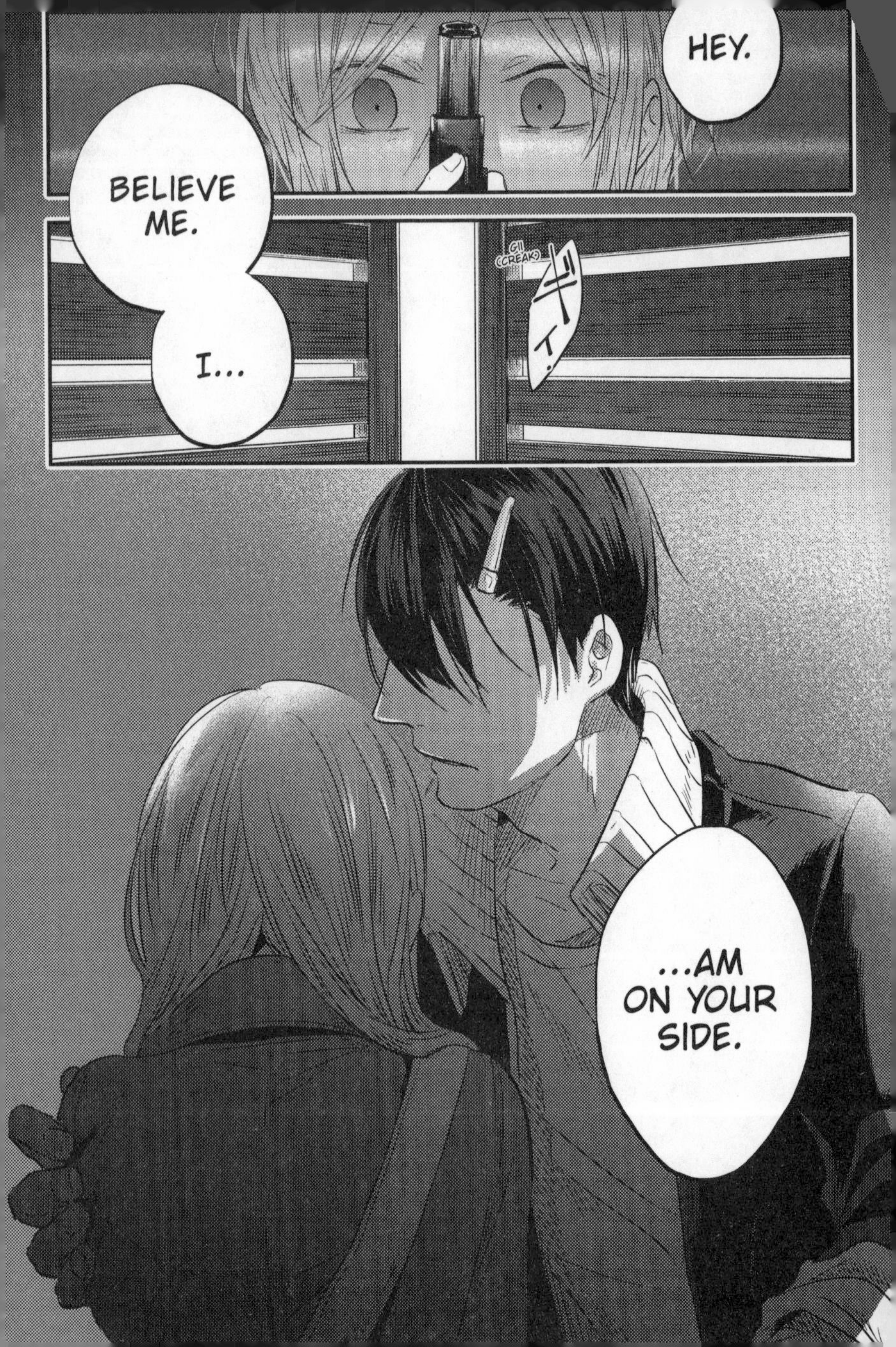
HEY.
BELIEVE ME.
GII (CREAK)
I...
...AM ON YOUR SIDE.

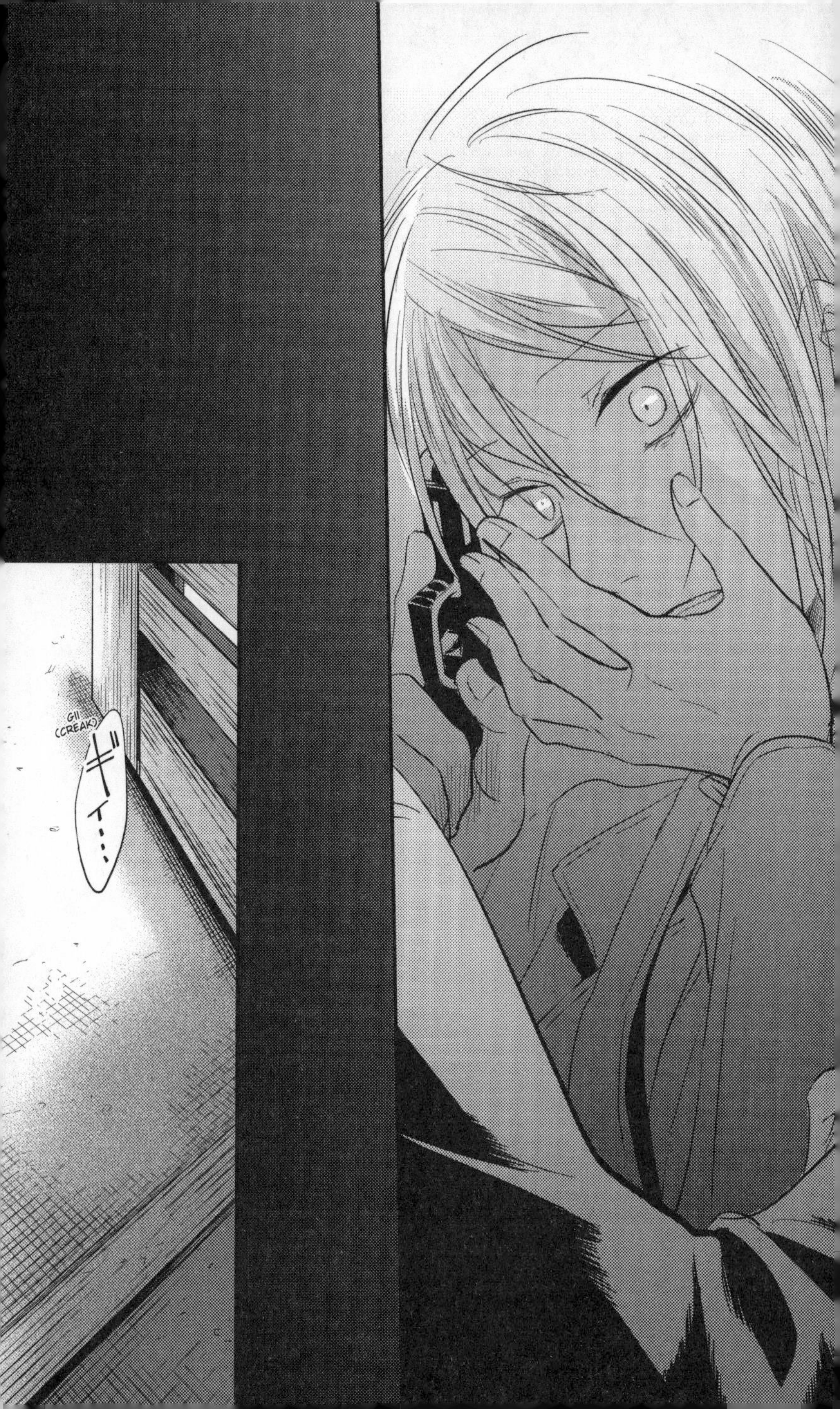
GII (CREAK)
ギィ…

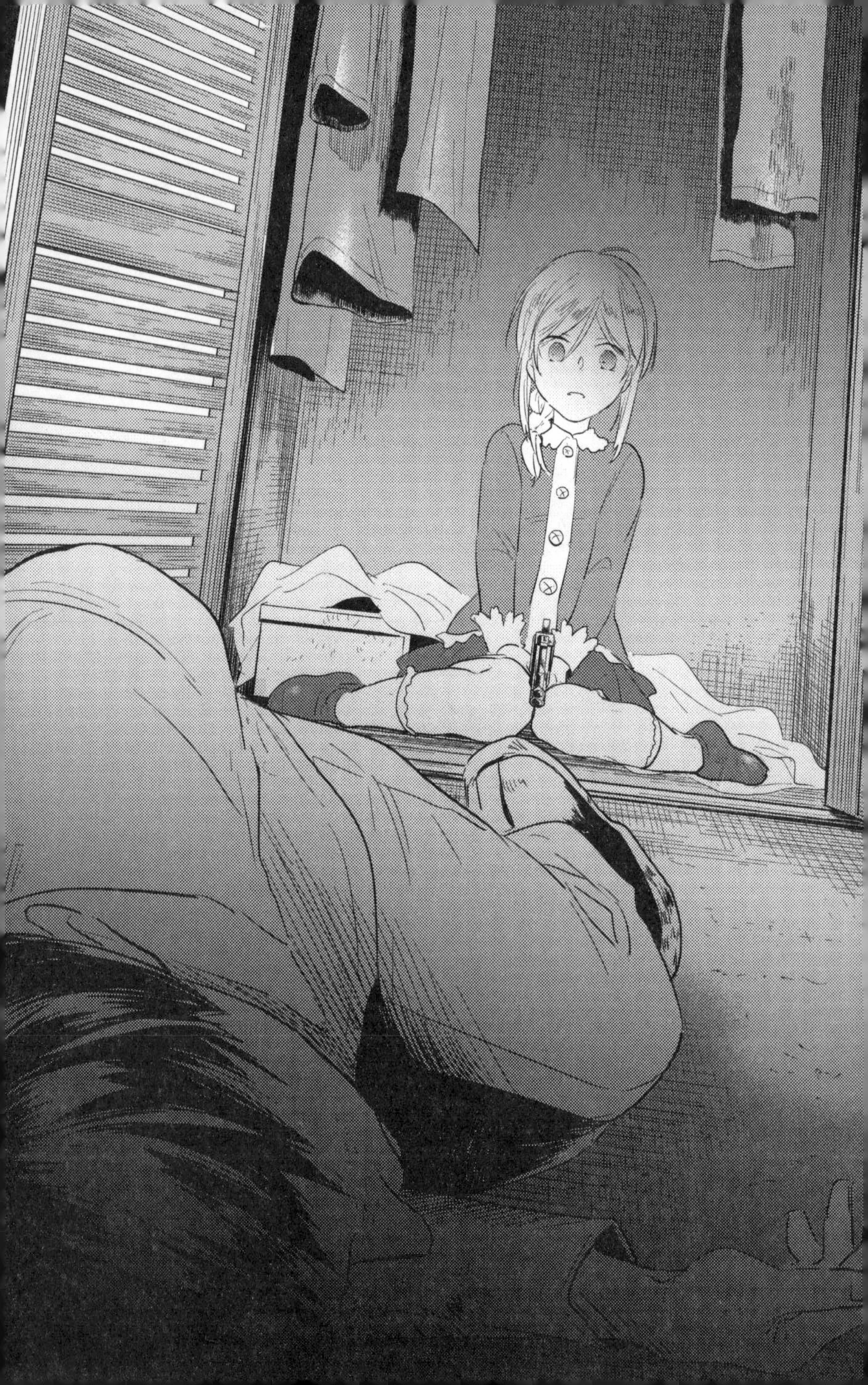

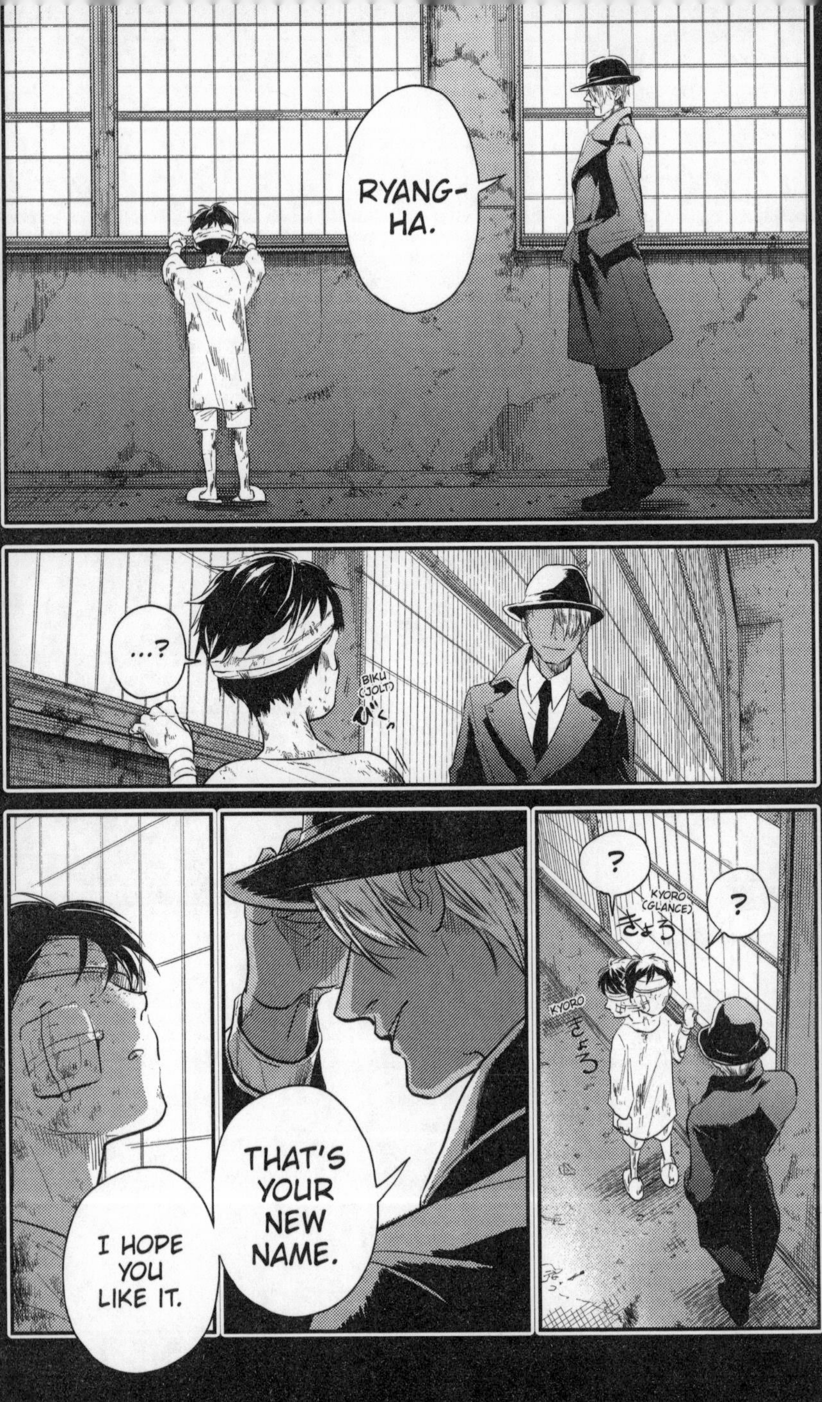
RYANG-HA.
...?
BIKU (JOLT)
びくっ
?
?
KYORO (GLANCE)
きょろ
KYORO
きょろ
THAT'S YOUR NEW NAME.
I HOPE YOU LIKE IT.

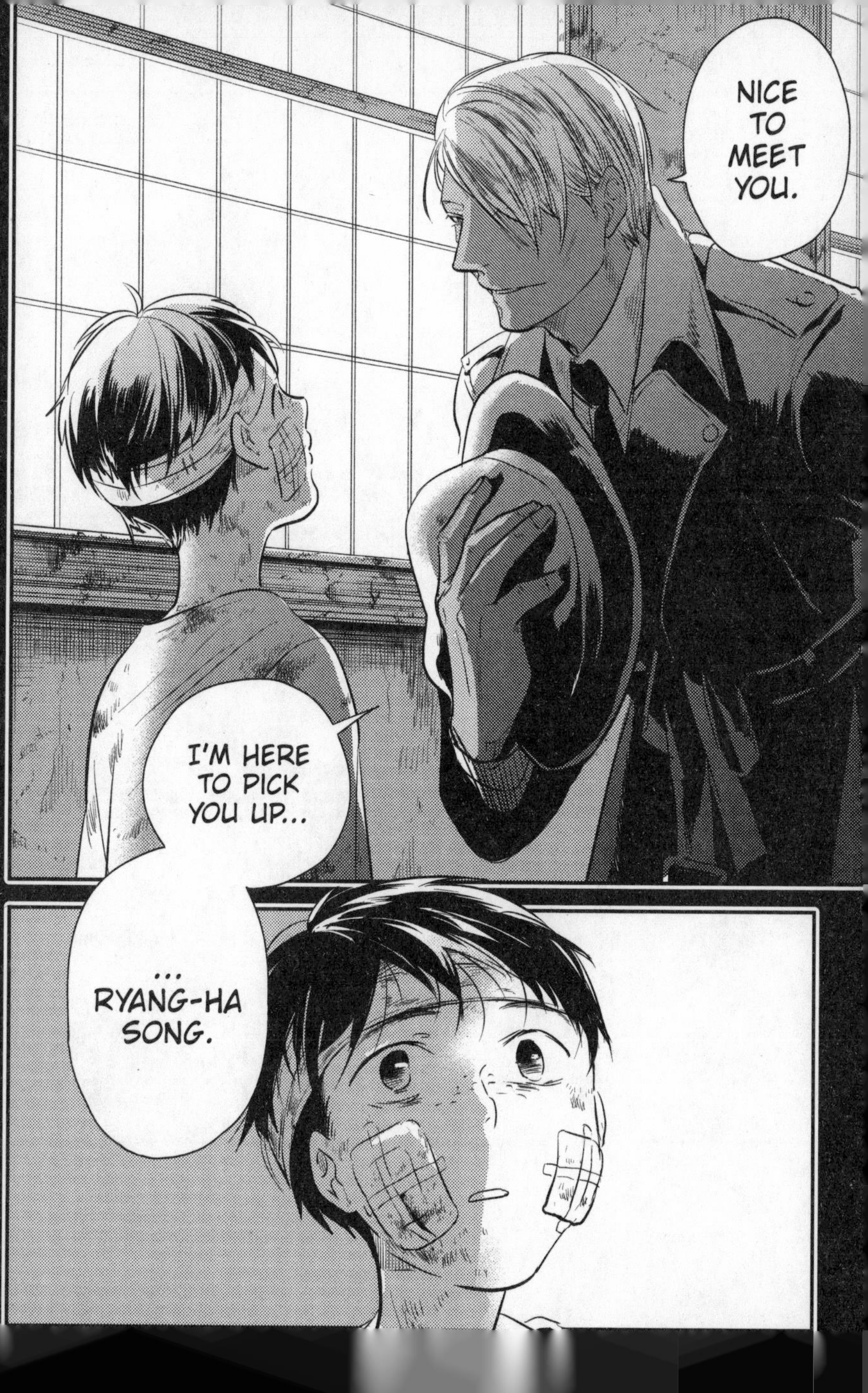
NICE TO MEET YOU.
I'M HERE TO PICK YOU UP...
... RYANG-HA SONG.

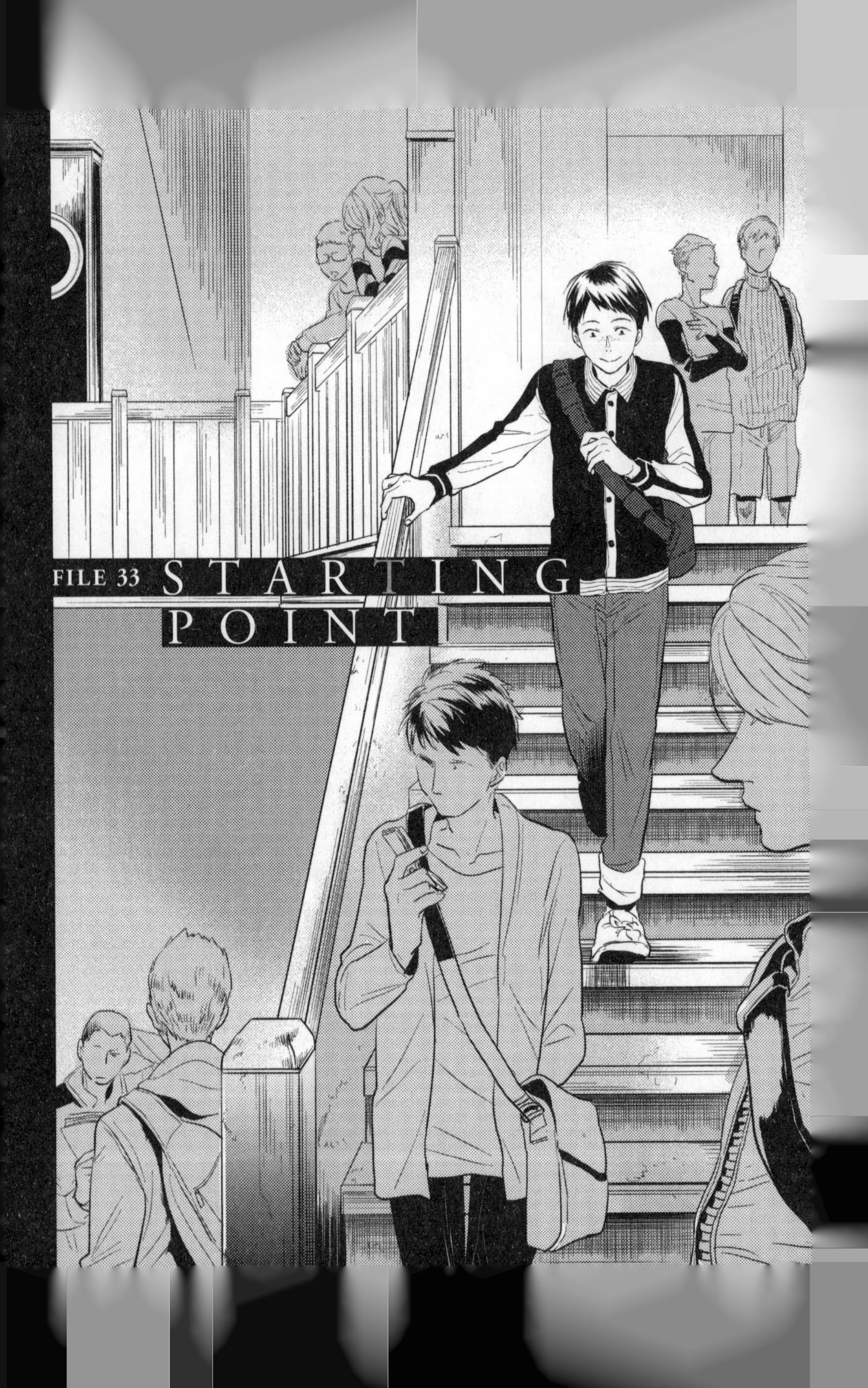
FILE 33
STARTING
POINT

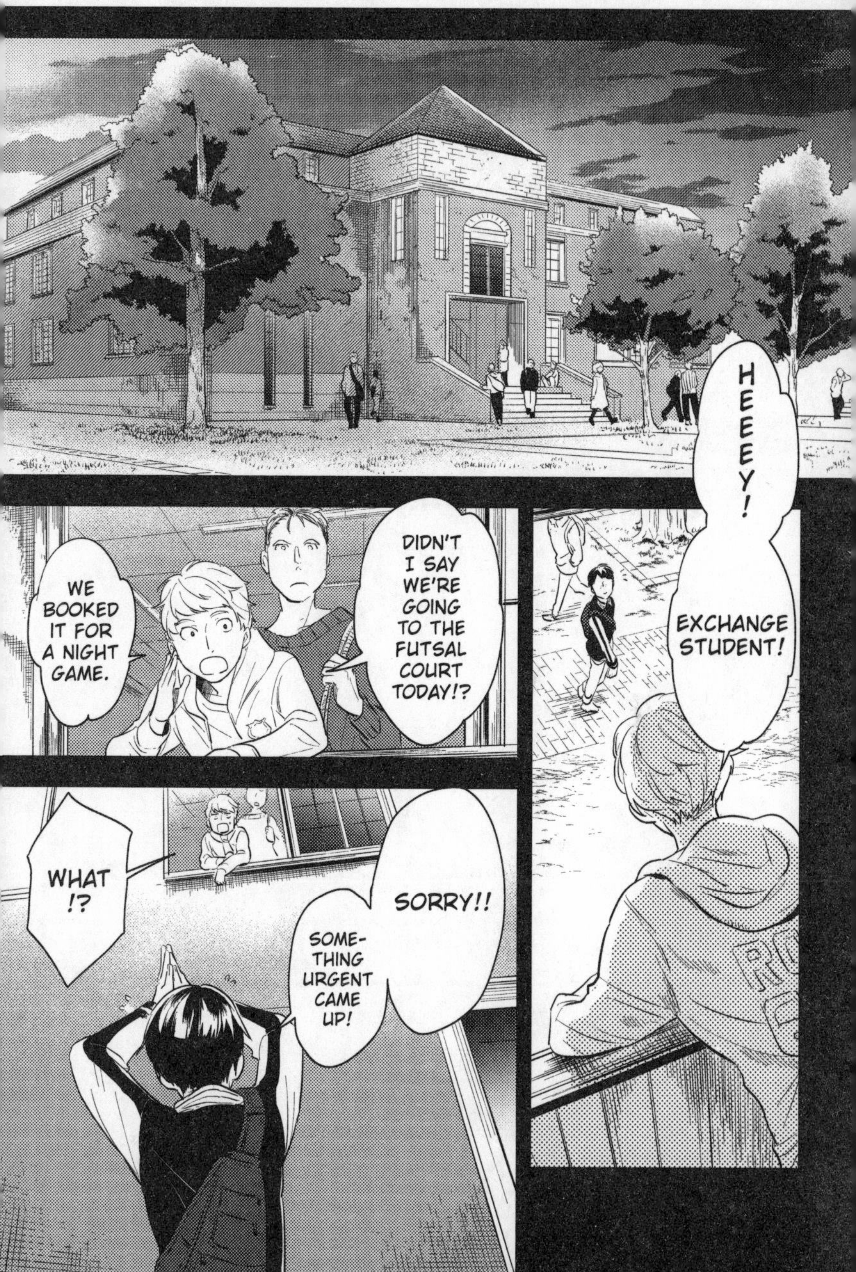
HEEEY!
EXCHANGE STUDENT!
DIDN'T I SAY WE'RE GOING TO THE FUTSAL COURT TODAY!?
WE BOOKED IT FOR A NIGHT GAME.
SORRY!!
SOME-THING URGENT CAME UP!
WHAT!?

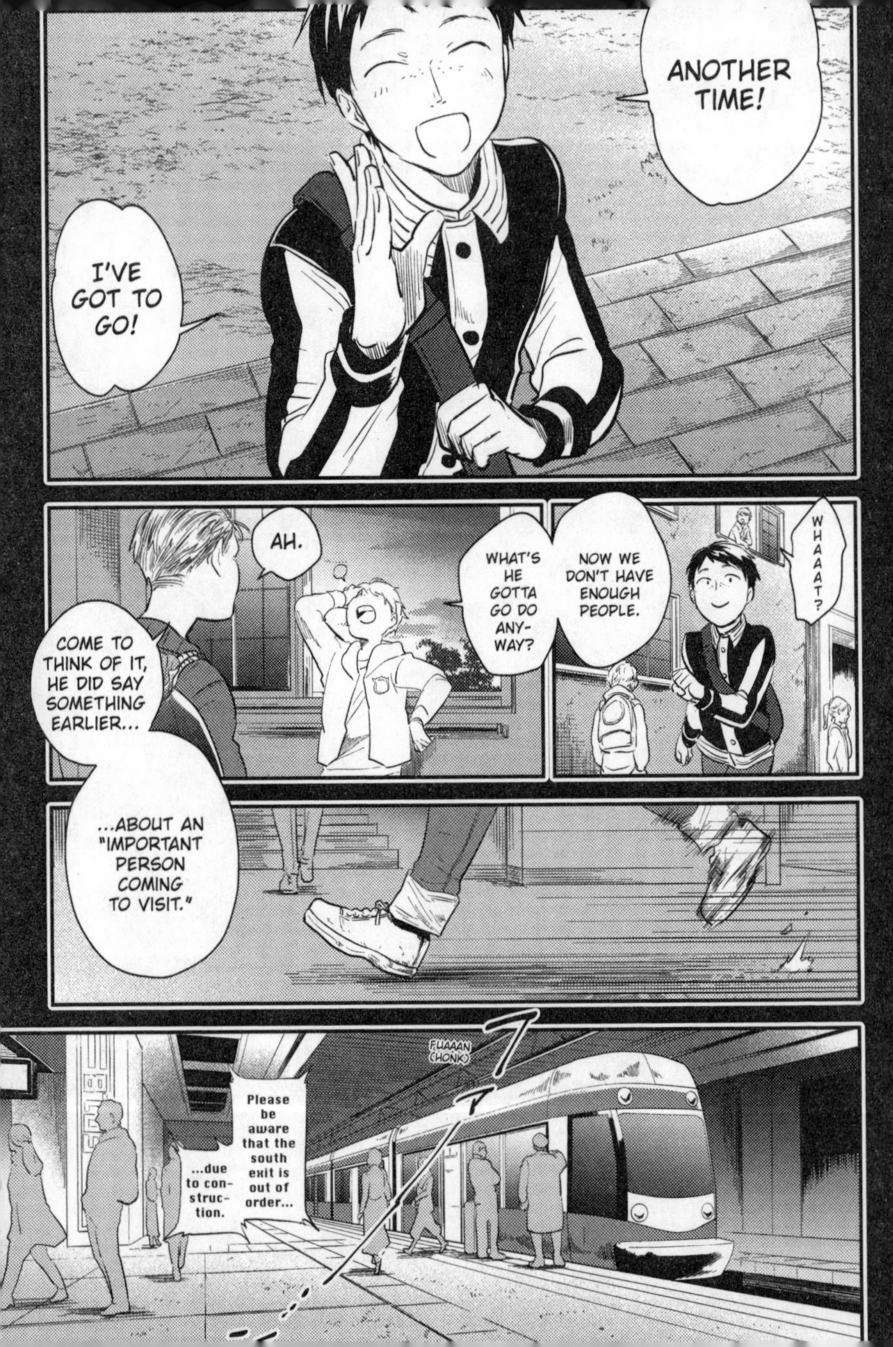
ANOTHER TIME!
I'VE GOT TO GO!
WHAAAAT?
NOW WE DON'T HAVE ENOUGH PEOPLE.
WHAT'S HE GOTTA GO DO ANY-WAY?
AH.
COME TO THINK OF IT, HE DID SAY SOMETHING EARLIER...
...ABOUT AN "IMPORTANT PERSON COMING TO VISIT."
FUAAAN (HONK)
Please be aware that the south exit is out of order...
...due to con-struc-tion.

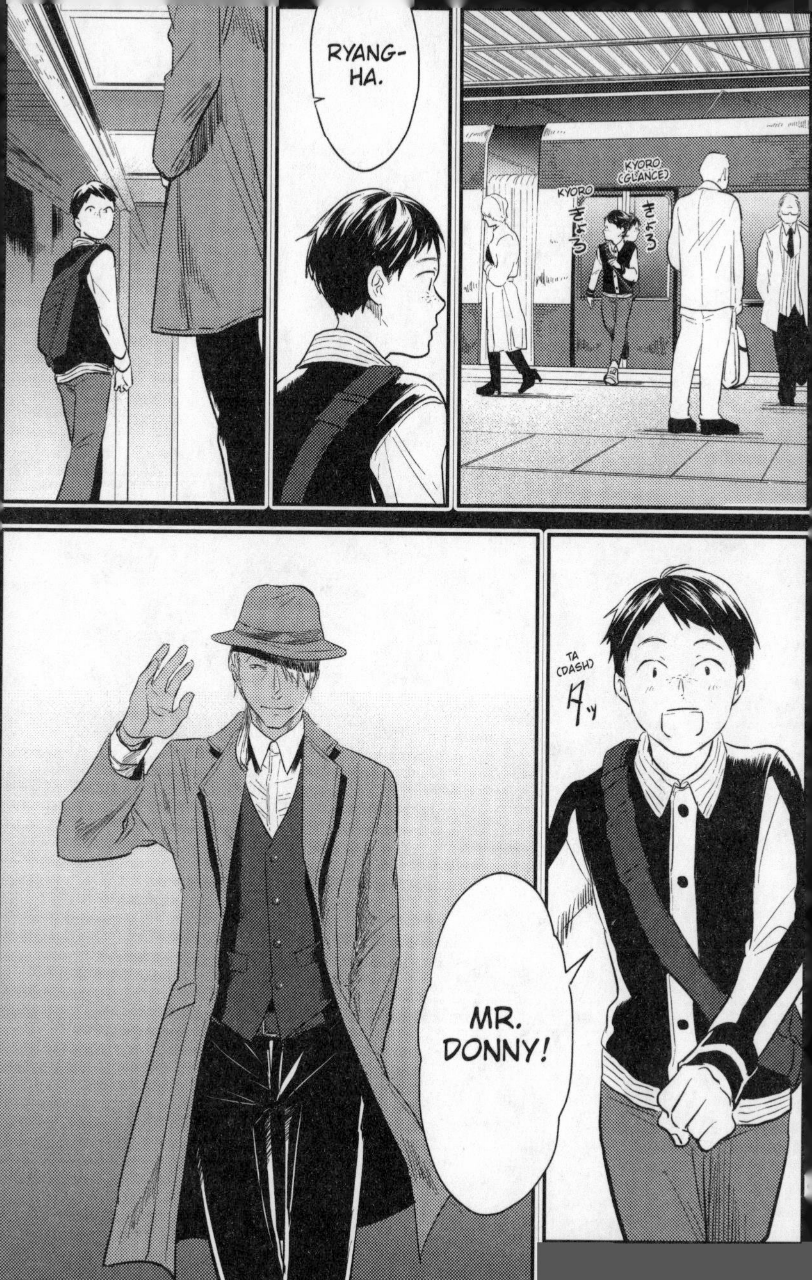
KYORO (GLANCE)
きょろ
KYORO
きょろ
RYANG-HA.
TA (DASH)
タッ
MR. DONNY!

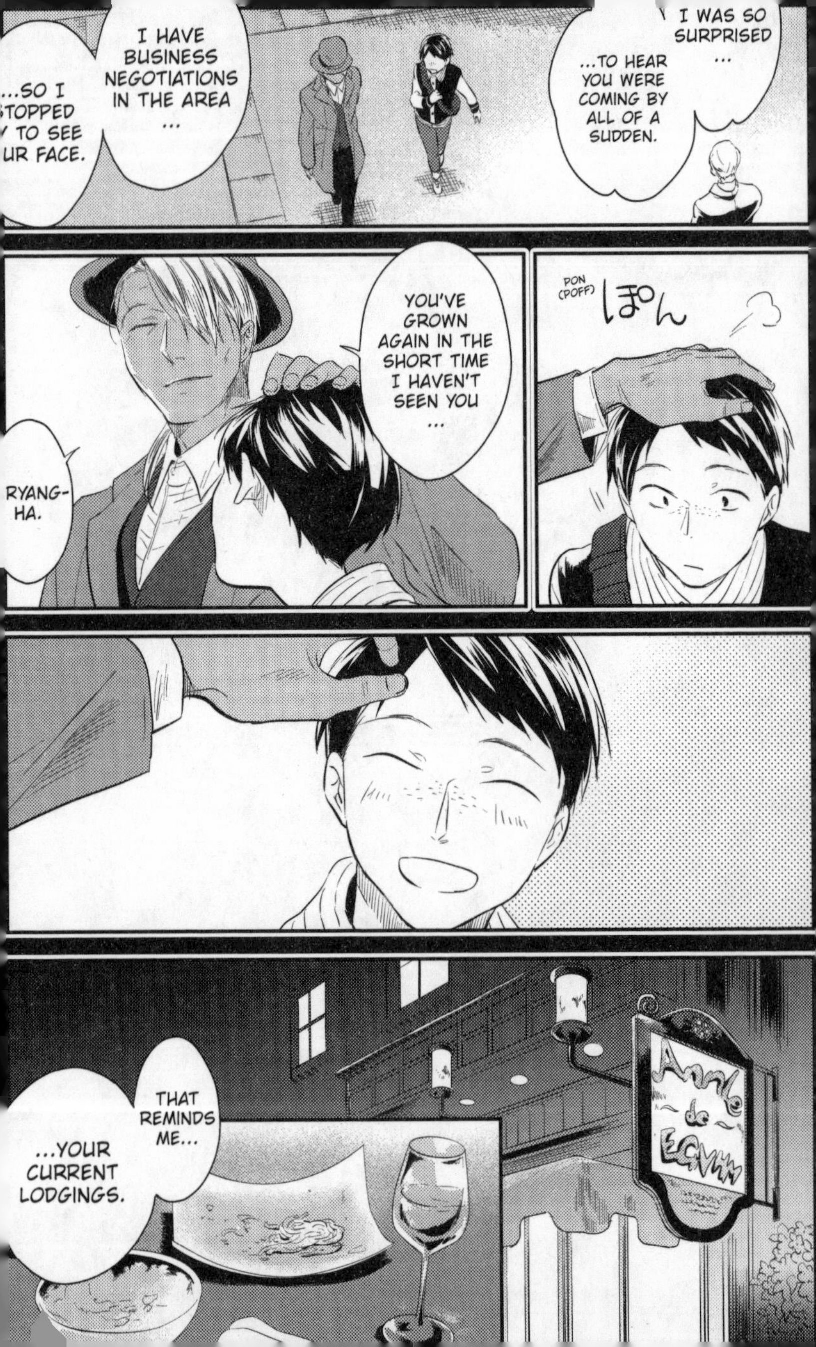
I WAS SO SURPRISED ...
...TO HEAR YOU WERE COMING BY ALL OF A SUDDEN.
I HAVE BUSINESS NEGOTIATIONS IN THE AREA ...
...SO I STOPPED Y TO SEE UR FACE.
PON (POFF)
ぽん
YOU'VE GROWN AGAIN IN THE SHORT TIME I HAVEN'T SEEN YOU ...
RYANG-HA.
THAT REMINDS ME...
...YOUR CURRENT LODGINGS.

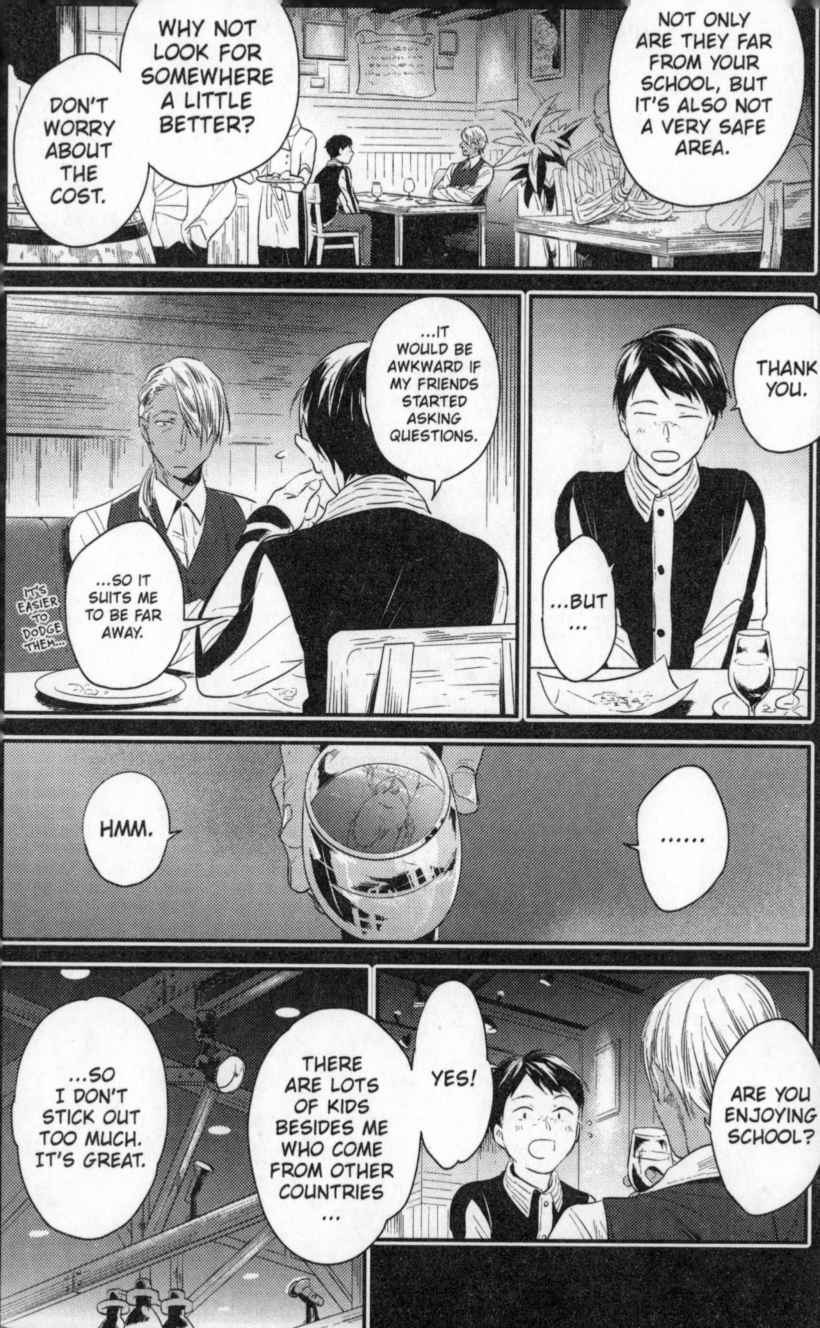
NOT ONLY ARE THEY FAR FROM YOUR SCHOOL, BUT IT'S ALSO NOT A VERY SAFE AREA.
WHY NOT LOOK FOR SOMEWHERE A LITTLE BETTER?
DON'T WORRY ABOUT THE COST.
THANK YOU.
...BUT ...
...IT WOULD BE AWKWARD IF MY FRIENDS STARTED ASKING QUESTIONS.
...SO IT SUITS ME TO BE FAR AWAY.
IT'S EASIER TO DODGE THEM...
......
HMM.
ARE YOU ENJOYING SCHOOL?
YES!
THERE ARE LOTS OF KIDS BESIDES ME WHO COME FROM OTHER COUNTRIES ...
...SO I DON'T STICK OUT TOO MUCH. IT'S GREAT.

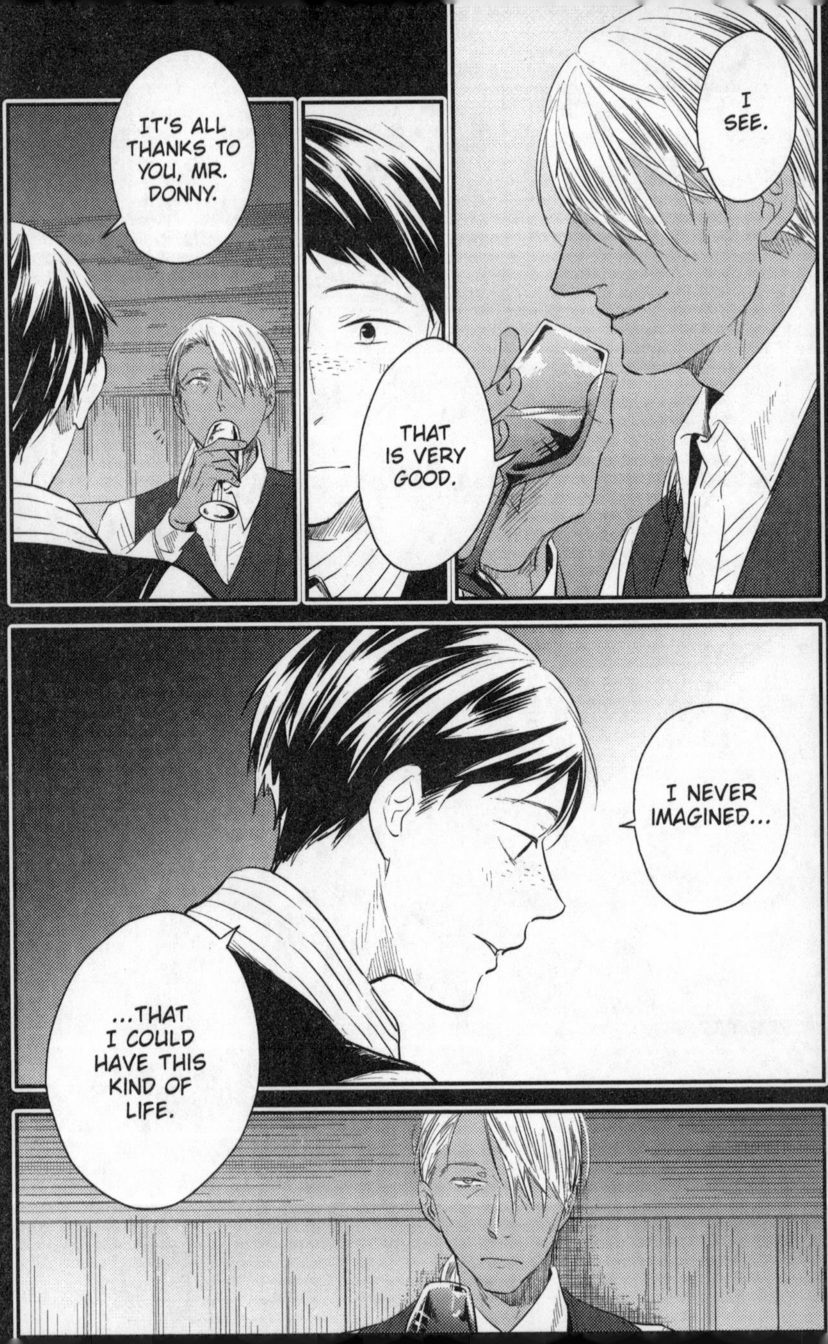
I SEE.
THAT IS VERY GOOD.
IT'S ALL THANKS TO YOU, MR. DONNY.
I NEVER IMAGINED...
...THAT I COULD HAVE THIS KIND OF LIFE.

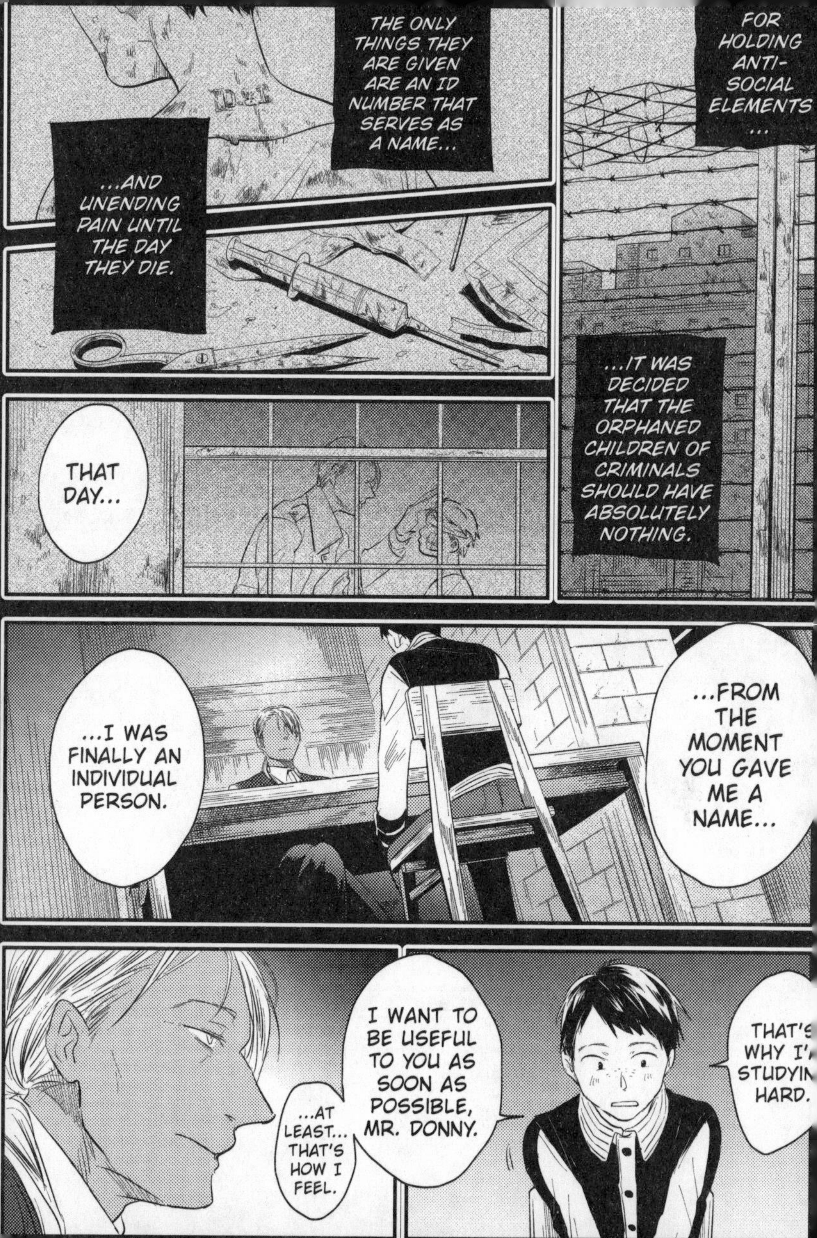
FOR HOLDING ANTI-SOCIAL ELEMENTS...
...IT WAS DECIDED THAT THE ORPHANED CHILDREN OF CRIMINALS SHOULD HAVE ABSOLUTELY NOTHING.
THE ONLY THINGS THEY ARE GIVEN ARE AN ID NUMBER THAT SERVES AS A NAME...
...AND UNENDING PAIN UNTIL THE DAY THEY DIE.
THAT DAY...
...FROM THE MOMENT YOU GAVE ME A NAME...
...I WAS FINALLY AN INDIVIDUAL PERSON.
THAT'S WHY I' STUDYIN HARD.
I WANT TO BE USEFUL TO YOU AS SOON AS POSSIBLE, MR. DONNY.
...AT LEAST... THAT'S HOW I FEEL.

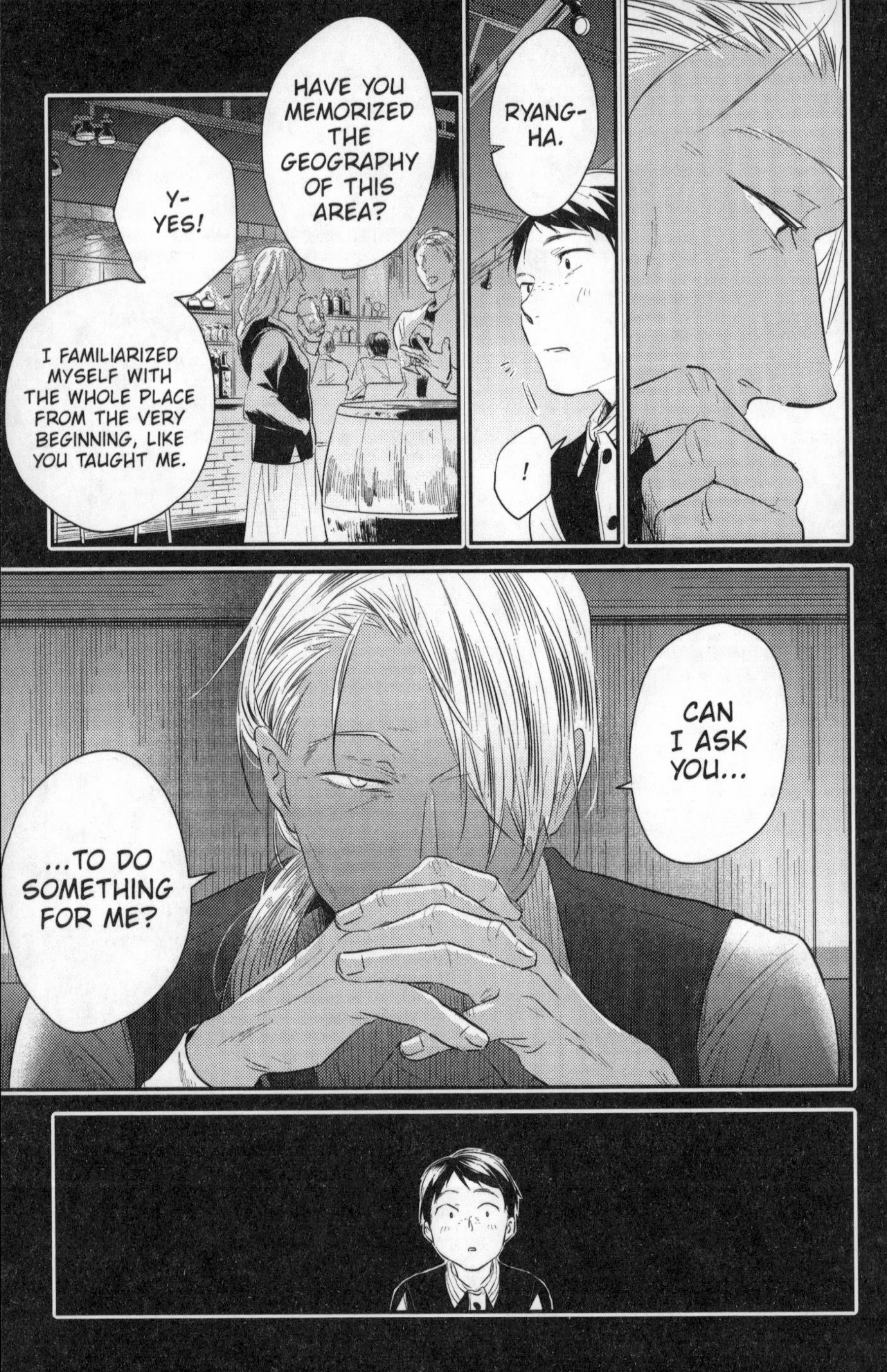
RYANG-HA.
!
HAVE YOU MEMORIZED THE GEOGRAPHY OF THIS AREA?
Y-YES!
I FAMILIARIZED MYSELF WITH THE WHOLE PLACE FROM THE VERY BEGINNING, LIKE YOU TAUGHT ME.
CAN I ASK YOU...
...TO DO SOMETHING FOR ME?

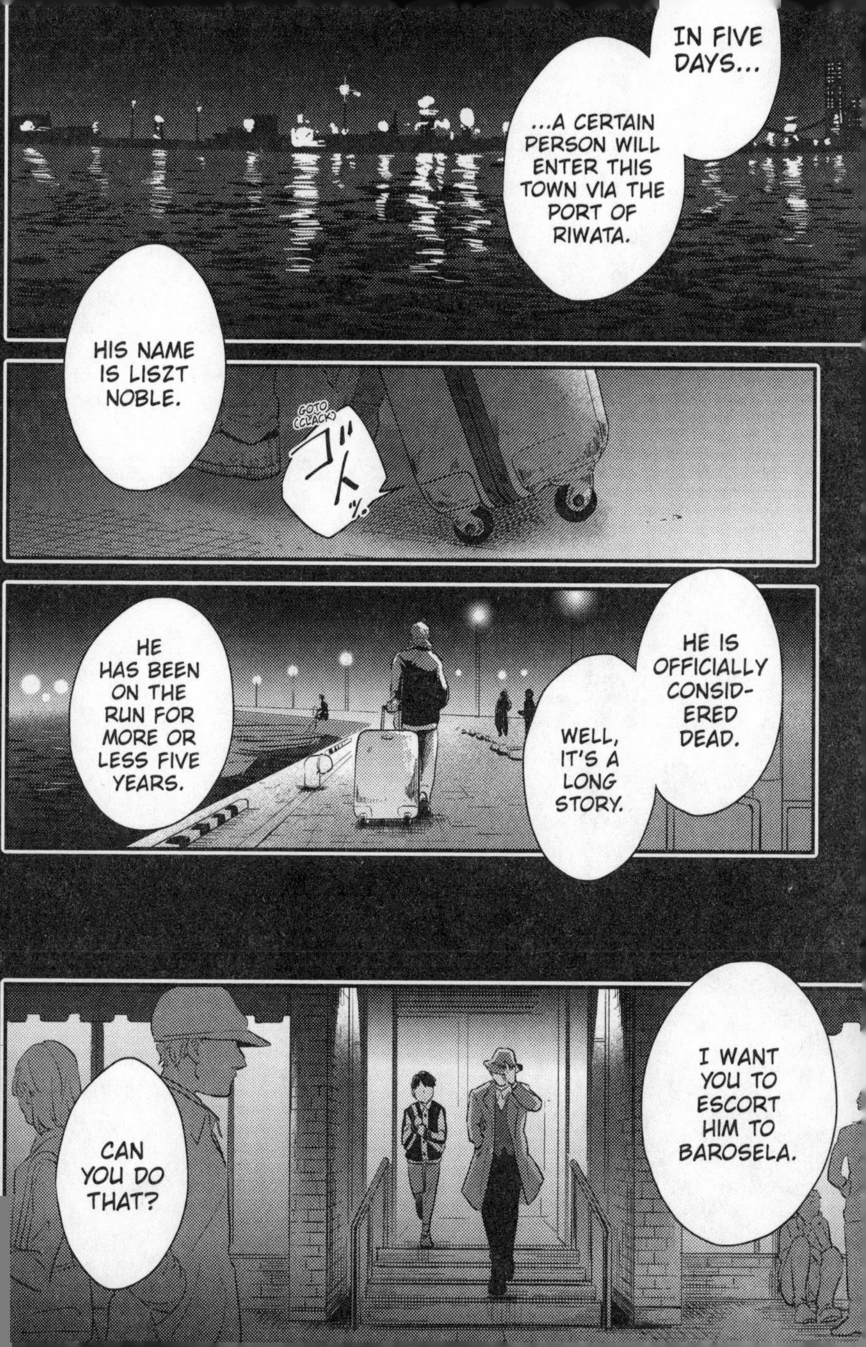
IN FIVE DAYS...
...A CERTAIN PERSON WILL ENTER THIS TOWN VIA THE PORT OF RIWATA.
HIS NAME IS LISZT NOBLE.
GOTO (CLACK)
ゴトッ
HE IS OFFICIALLY CONSID-ERED DEAD.
WELL, IT'S A LONG STORY.
HE HAS BEEN ON THE RUN FOR MORE OR LESS FIVE YEARS.
I WANT YOU TO ESCORT HIM TO BAROSELA.
CAN YOU DO THAT?

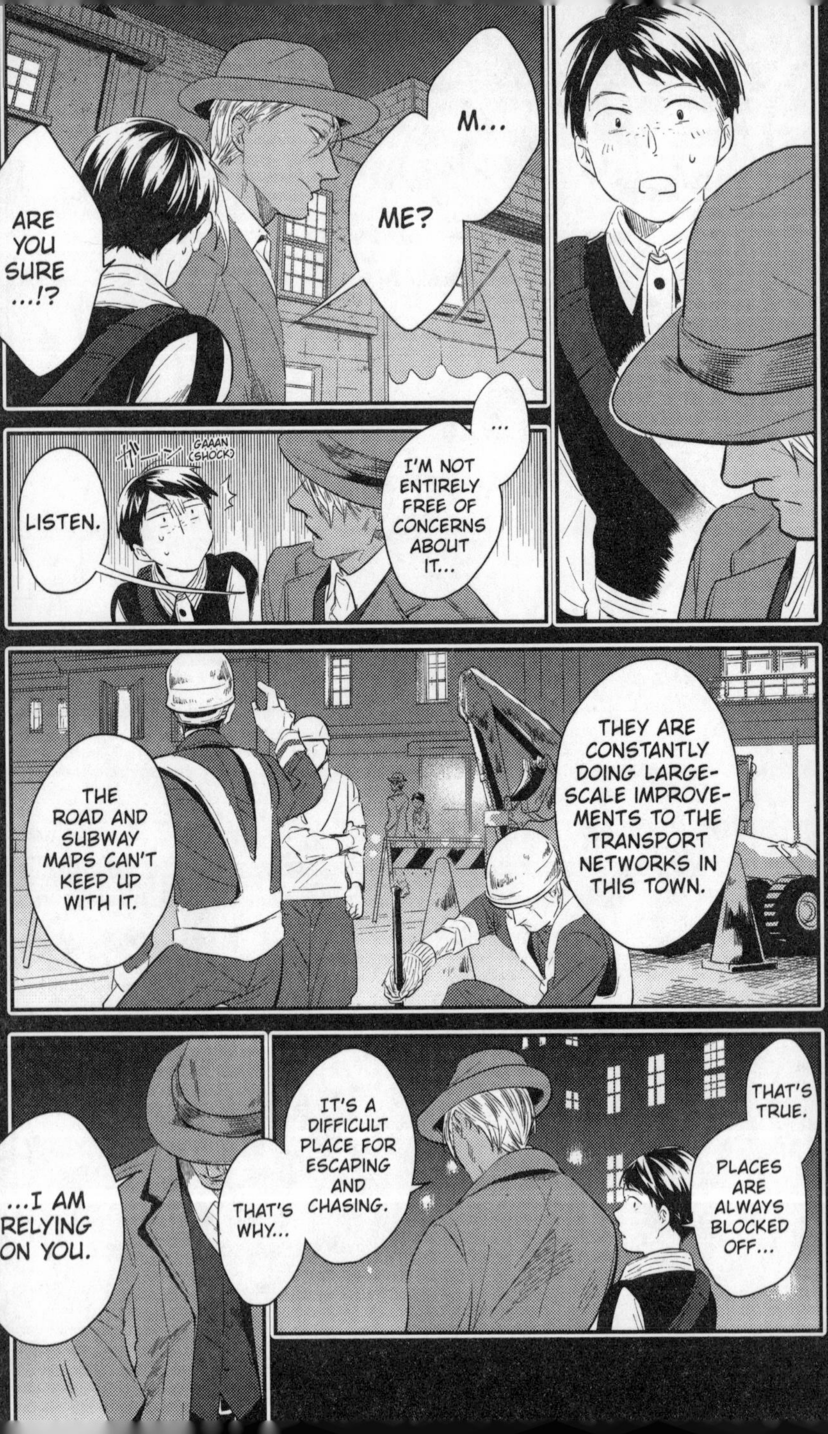
...
M...
ME?
ARE YOU SURE ...!?
I'M NOT ENTIRELY FREE OF CONCERNS ABOUT IT...
ガーン
GAAAN (SHOCK)
LISTEN.
THEY ARE CONSTANTLY DOING LARGE-SCALE IMPROVEMENTS TO THE TRANSPORT NETWORKS IN THIS TOWN.
THE ROAD AND SUBWAY MAPS CAN'T KEEP UP WITH IT.
THAT'S TRUE.
PLACES ARE ALWAYS BLOCKED OFF...
IT'S A DIFFICULT PLACE FOR ESCAPING AND CHASING.
THAT'S WHY...
...I AM RELYING ON YOU.

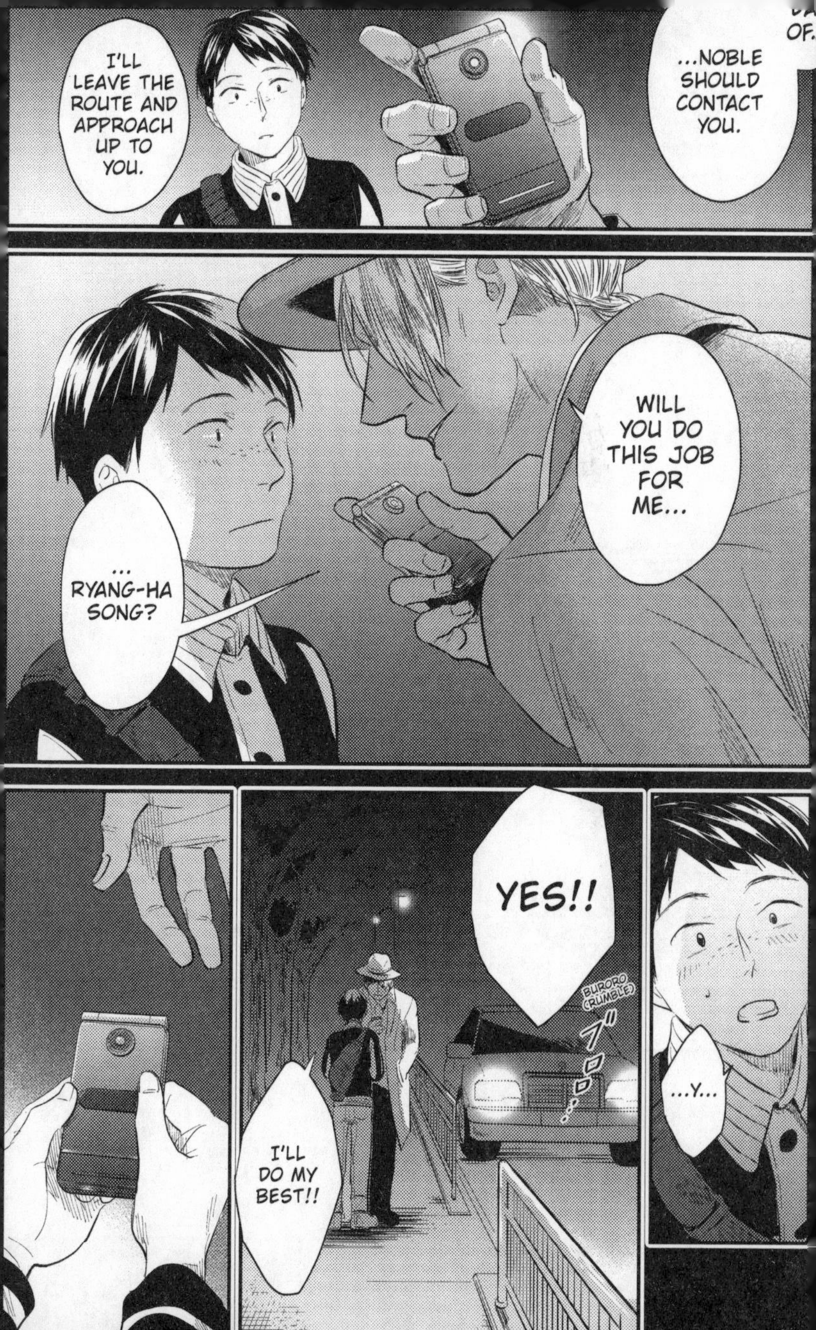
...NOBLE SHOULD CONTACT YOU.
I'LL LEAVE THE ROUTE AND APPROACH UP TO YOU.
WILL YOU DO THIS JOB FOR ME...
... RYANG-HA SONG?
...Y...
YES!!
BURORO (RUMBLE)
I'LL DO MY BEST!!

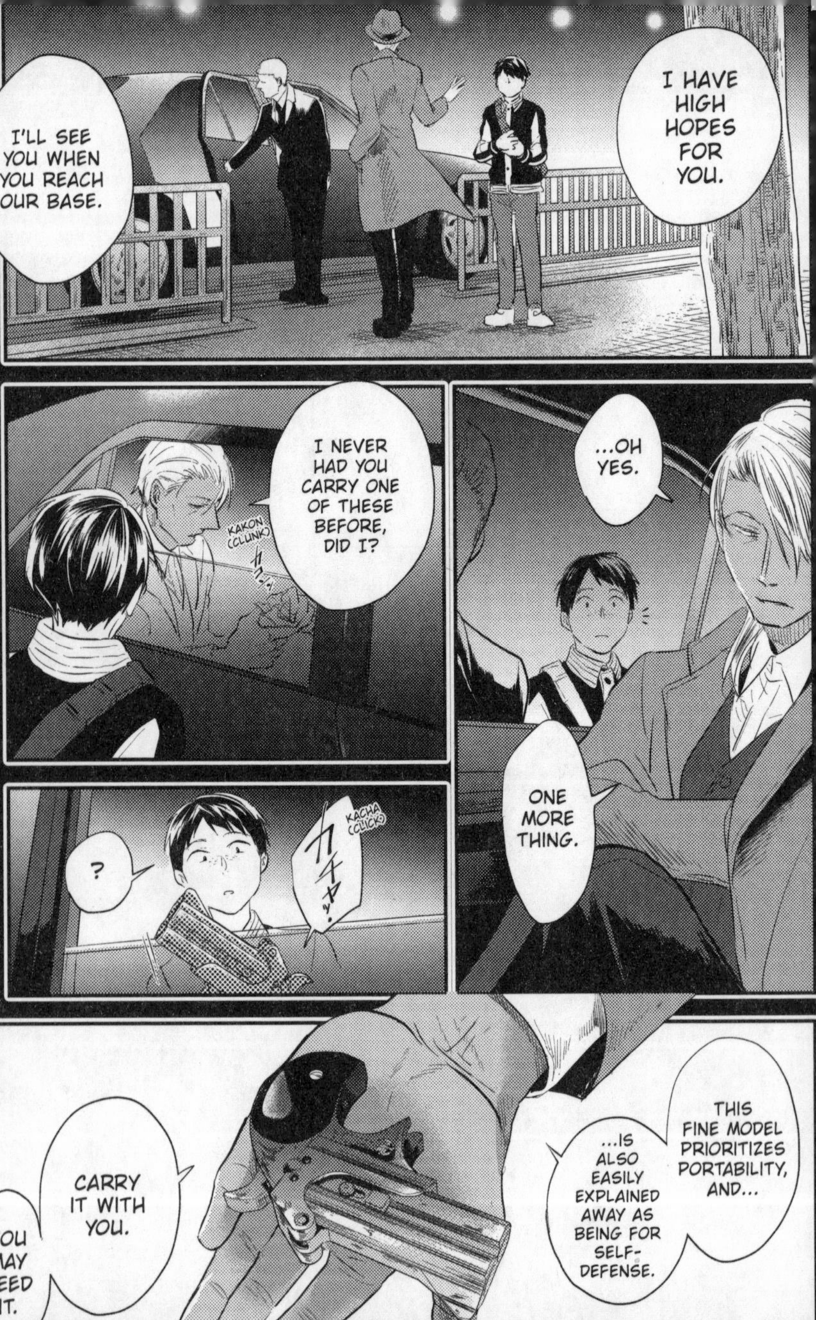
I HAVE HIGH HOPES FOR YOU.
I'LL SEE YOU WHEN YOU REACH OUR BASE.
...OH YES.
ONE MORE THING.
I NEVER HAD YOU CARRY ONE OF THESE BEFORE, DID I?
KAKON (CLUNK)
KACHA (CLICK)
?
THIS FINE MODEL PRIORITIZES PORTABILITY, AND...
...IS ALSO EASILY EXPLAINED AWAY AS BEING FOR SELF-DEFENSE.
CARRY IT WITH YOU.
YOU MAY NEED IT.

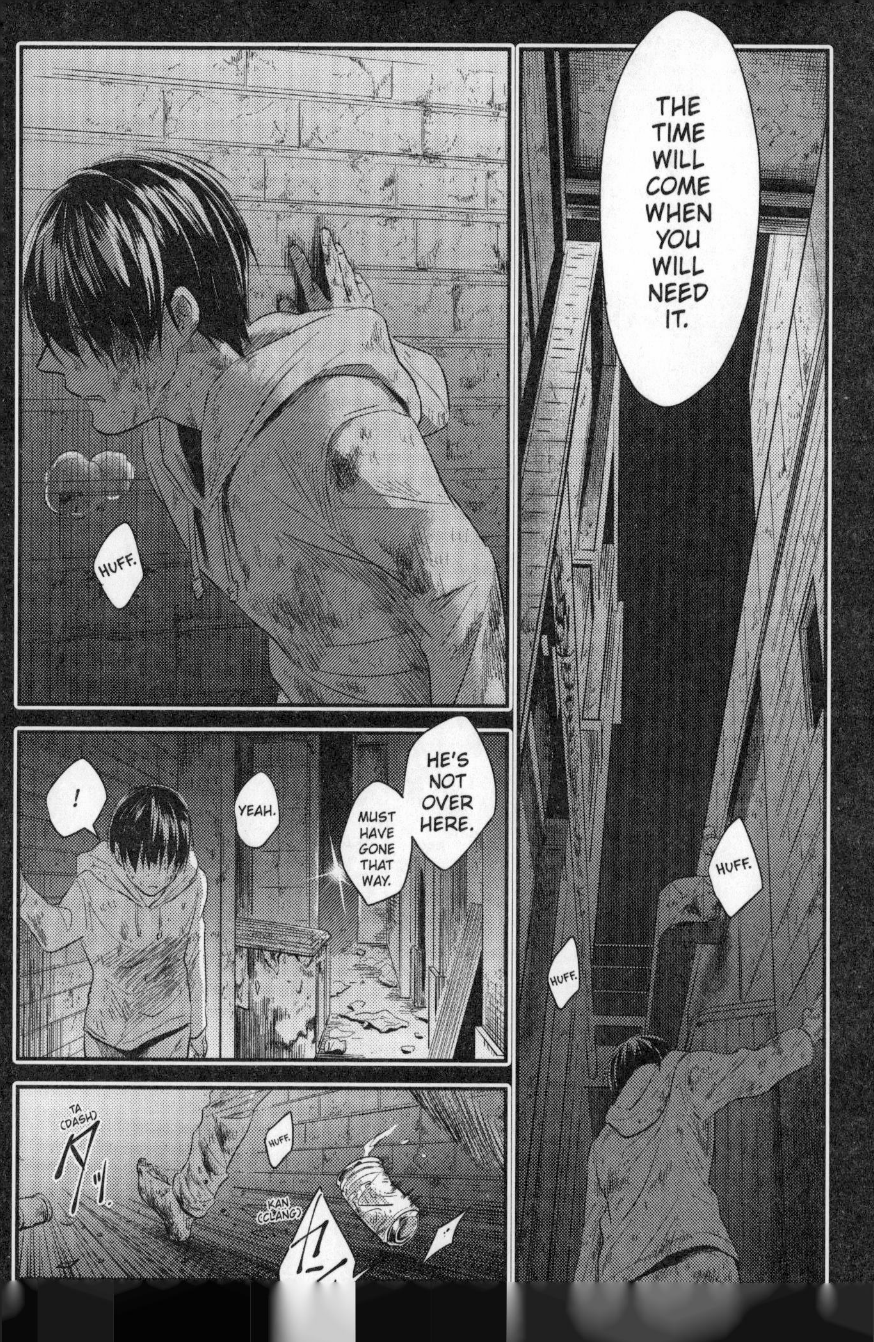
THE TIME WILL COME WHEN YOU WILL NEED IT.
HUFF.
HUFF.
HUFF.
HE'S NOT OVER HERE.
MUST HAVE GONE THAT WAY.
YEAH.
!
TA (DASH)
HUFF.
KAN (CLANG)

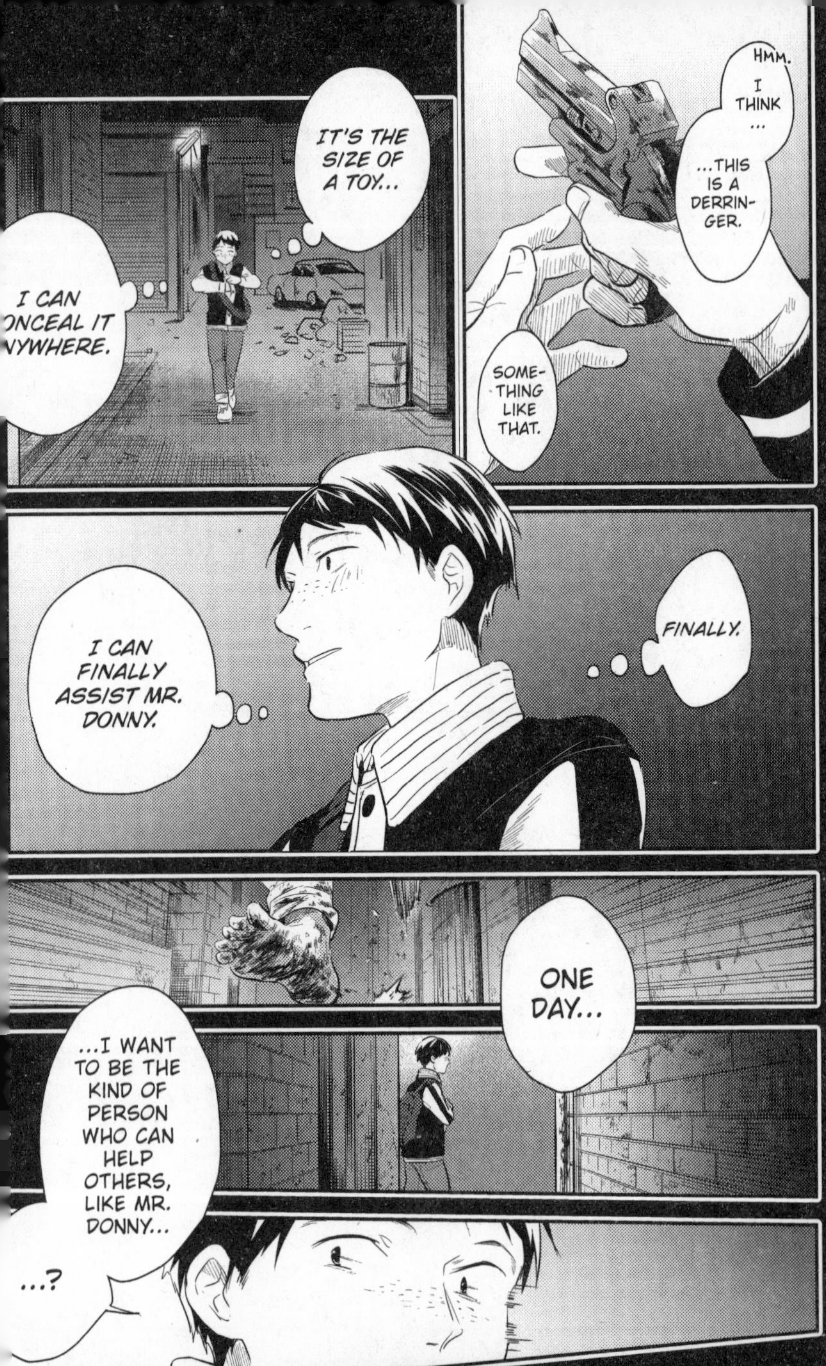
HMM.
I THINK ...
...THIS IS A DERRIN-GER.
SOME-THING LIKE THAT.
IT'S THE SIZE OF A TOY...
I CAN ONCEAL IT NYWHERE.
FINALLY.
I CAN FINALLY ASSIST MR. DONNY.
ONE DAY...
...I WANT TO BE THE KIND OF PERSON WHO CAN HELP OTHERS, LIKE MR. DONNY...
...?

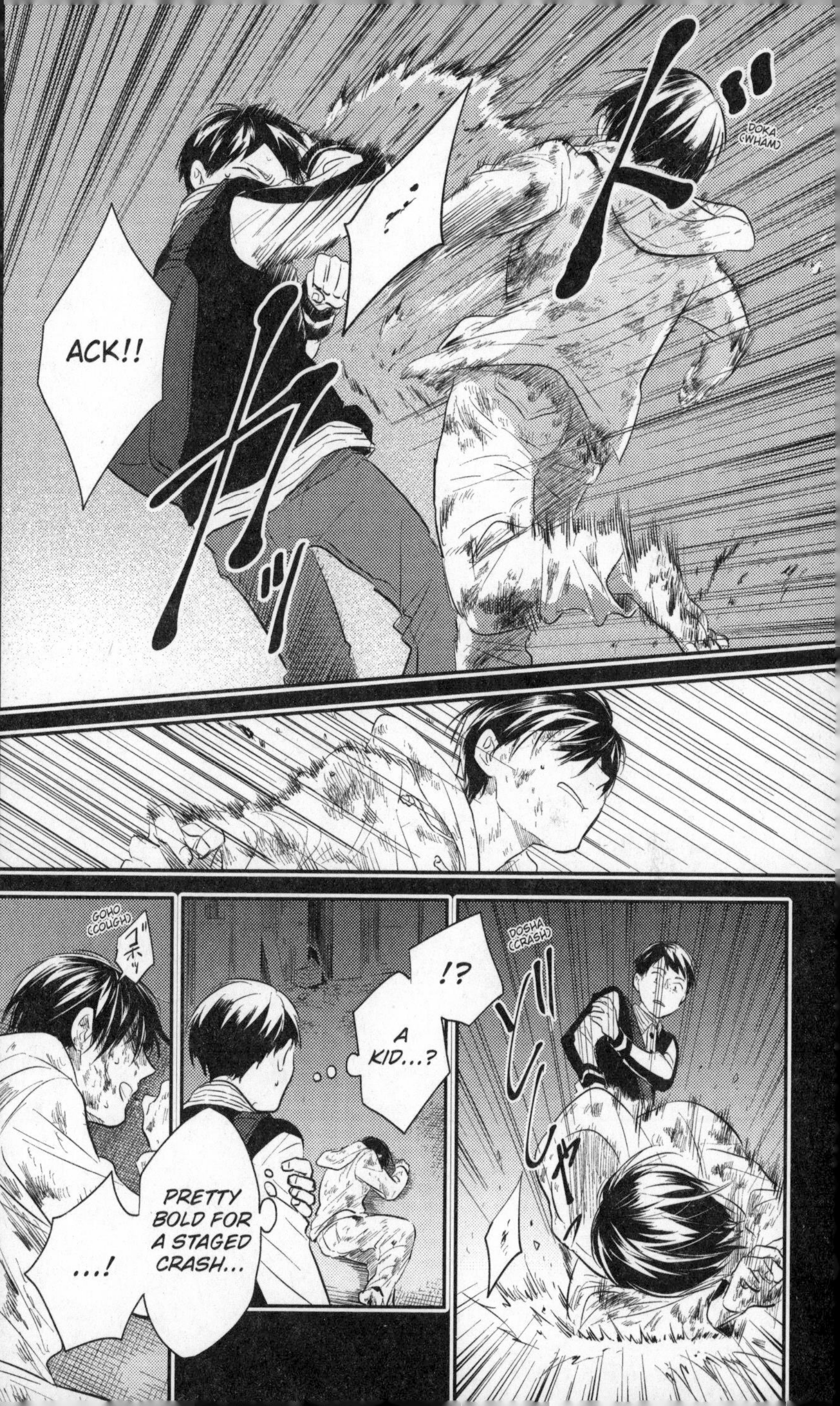
DOKA (WHAM)
...
ACK!!
DOSHA (CRASH)
!?
A KID...?
PRETTY BOLD FOR A STAGED CRASH...
GOHO (COUGH)
...!

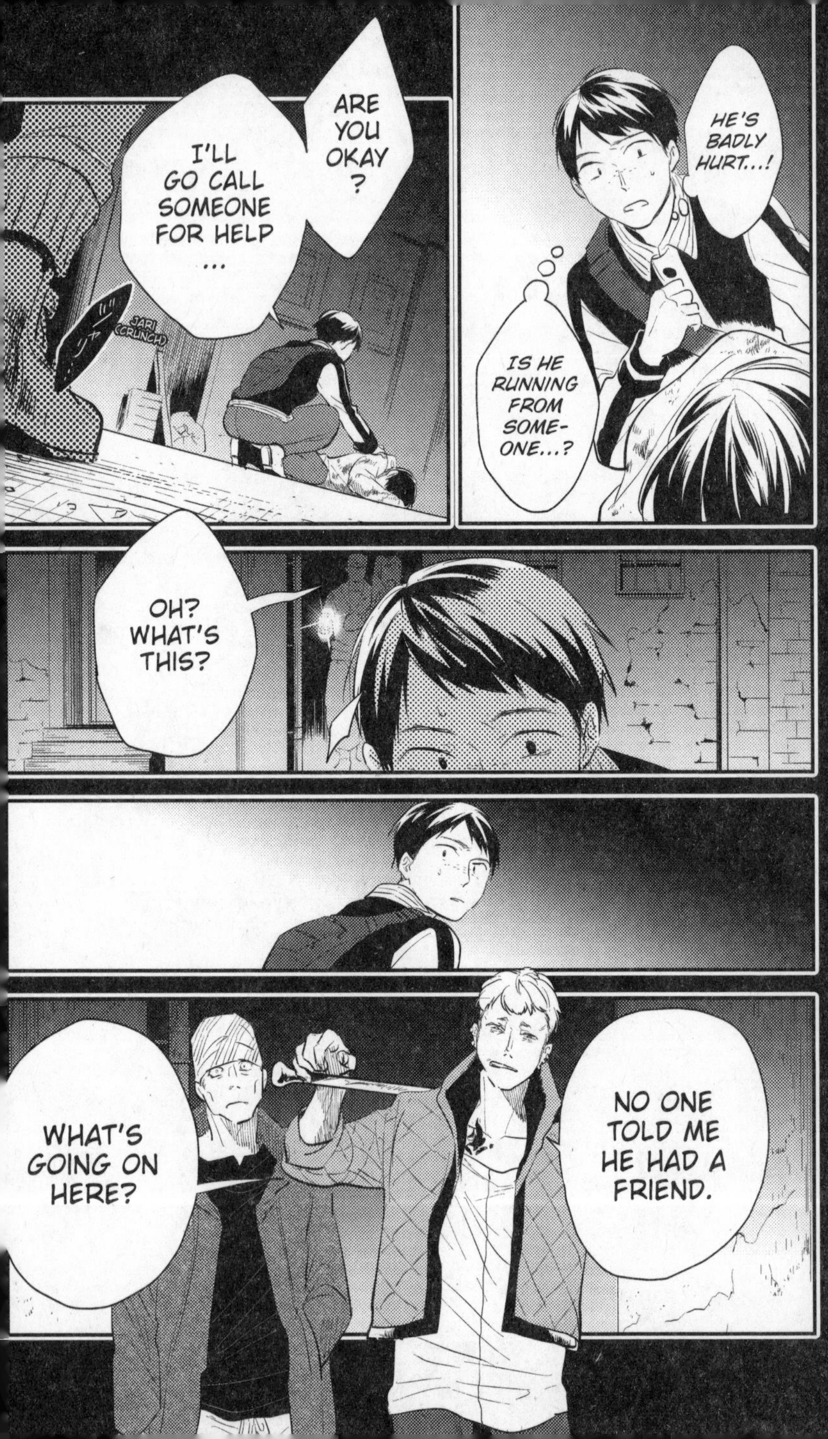
HE'S BADLY HURT...!
IS HE RUNNING FROM SOME-ONE...?
ARE YOU OKAY?
I'LL GO CALL SOMEONE FOR HELP...
JARI (CRUNCH)
OH? WHAT'S THIS?
NO ONE TOLD ME HE HAD A FRIEND.
WHAT'S GOING ON HERE?

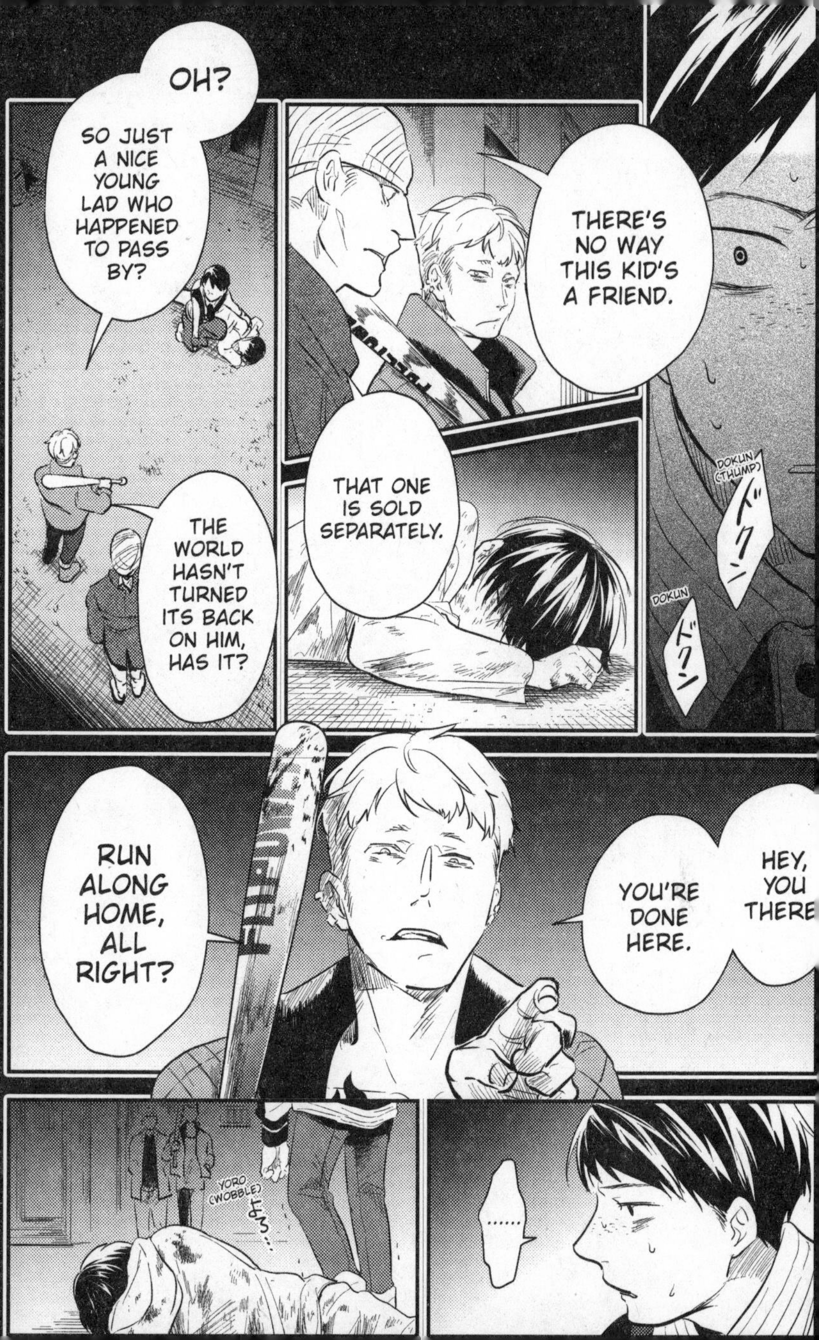
DOKUN (THUMP)
ドクン
DOKUN
ドクン
THERE'S NO WAY THIS KID'S A FRIEND.
THAT ONE IS SOLD SEPARATELY.
OH?
SO JUST A NICE YOUNG LAD WHO HAPPENED TO PASS BY?
THE WORLD HASN'T TURNED ITS BACK ON HIM, HAS IT?
HEY, YOU THERE
YOU'RE DONE HERE.
RUN ALONG HOME, ALL RIGHT?
……
YORO (WOBBLE)
よろ…

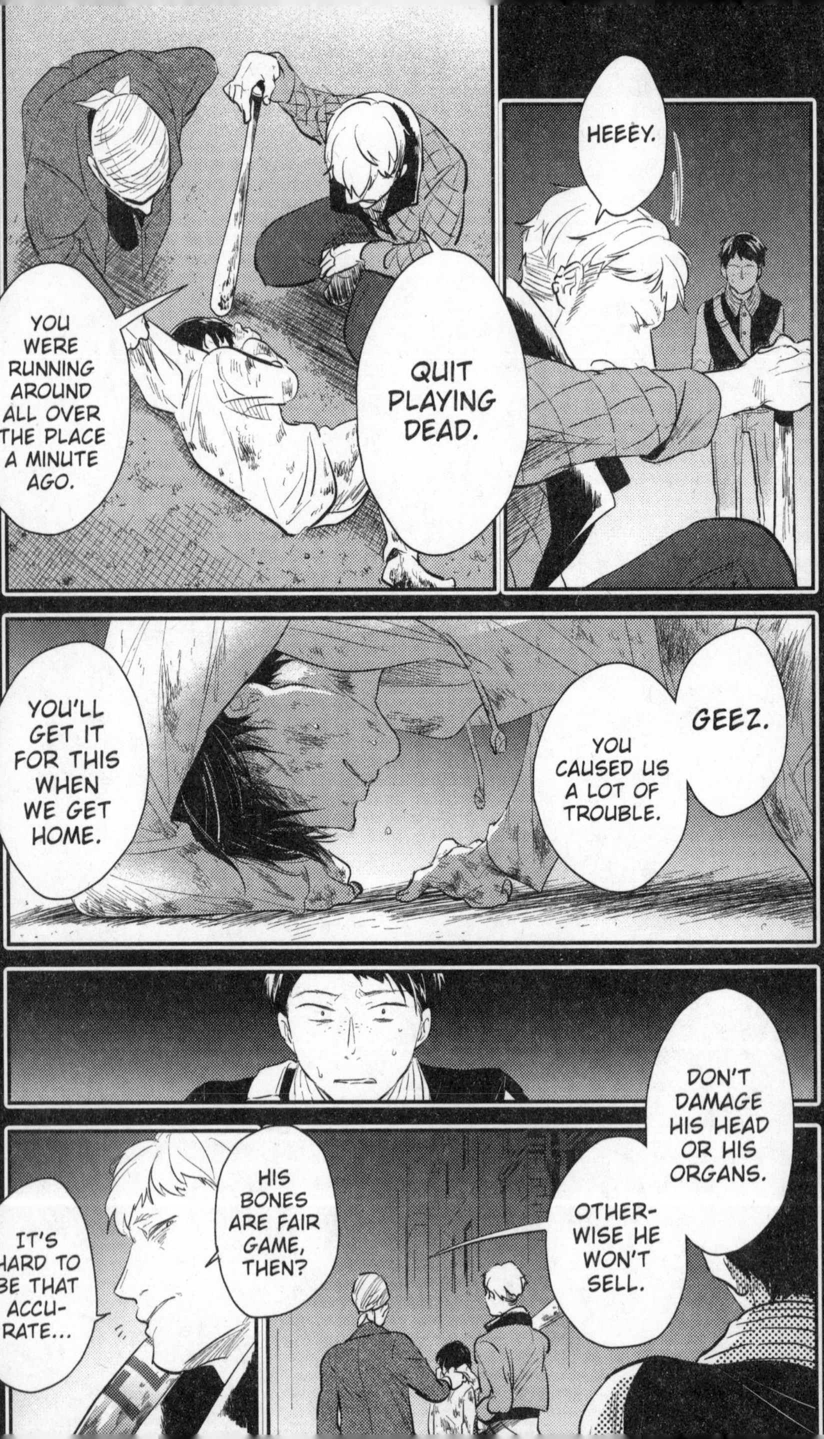
HEEEY.
QUIT PLAYING DEAD.
YOU WERE RUNNING AROUND ALL OVER THE PLACE A MINUTE AGO.
GEEZ.
YOU CAUSED US A LOT OF TROUBLE.
YOU'LL GET IT FOR THIS WHEN WE GET HOME.
DON'T DAMAGE HIS HEAD OR HIS ORGANS.
OTHER-WISE HE WON'T SELL.
HIS BONES ARE FAIR GAME, THEN?
IT'S HARD TO BE THAT ACCU-RATE...

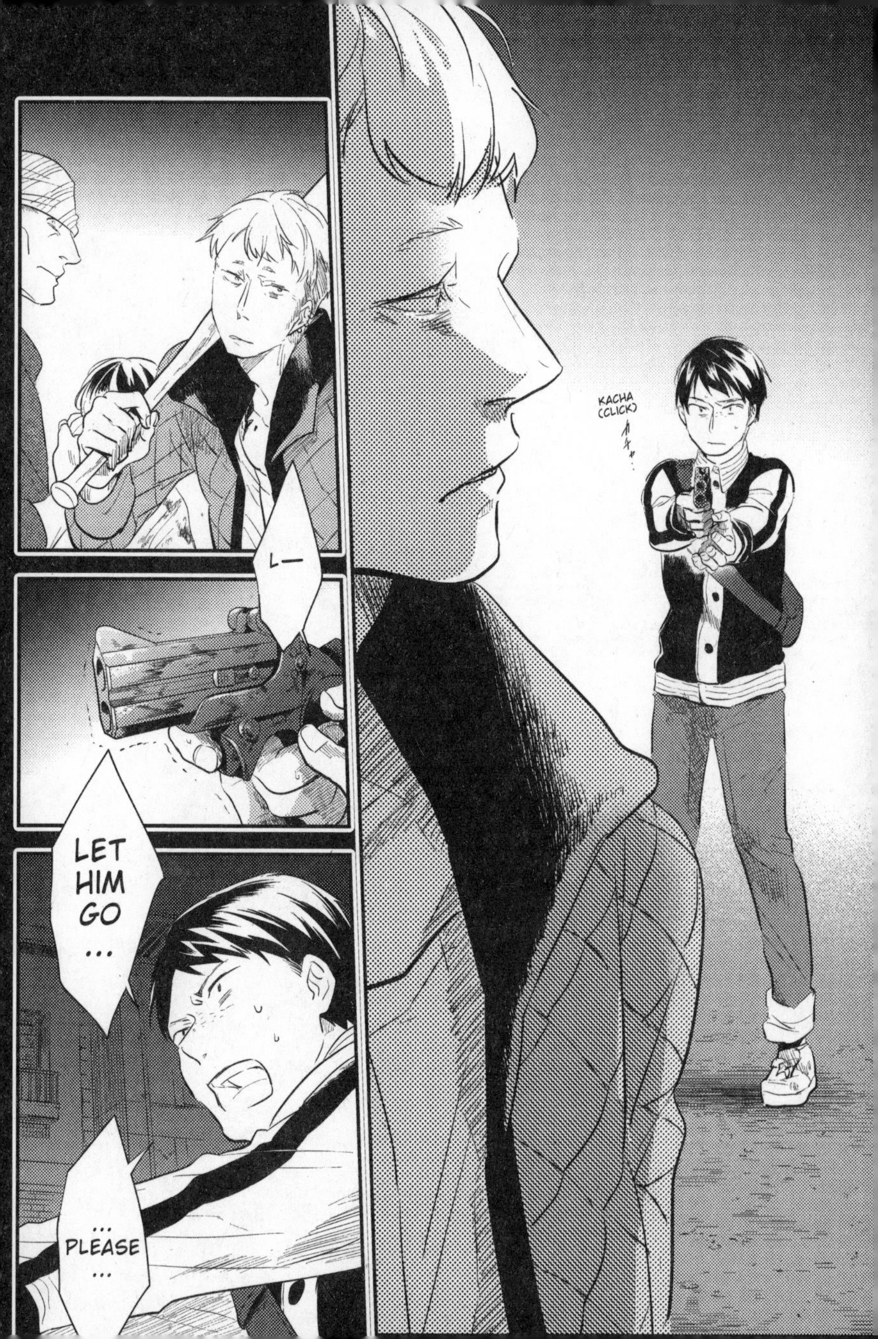
KACHA (CLICK)
カチャ
L—
LET HIM GO ...
... PLEASE ...

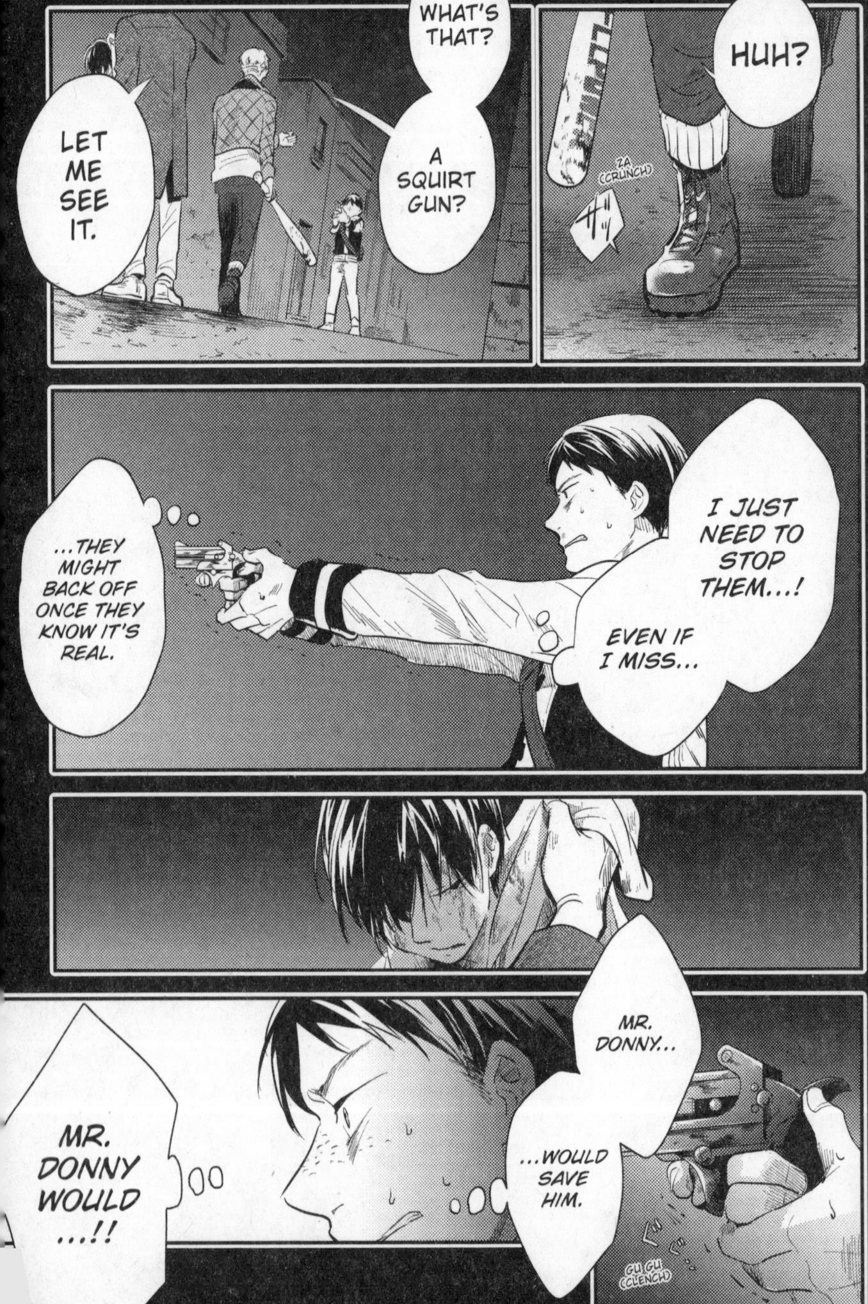
HUH?
ZA (CRUNCH)
ザッ
WHAT'S THAT?
A SQUIRT GUN?
LET ME SEE IT.
I JUST NEED TO STOP THEM...!
EVEN IF I MISS...
...THEY MIGHT BACK OFF ONCE THEY KNOW IT'S REAL.
MR. DONNY...
...WOULD SAVE HIM.
GU GU (CLENCH)
MR. DONNY WOULD ...!!

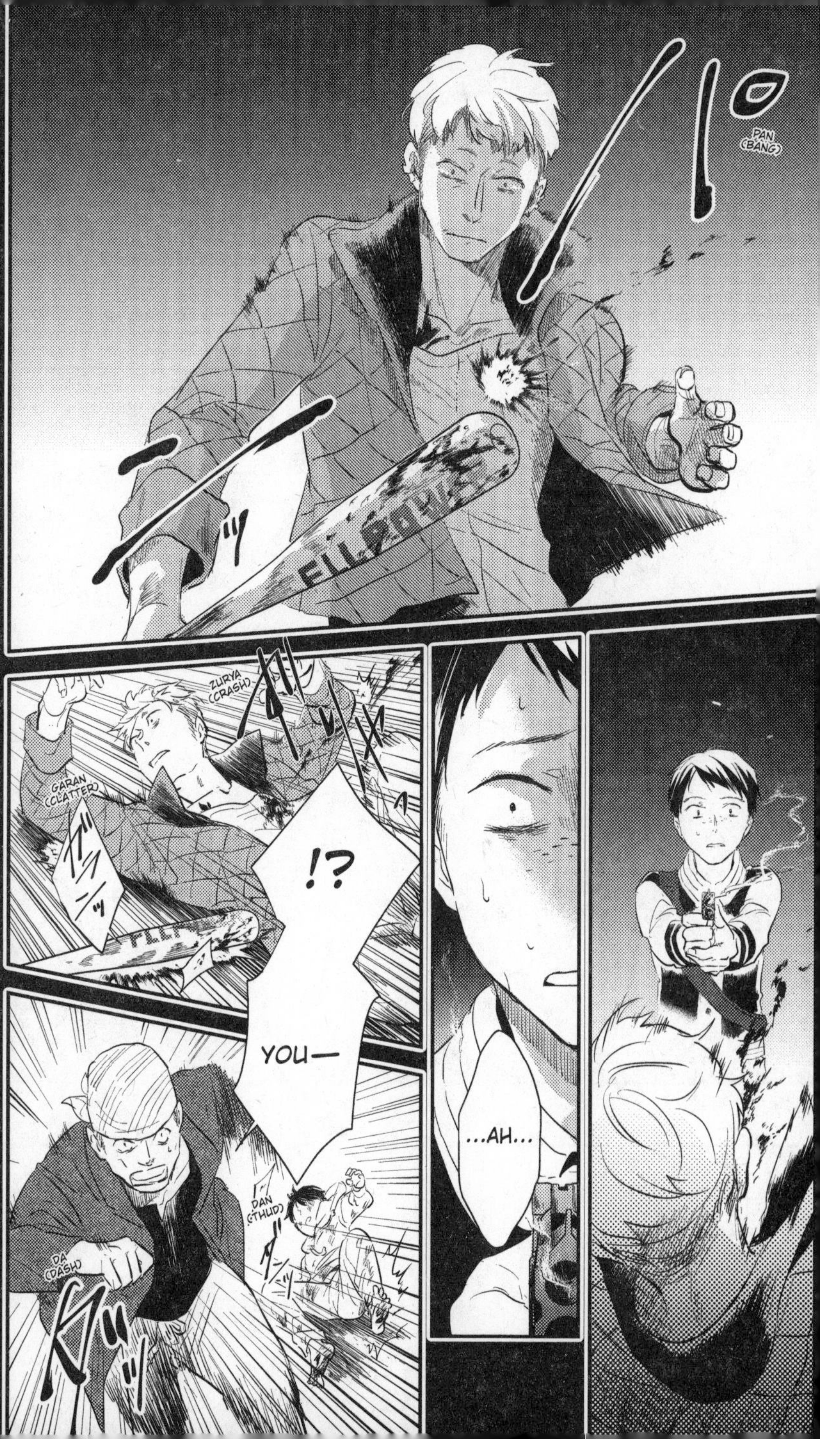
PAN (BANG)
...AH...
ZURYA (CRASH)
GARAN (CLATTER)
!?
YOU—
DAN (THUD)
DA (DASH)

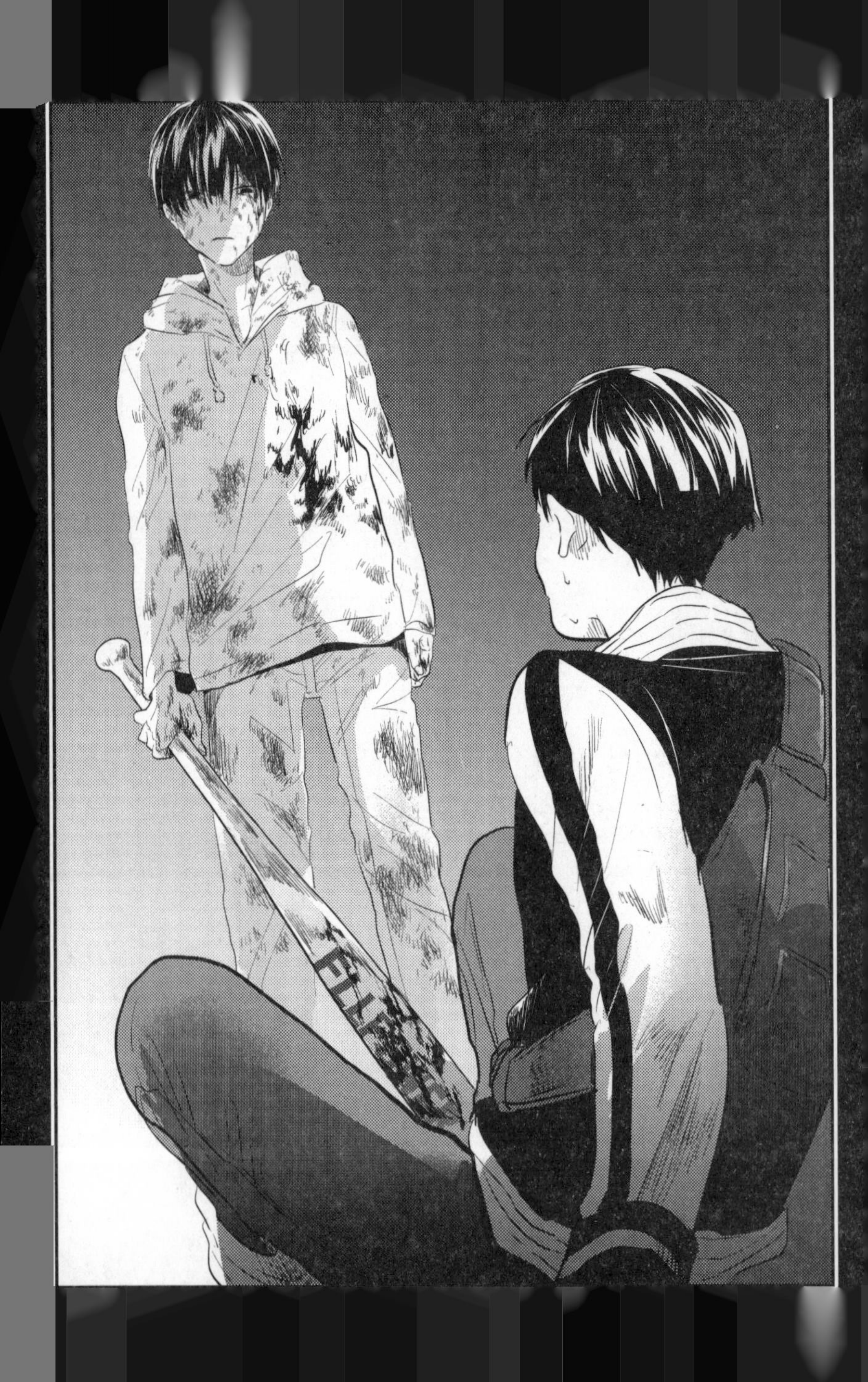

# FILE 31: THANK YOU

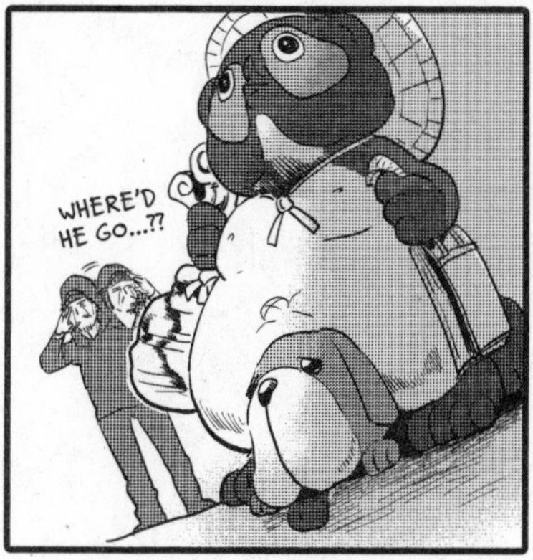
WHERE'D HE GO...??

THIS IS THE MOST PEACEFUL CHAPTER WE'VE HAD RECENTLY. THE THING ABOUT THE DOG THAT APPEARS IN THIS BIT IS THAT—POSSIBLY THANKS IN PART TO THE SCREENTONES—I CAN'T SEE THE SHAPE OF THE AREA BETWEEN HIS NOSE AND MOUTH AS ANYTHING EXCEPT THE THINGS THAT HANG BETWEEN A SHIGARAKI CERAMIC TANUKI'S LEGS. IN MY HEAD, I NAMED HIM "THE B*LL-FACED DOG"...

# FILE 32: ALLY

I RECEIVED COMMENTS FROM MANY PEOPLE ABOUT THIS CHAPTER, ASKING ME, "WHAT'S WITH RYANG-HA'S HAIR CLIP?" IT'S...UM...Y'KNOW...LIKE...

A DISGUISE...SO...UM...I'M SORRY...

IN THEIR WORLD, RYANG-HA'S OUTWARD APPEARANCE SEEMS TO STRIKE OTHER PEOPLE AS THAT OF A GENERIC-LOOKING YOUNG CHINESE OR KOREAN MAN. SO, AS LONG AS THEY ARE IN A PLACE WHERE ASIAN PEOPLE IN GENERAL ARE NOT UNUSUAL, HE CAN BLEND IN.

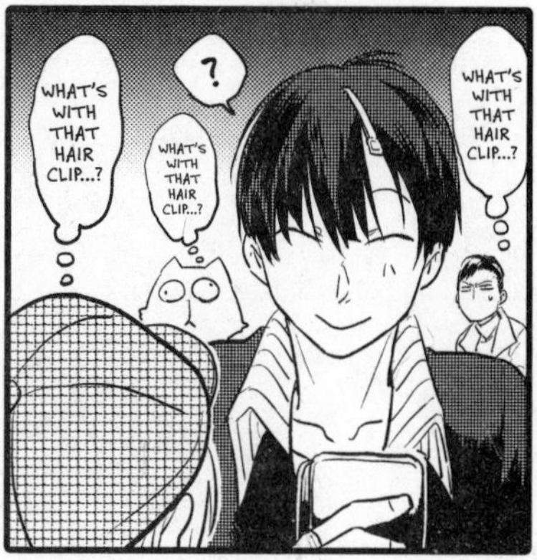
WHAT'S WITH THAT HAIR CLIP...?
?
WHAT'S WITH THAT HAIR CLIP...?
WHAT'S WITH THAT HAIR CLIP...?

DOESN'T THAT MEAN HIS HAIR CLIP DEFEATS ITS OWN PURPOSE...? LOL.

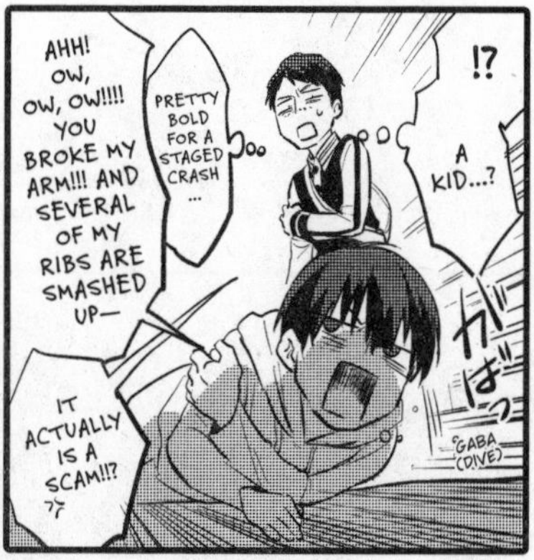
!?
A KID...?
PRETTY BOLD FOR A STAGED CRASH ...
AHH! OW, OW, OW!!!! YOU BROKE MY ARM!!! AND SEVERAL OF MY RIBS ARE SMASHED UP—
IT ACTUALLY IS A SCAM!!?
GABA (DIVE)

# FILE 33: STARTING POINT

WE PLUNGE INTO THE PAST. WOULD THE FOOL WHO THOUGHT "I CAN TOTALLY FINISH THE WHOLE FLASHBACK WITHIN THE SPAN OF VOLUME 6" WHEN THEY STARTED WRITING THIS SECTION PLEASE RAISE THEIR HAND?!

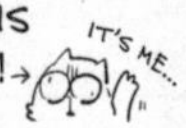
IT'S ME...

WITH THE APPEARANCE OF THE ORIGINAL RYANG-HA, PHONE CALLS WITH MY EDITOR HAVE BECOME CONFUSING, LOL.

FE: "SO HERE RYANG-HA IS LIKE—"

EDITOR: "WHICH ONE?"

I NOW MAKE IT A POINT TO CALL THEM "OLD RYANG-HA" AND "CURRENT RYANG-HA"...

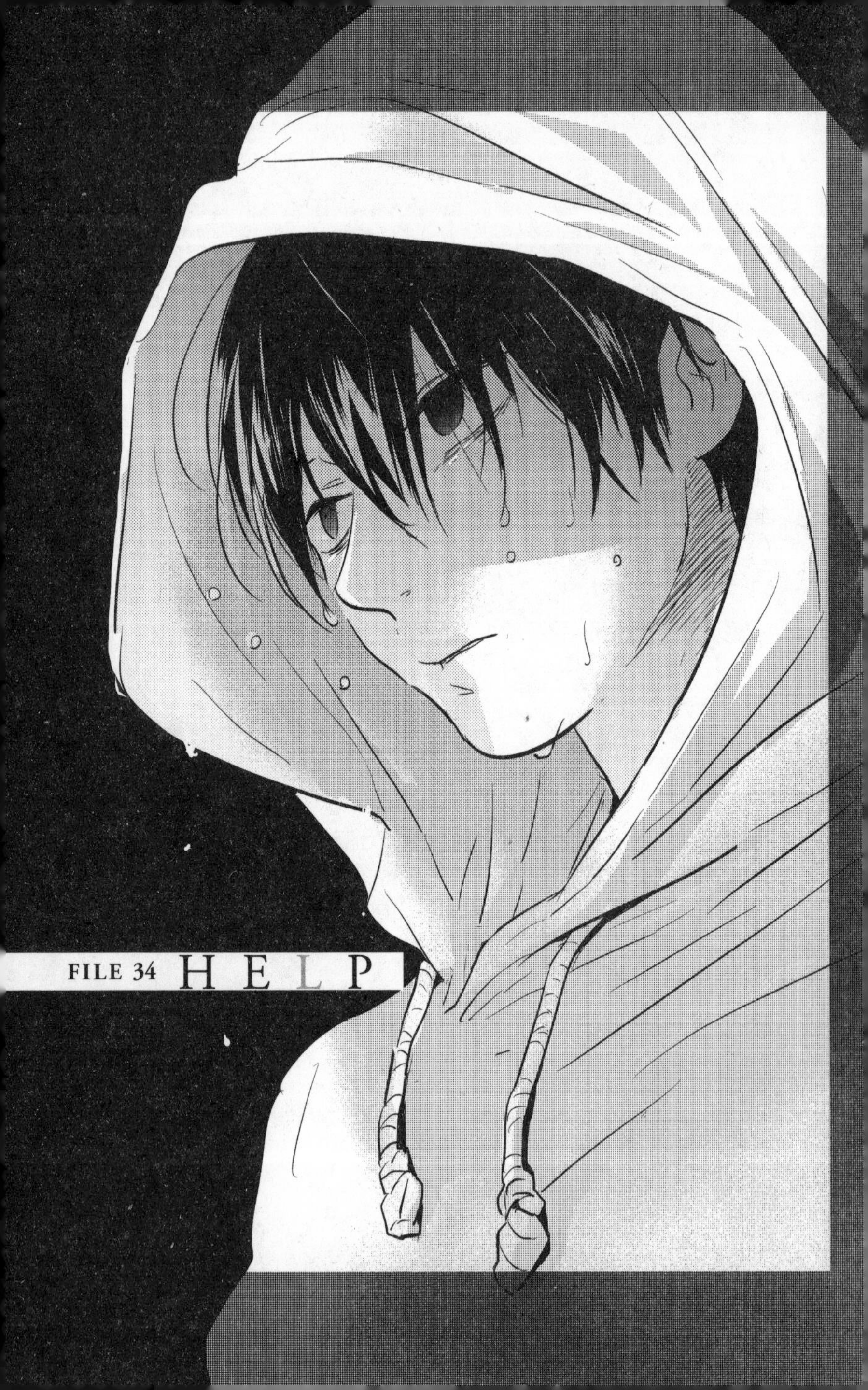
FILE 34 HELP

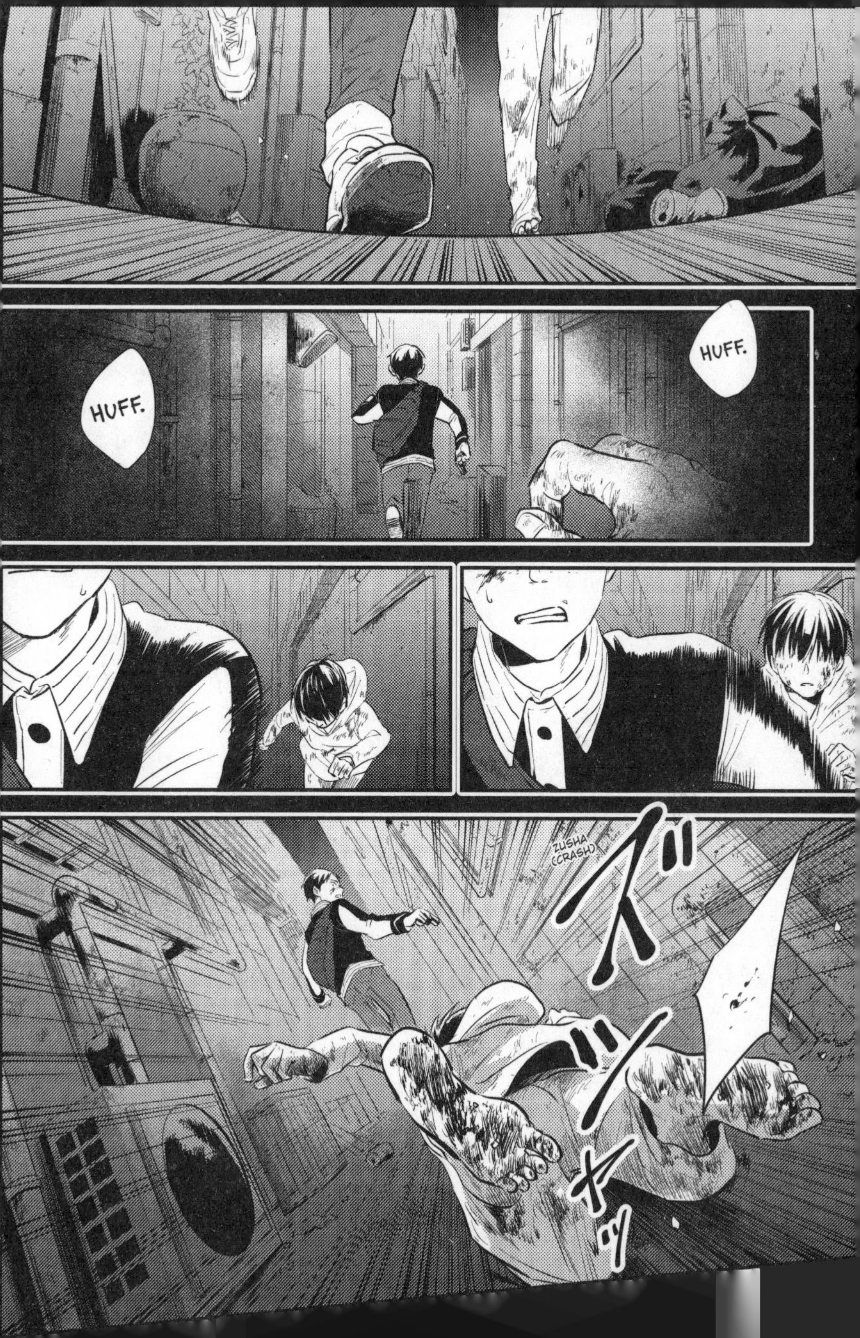
HUFF.
HUFF.
ZUSHA (CRASH)

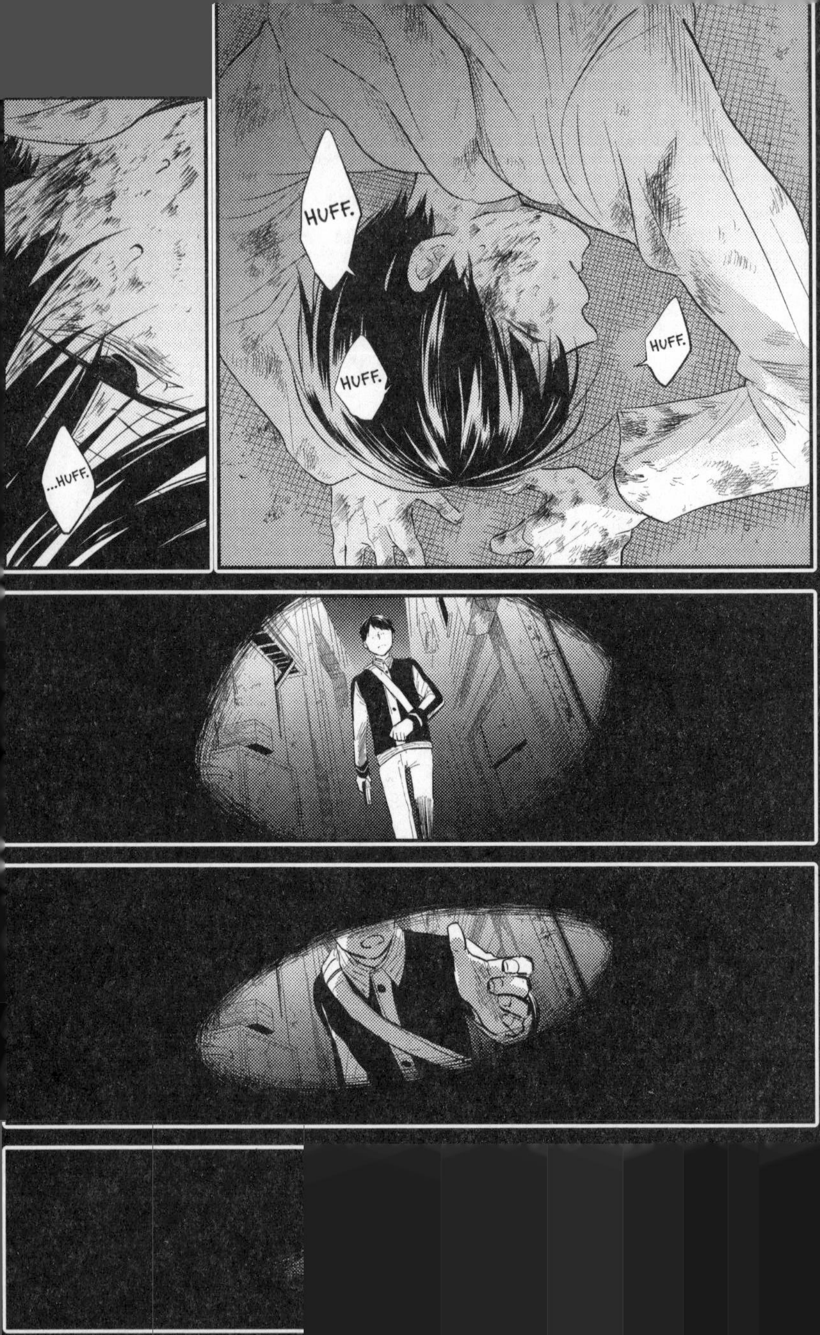
HUFF.
HUFF.
HUFF.
...HUFF.

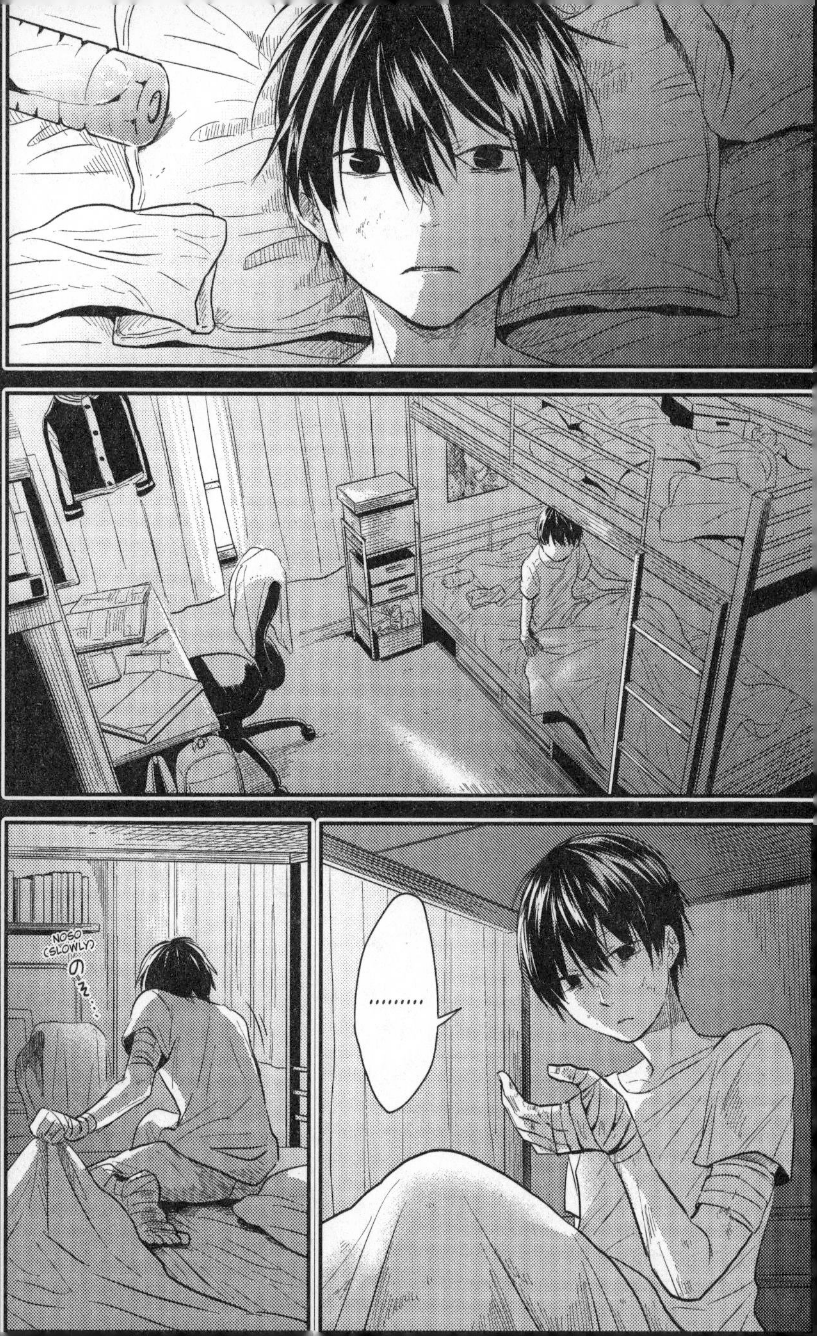
.........
のそ…
NOSO (SLOWLY)

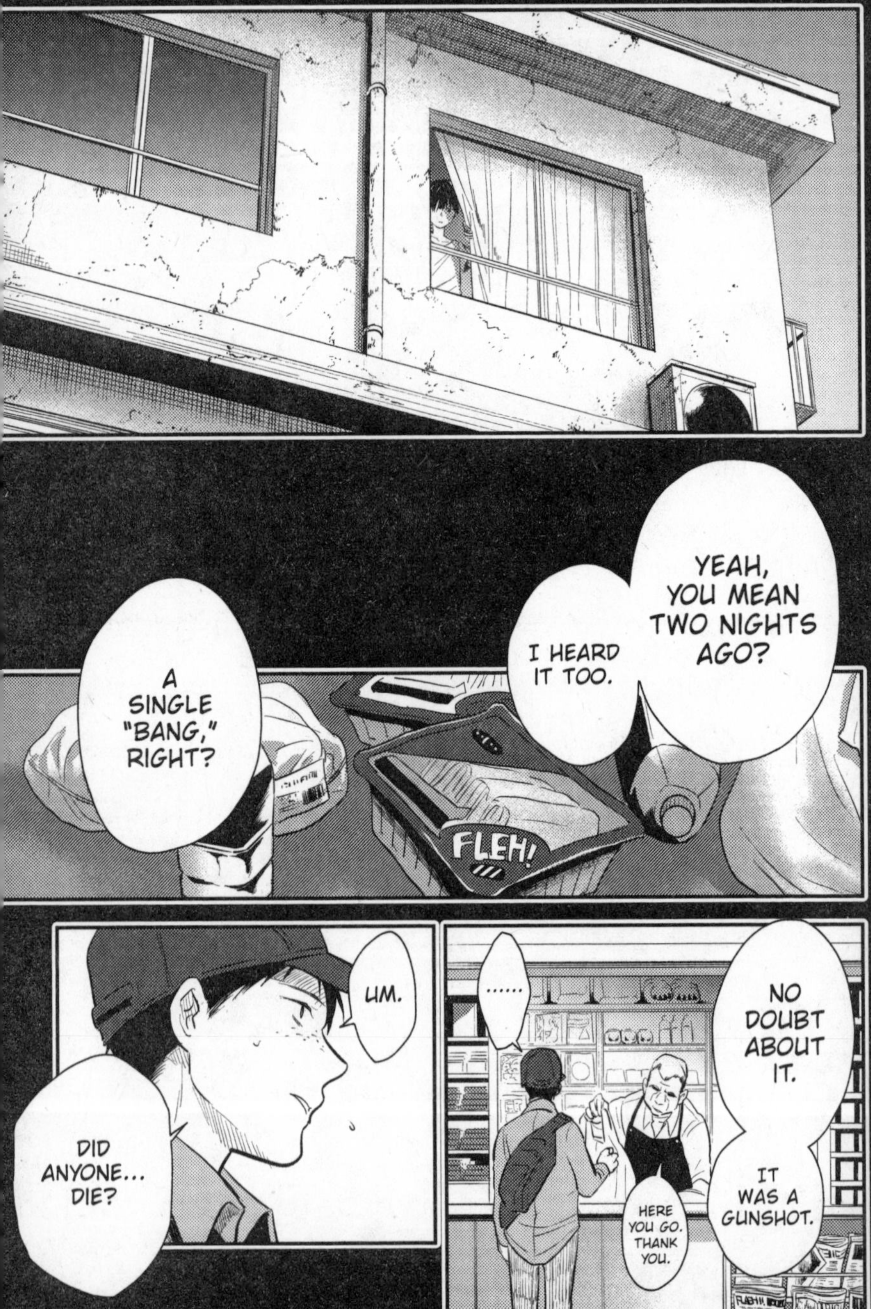
YEAH, YOU MEAN TWO NIGHTS AGO?
I HEARD IT TOO.
A SINGLE "BANG," RIGHT?
FLEH!
NO DOUBT ABOUT IT.
......
IT WAS A GUNSHOT.
HERE YOU GO. THANK YOU.
UM.
DID ANYONE... DIE?

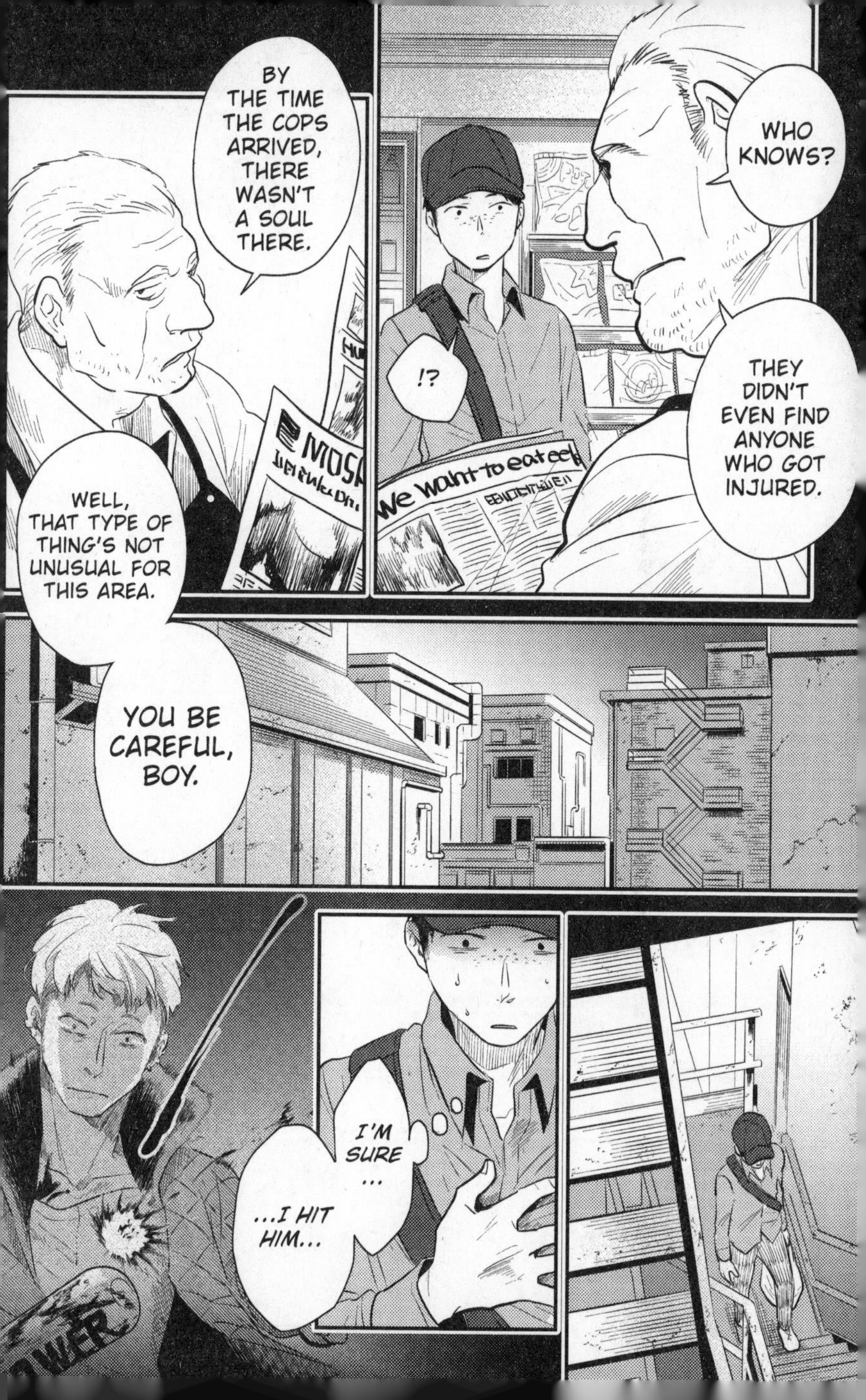
WHO KNOWS?
!?
THEY DIDN'T EVEN FIND ANYONE WHO GOT INJURED.
BY THE TIME THE COPS ARRIVED, THERE WASN'T A SOUL THERE.
WELL, THAT TYPE OF THING'S NOT UNUSUAL FOR THIS AREA.
YOU BE CAREFUL, BOY.
I'M SURE...
...I HIT HIM...

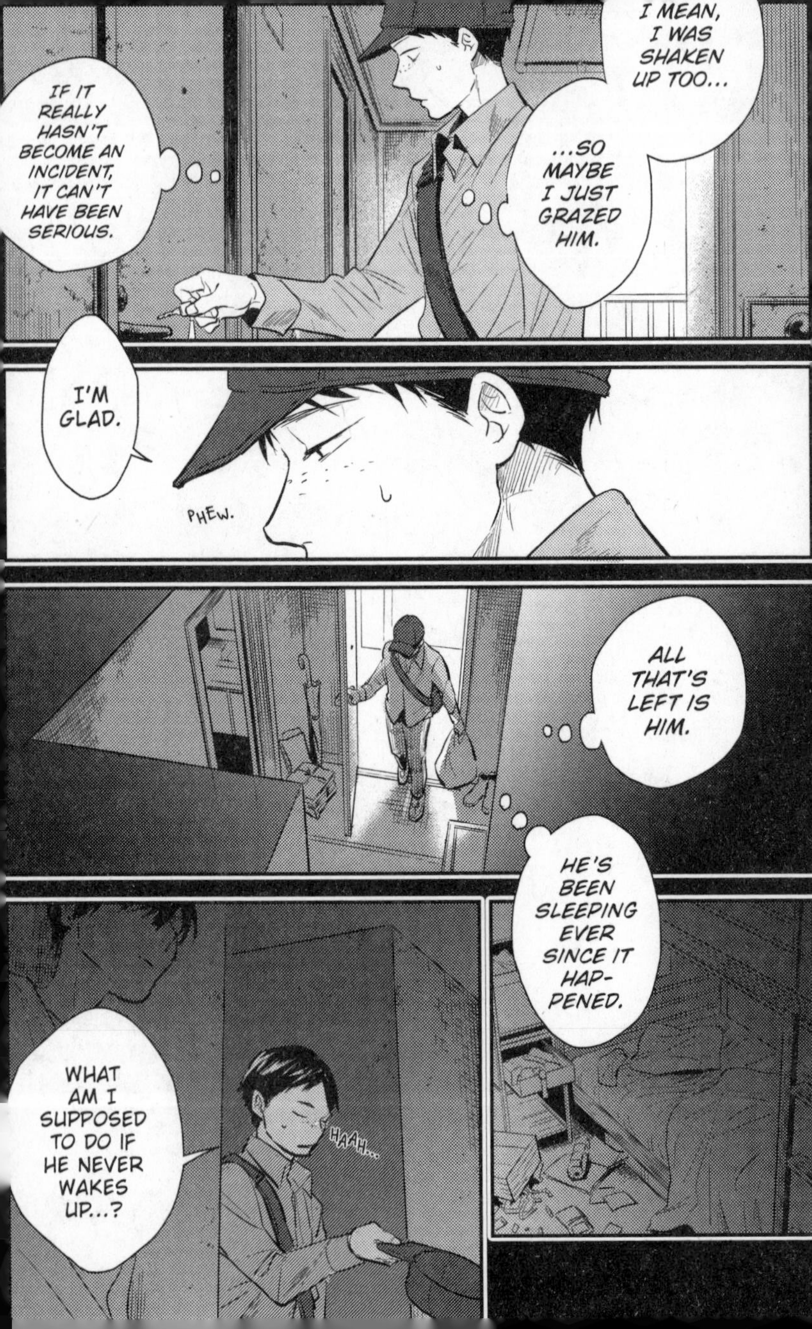
I MEAN, I WAS SHAKEN UP TOO...
...SO MAYBE I JUST GRAZED HIM.
IF IT REALLY HASN'T BECOME AN INCIDENT, IT CAN'T HAVE BEEN SERIOUS.
I'M GLAD.
PHEW.
ALL THAT'S LEFT IS HIM.
HE'S BEEN SLEEPING EVER SINCE IT HAP-PENED.
WHAT AM I SUPPOSED TO DO IF HE NEVER WAKES UP...?
HAAH...

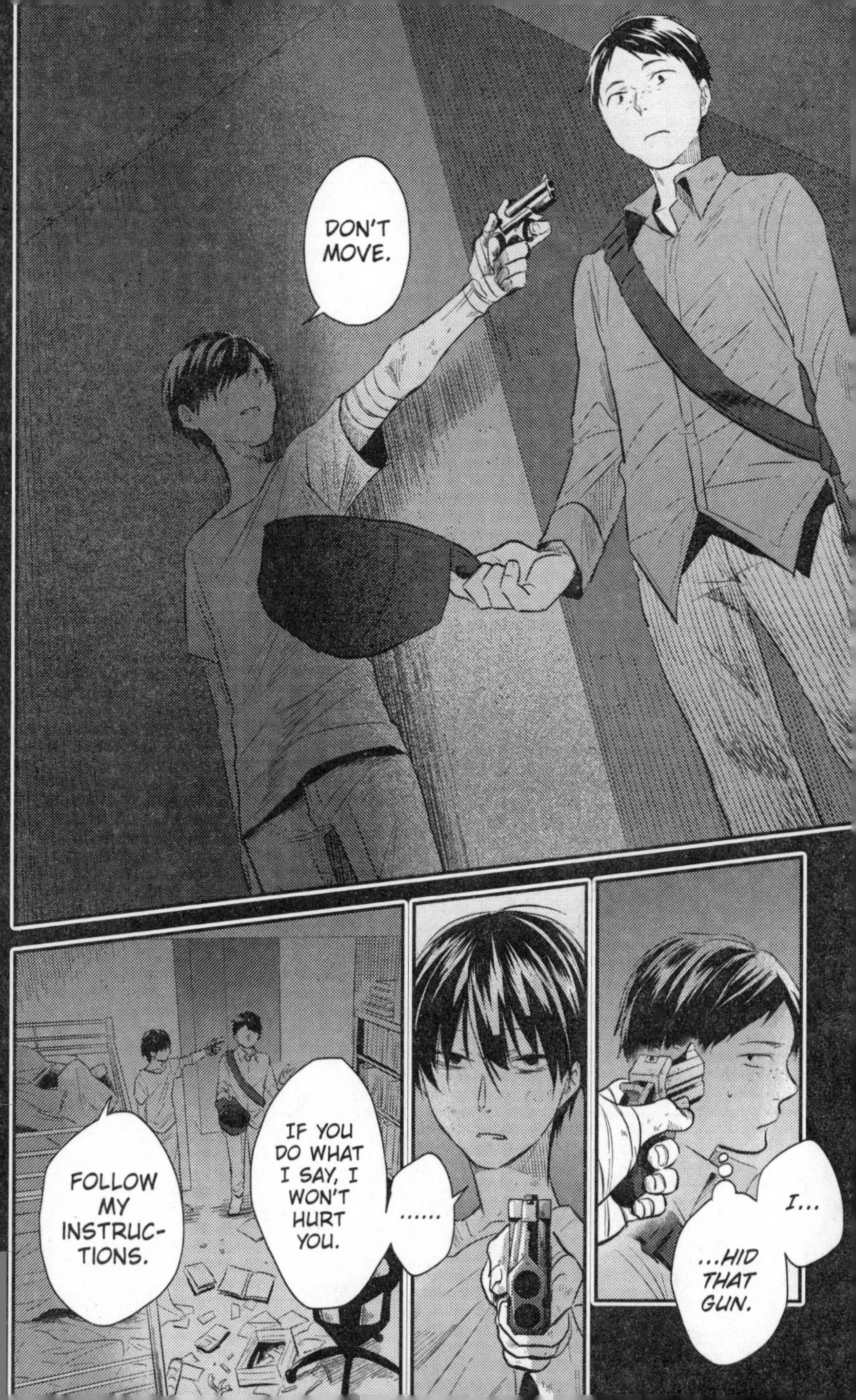
DON'T MOVE.
I...
...HID THAT GUN.
......
IF YOU DO WHAT I SAY, I WON'T HURT YOU.
FOLLOW MY INSTRUC-TIONS.

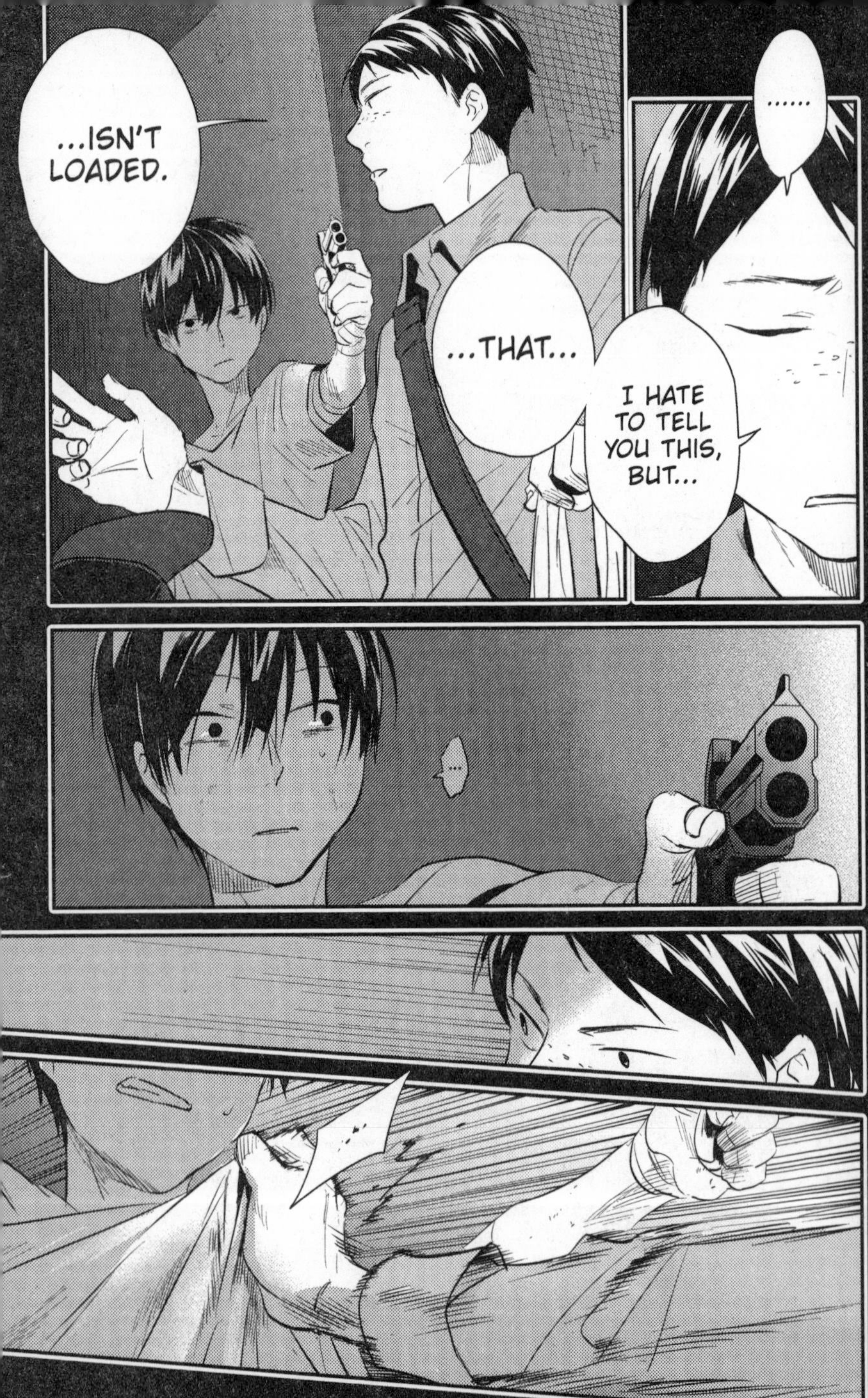
......
I HATE TO TELL YOU THIS, BUT...
...THAT...
...ISN'T LOADED.
...

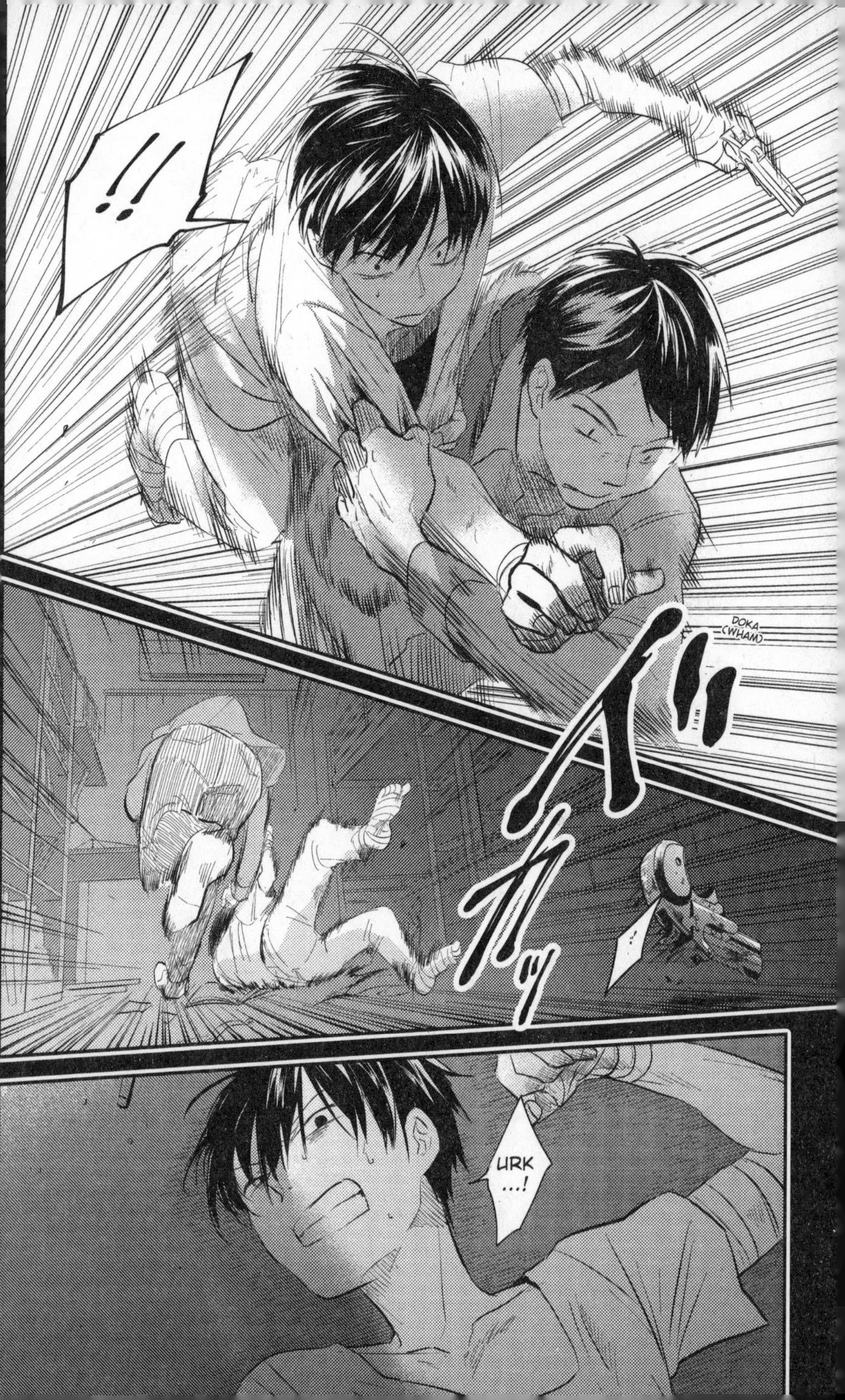
!!
DOKA (WHAM)
URK ...!

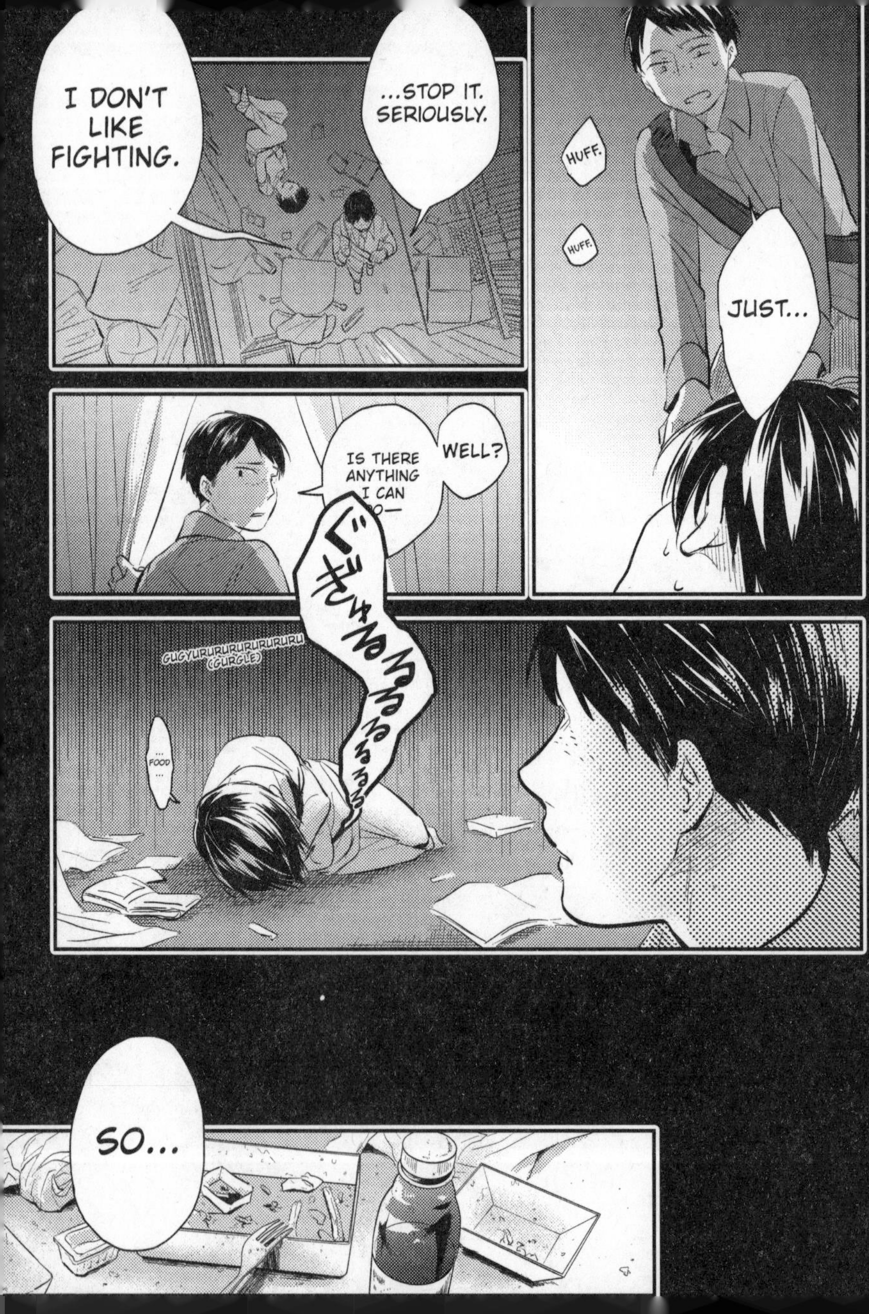
HUFF.
HUFF.
JUST...
...STOP IT. SERIOUSLY.
I DON'T LIKE FIGHTING.
WELL?
IS THERE ANYTHING I CAN DO—
GUGYURURURURURURURU (GURGLE)
...FOOD...
SO...

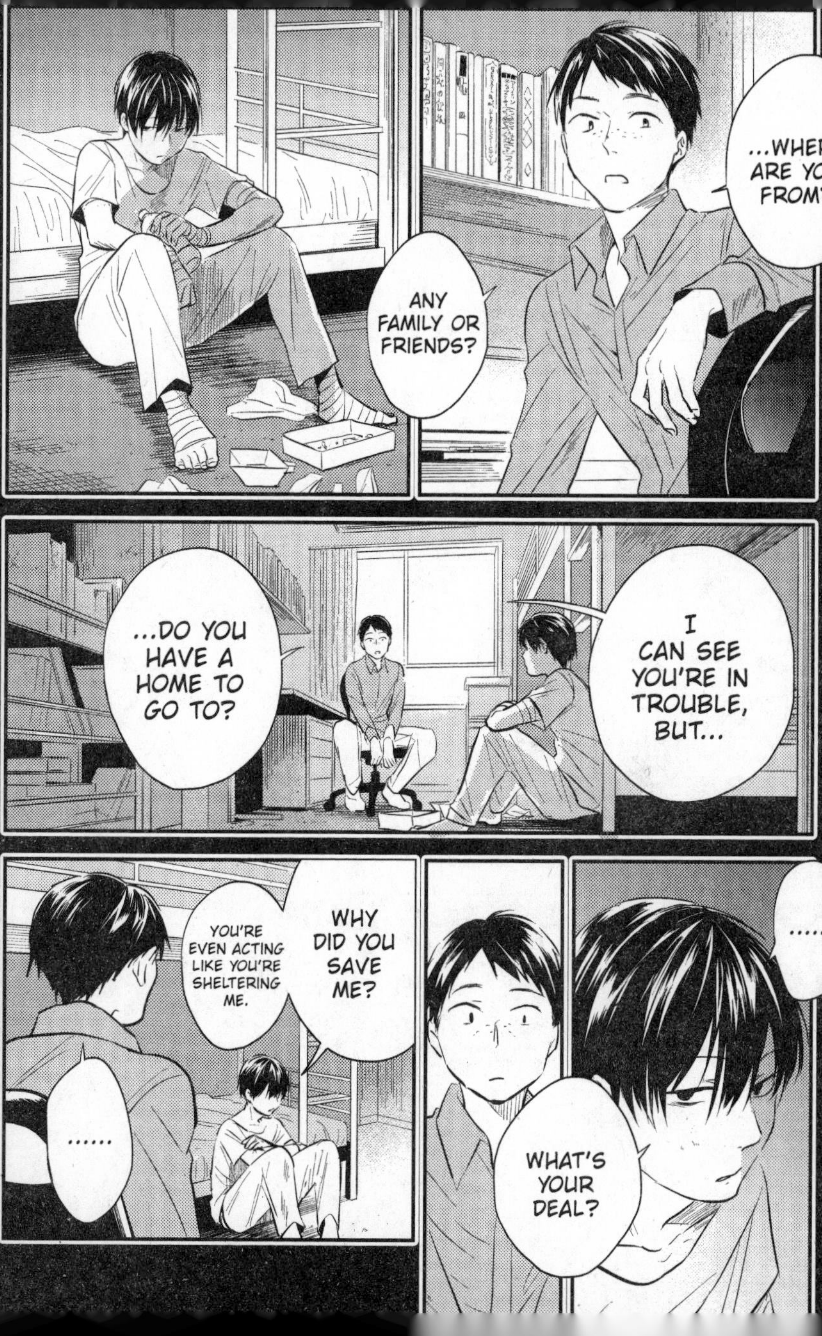
...WHERE ARE YOU FROM?
ANY FAMILY OR FRIENDS?
I CAN SEE YOU'RE IN TROUBLE, BUT...
...DO YOU HAVE A HOME TO GO TO?
......
WHAT'S YOUR DEAL?
WHY DID YOU SAVE ME?
YOU'RE EVEN ACTING LIKE YOU'RE SHELTERING ME.
......

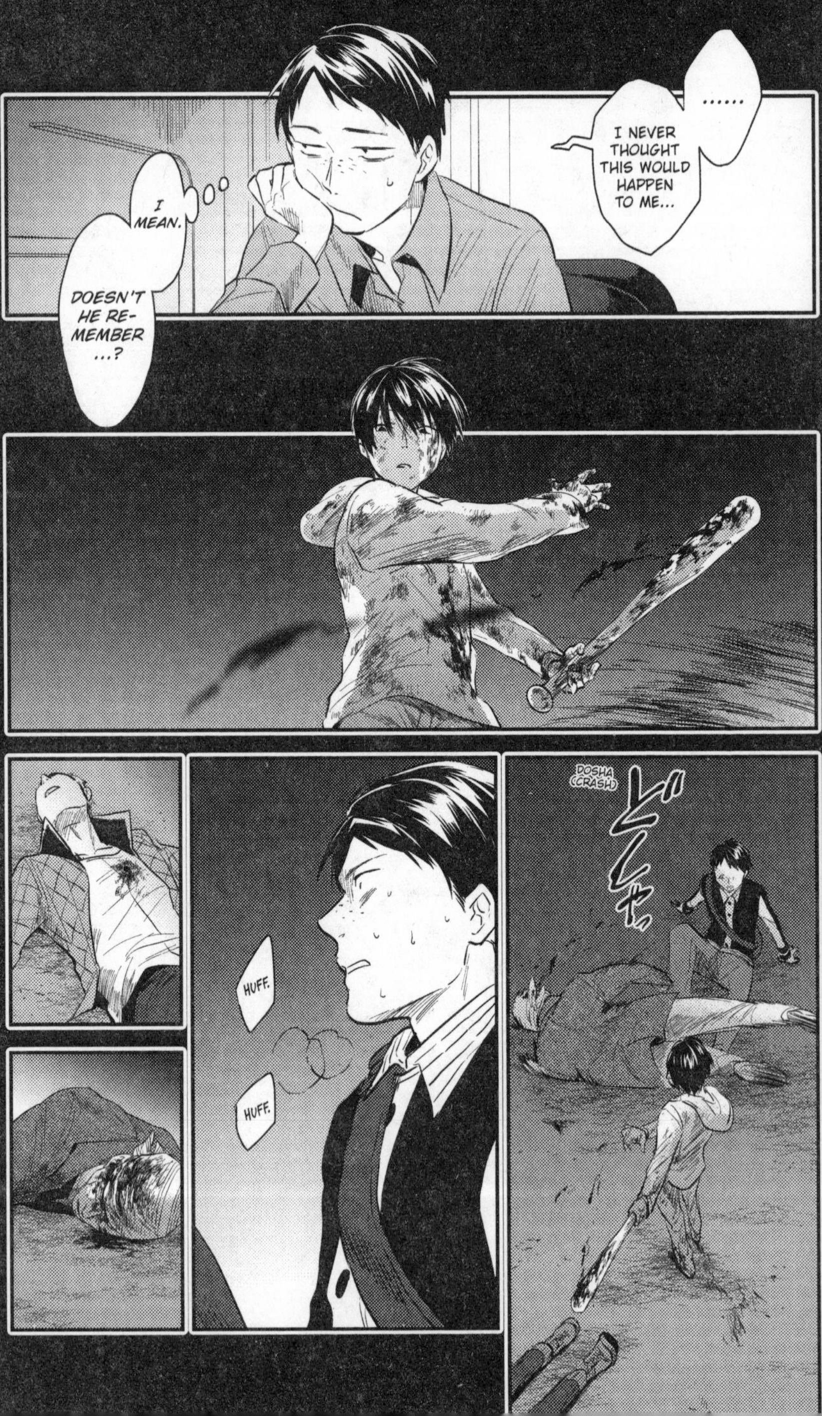
......
I NEVER THOUGHT THIS WOULD HAPPEN TO ME...
I MEAN.
DOESN'T HE RE-MEMBER ...?
DOSHA (CRASH)
どしゃ
HUFF.
HUFF.

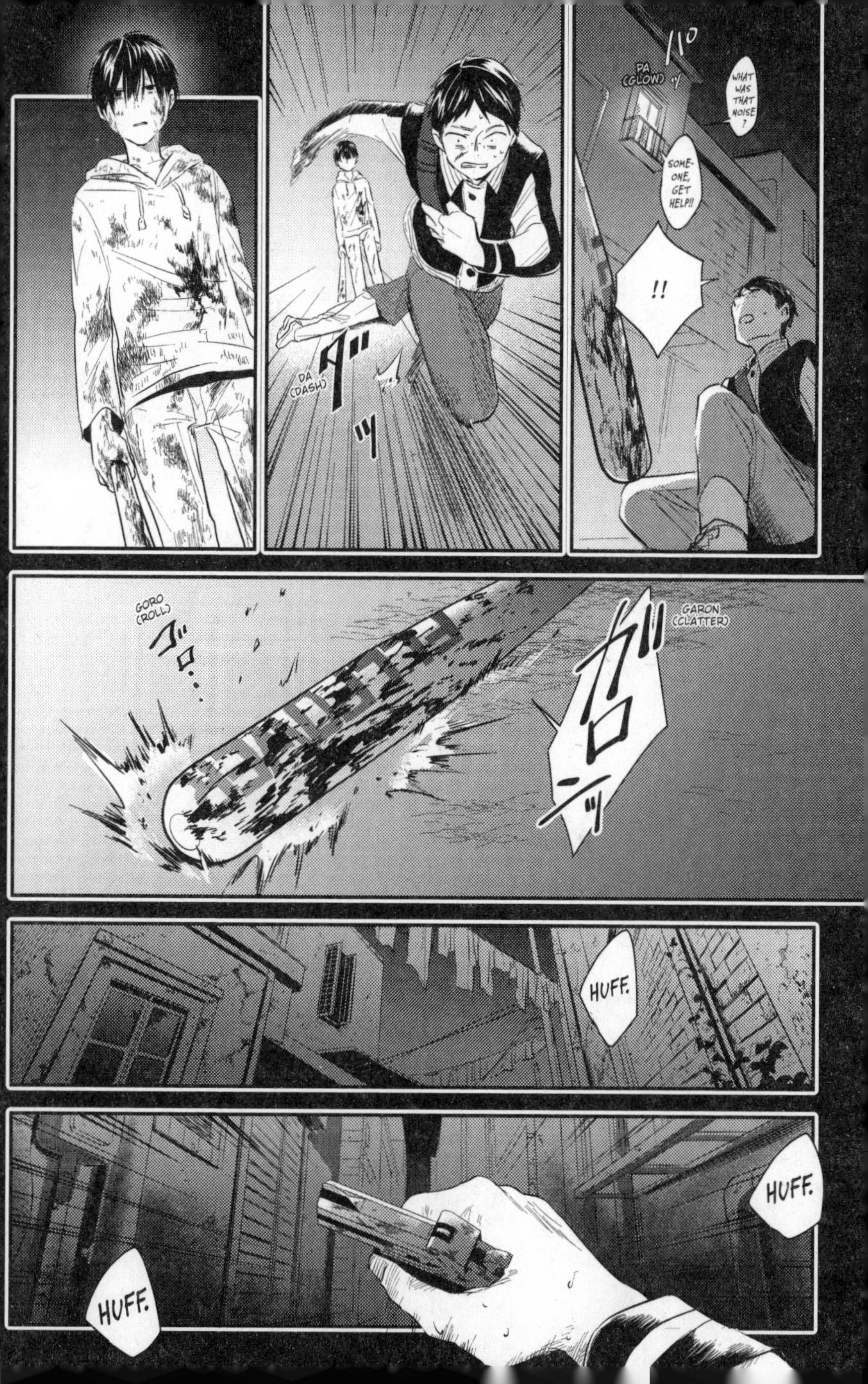
PA (GLOW)
WHAT WAS THAT NOISE?
SOME-ONE, GET HELP!!
!!
DA (DASH)
GARON (CLATTER)
GORO (ROLL)
HUFF.
HUFF.
HUFF.

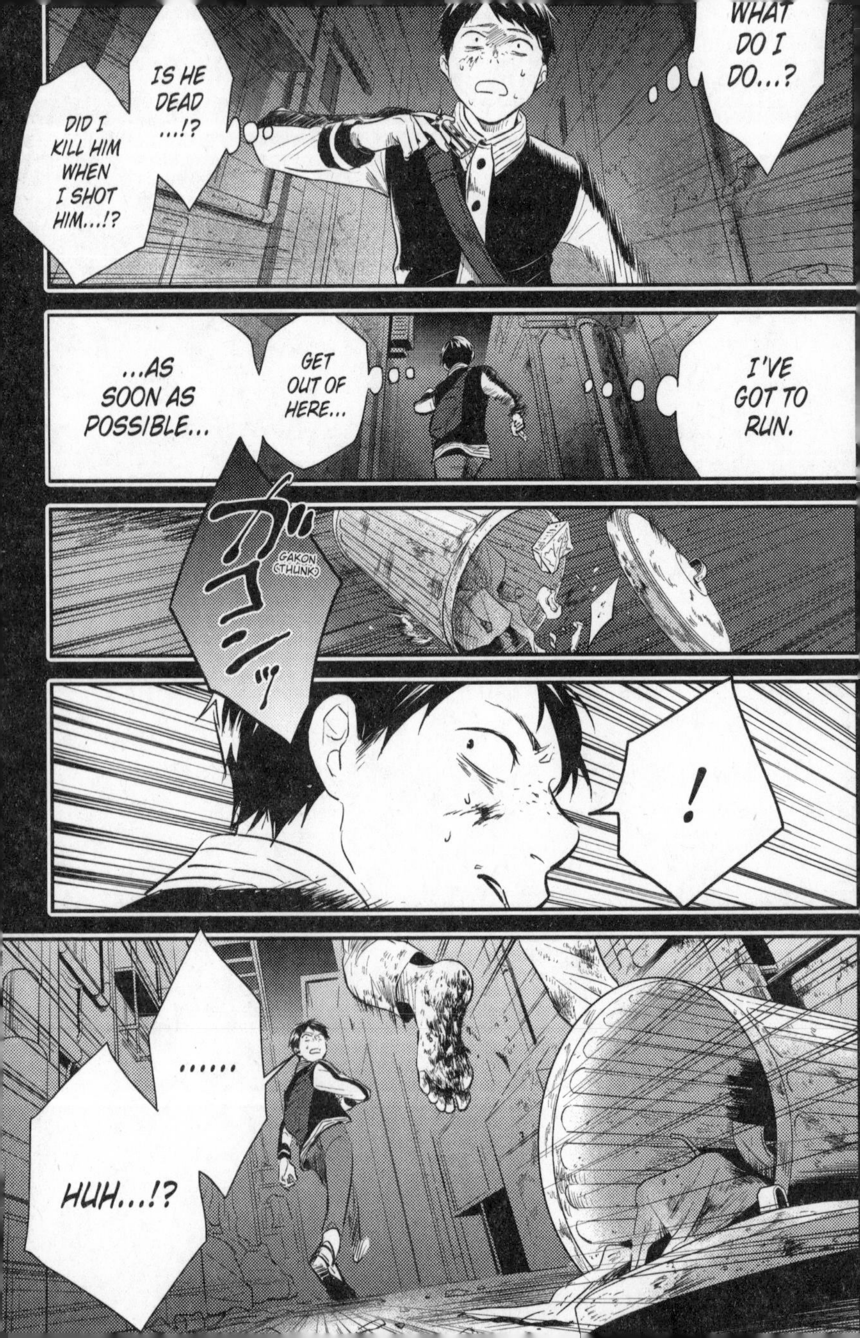
WHAT DO I DO...?
IS HE DEAD ...!?
DID I KILL HIM WHEN I SHOT HIM...!?
I'VE GOT TO RUN.
GET OUT OF HERE...
...AS SOON AS POSSIBLE...
GAKON (THUNK)
!
......
HUH...!?

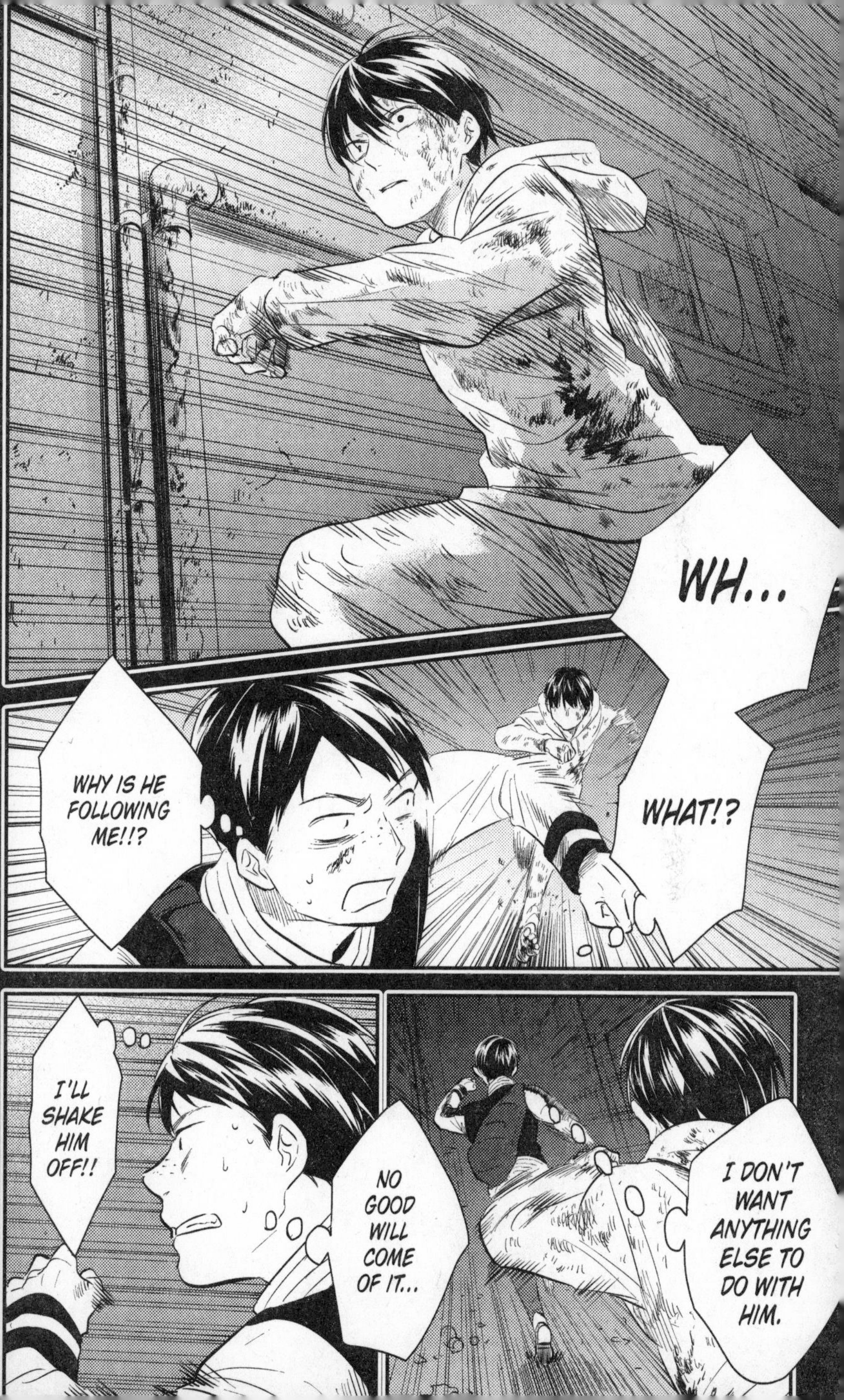
WH...
WHAT!?
WHY IS HE FOLLOWING ME!!?
I DON'T WANT ANYTHING ELSE TO DO WITH HIM.
NO GOOD WILL COME OF IT...
I'LL SHAKE HIM OFF!!

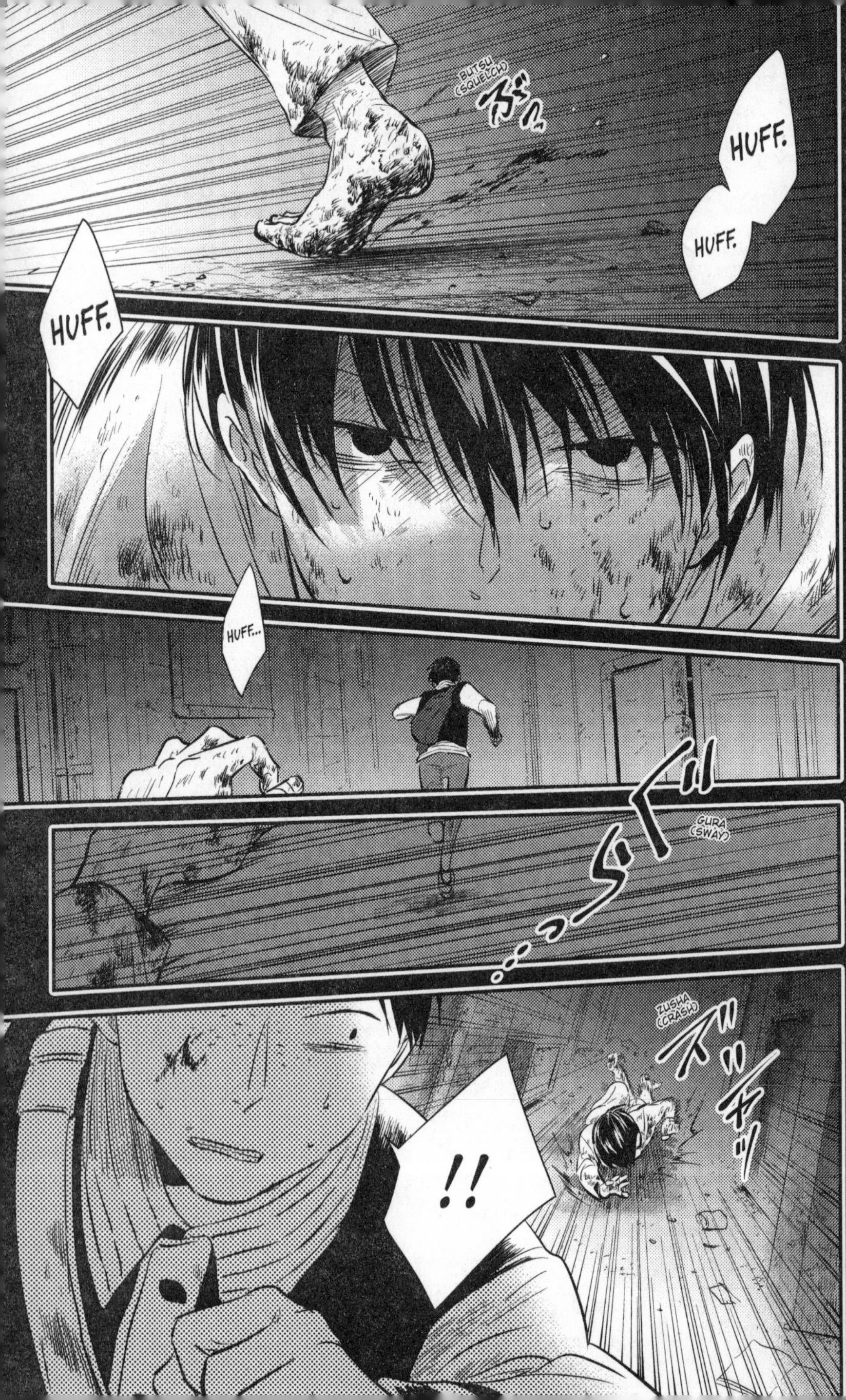
HUFF.
HUFF.
BUTSU (SQUELCH)
HUFF.
HUFF...
GURA (SWAY)
ZUSHA (CRASH)
!!

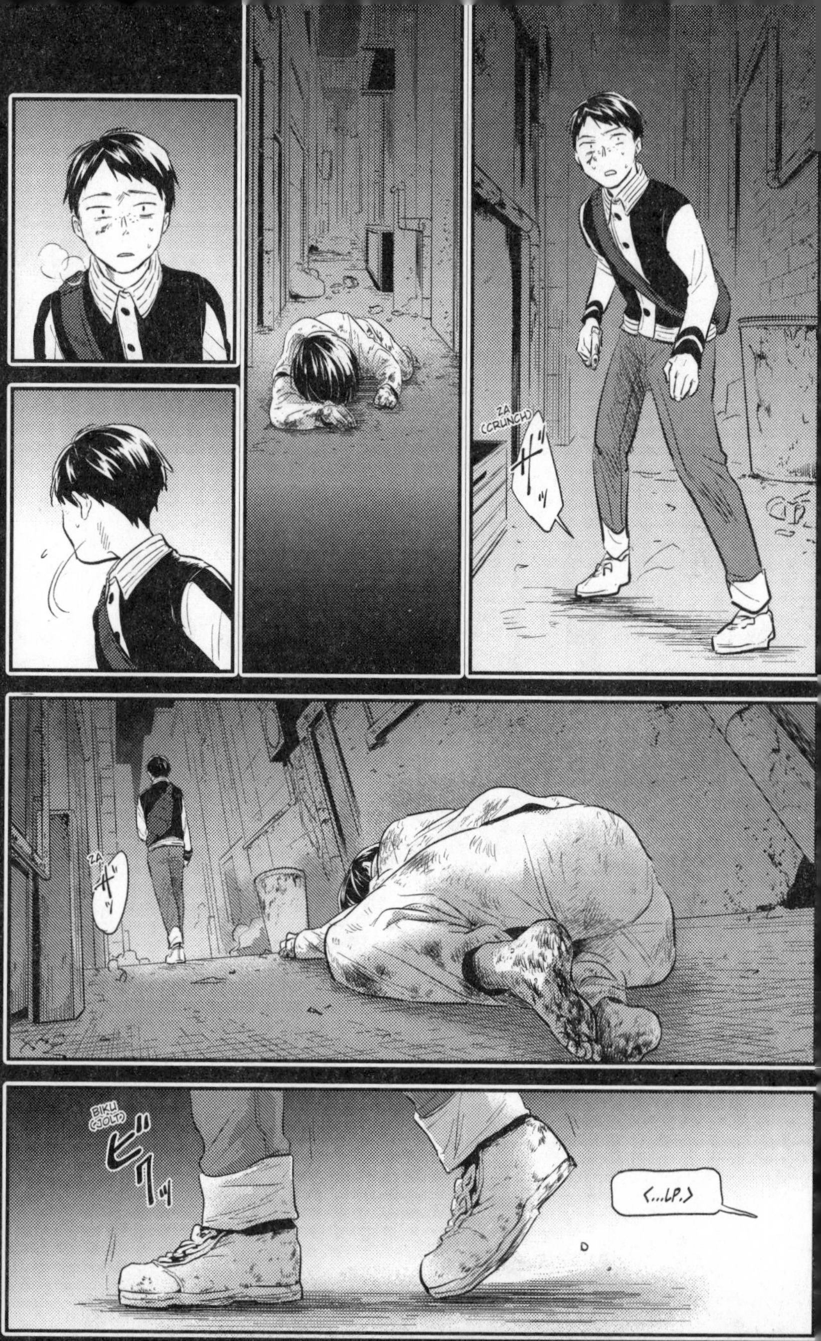
ZA (CRUNCH)
ザッ
ZA
ザッ
BIKU (JOLT)
ビクッ
<...LP.>

〈SOMEONE...〉

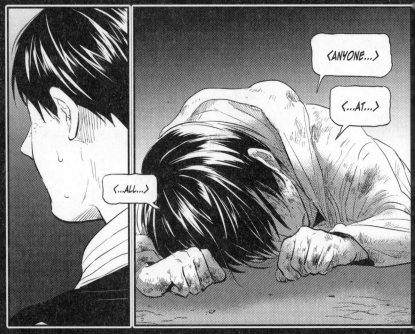

〈ANYONE...〉

〈...AT....〉

〈...ALL....〉

タ
ッ
TA

タ
ッ
TA

TA
(STEP)

タ
ッ

ZARI
(CRUNCH)

ザリッ

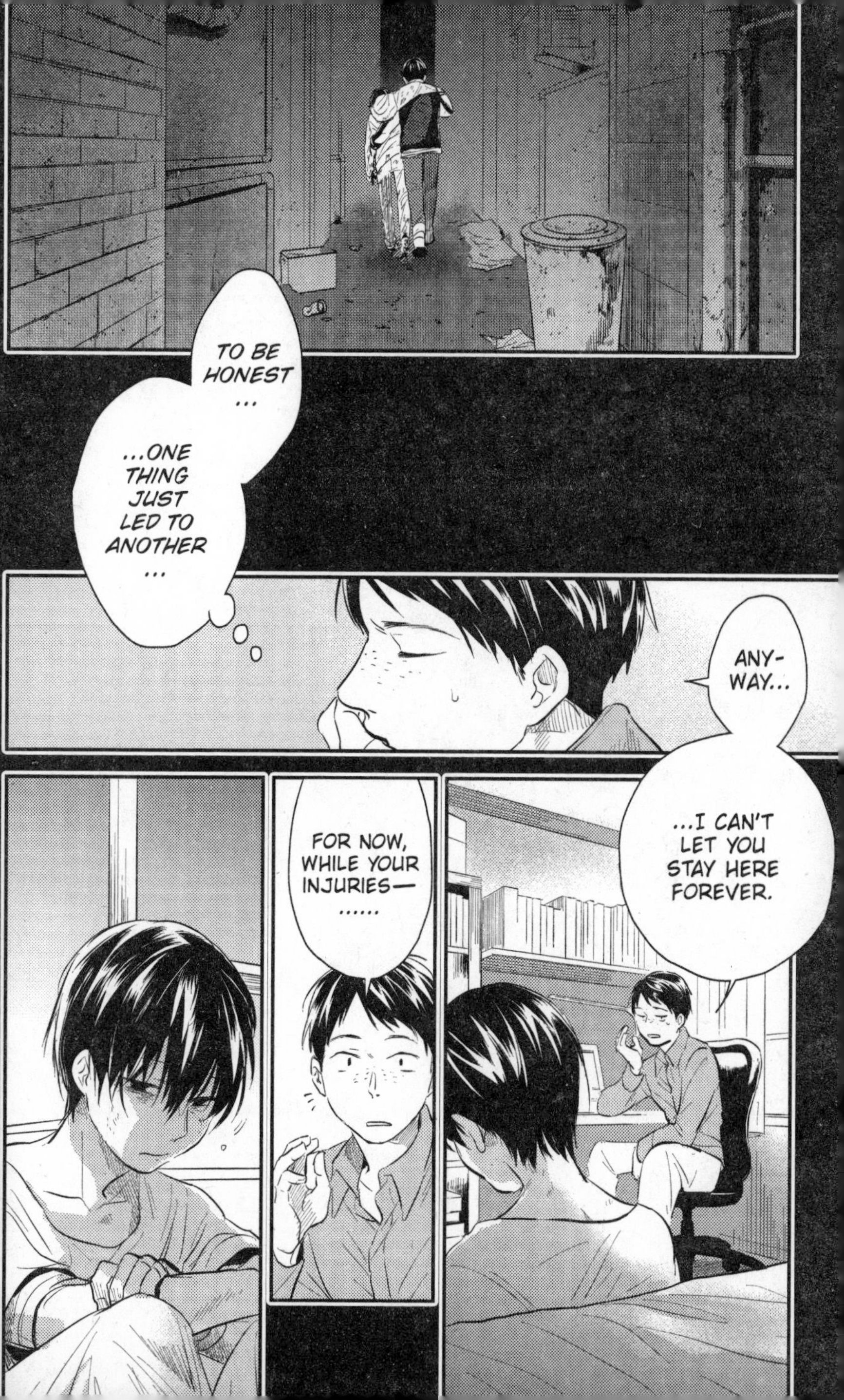
TO BE HONEST ...
...ONE THING JUST LED TO ANOTHER ...
ANY-WAY...
...I CAN'T LET YOU STAY HERE FOREVER.
FOR NOW, WHILE YOUR INJURIES—
......

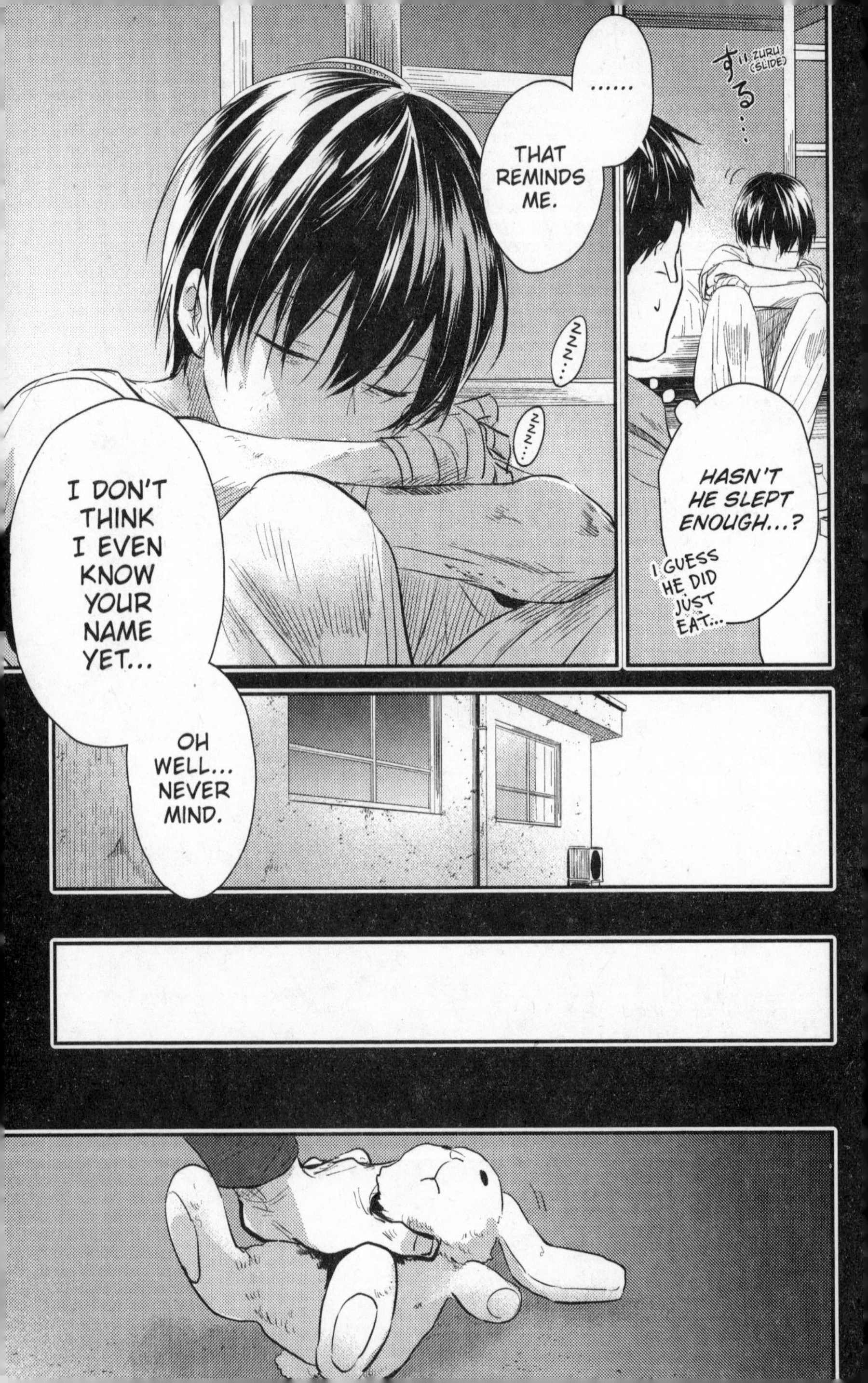

する… ZURU (SLIDE)
HASN'T HE SLEPT ENOUGH...?
I GUESS HE DID JUST EAT...
......
THAT REMINDS ME.
ZZZ...
ZZZ...
I DON'T THINK I EVEN KNOW YOUR NAME YET...
OH WELL... NEVER MIND.

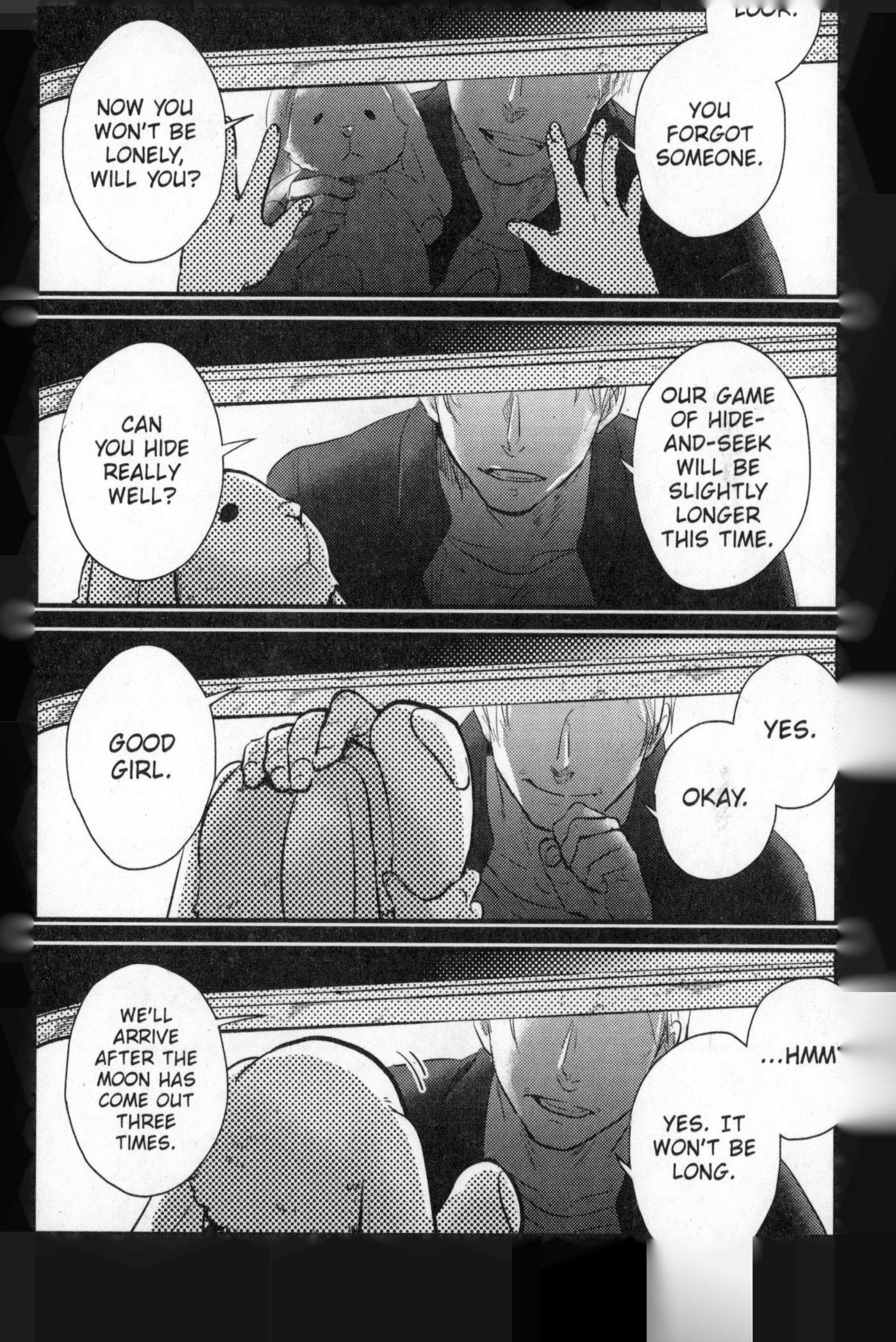
YOU FORGOT SOMEONE.
NOW YOU WON'T BE LONELY, WILL YOU?
OUR GAME OF HIDE-AND-SEEK WILL BE SLIGHTLY LONGER THIS TIME.
CAN YOU HIDE REALLY WELL?
YES.
OKAY.
GOOD GIRL.
...HMM
YES. IT WON'T BE LONG.
WE'LL ARRIVE AFTER THE MOON HAS COME OUT THREE TIMES.

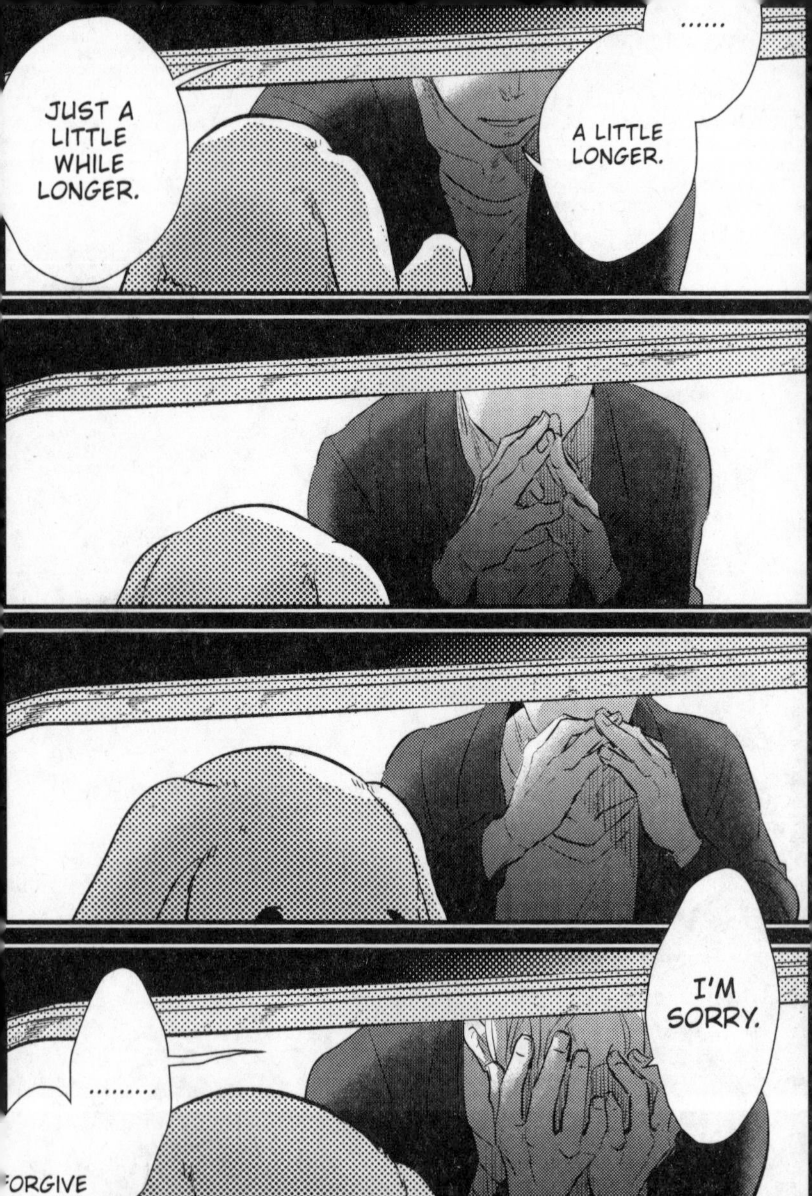
......
A LITTLE LONGER.
JUST A LITTLE WHILE LONGER.
I'M SORRY.
........
FORGIVE ME.

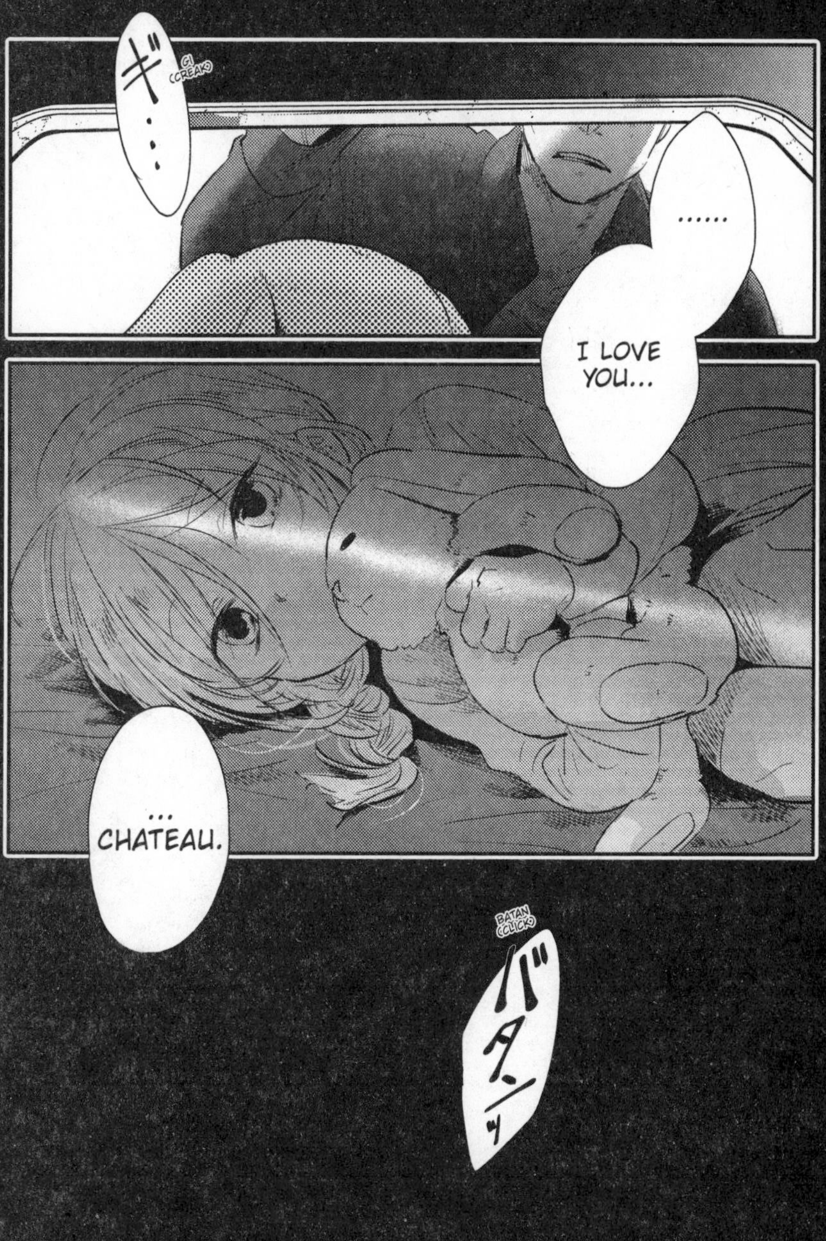
ギ…
GI (CREAK)
......
I LOVE YOU...
... CHATEAU.
バタン ッ
BATAN (CLICK)

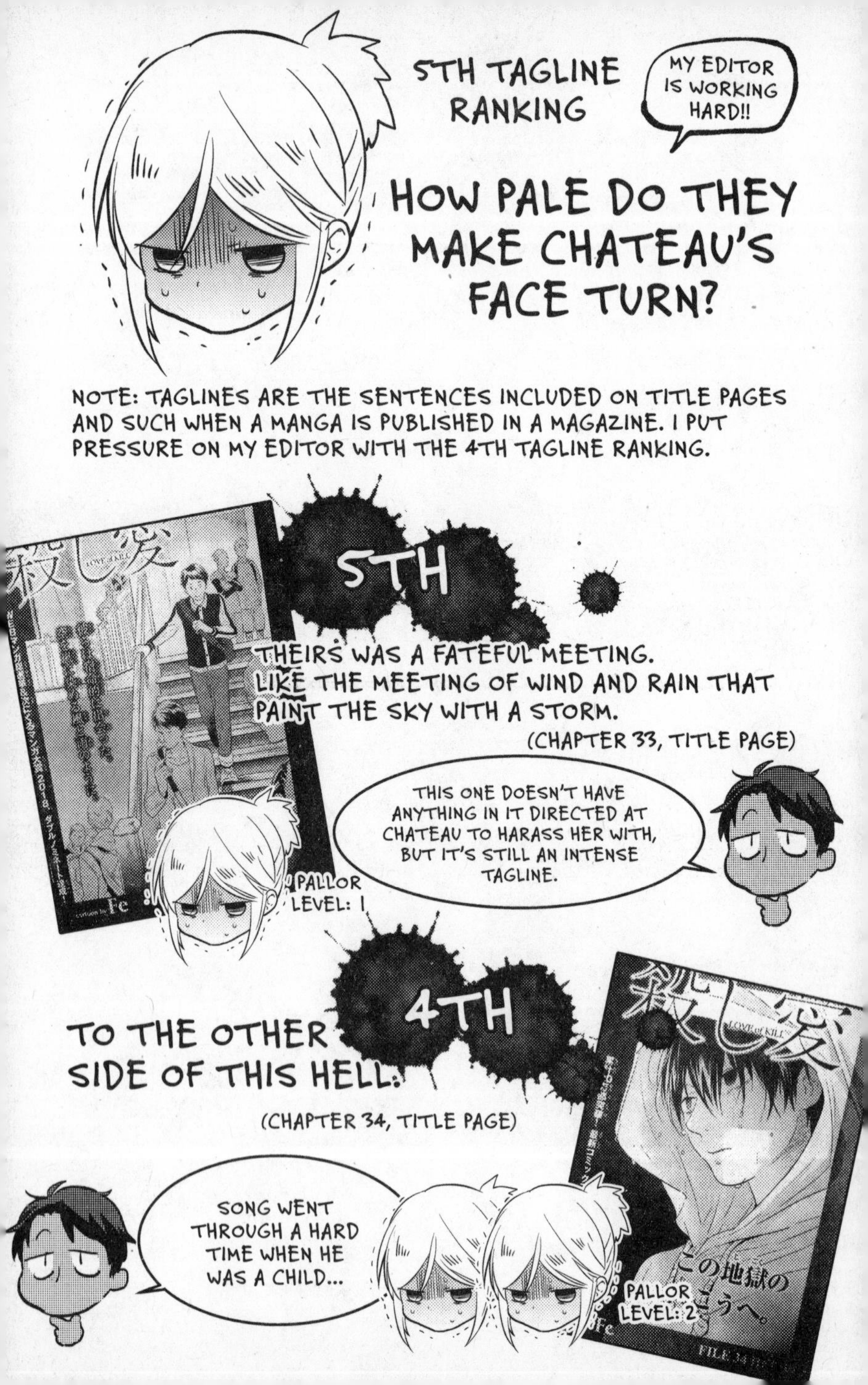
MY EDITOR IS WORKING HARD!!
5TH TAGLINE RANKING
HOW PALE DO THEY MAKE CHATEAU'S FACE TURN?
NOTE: TAGLINES ARE THE SENTENCES INCLUDED ON TITLE PAGES AND SUCH WHEN A MANGA IS PUBLISHED IN A MAGAZINE. I PUT PRESSURE ON MY EDITOR WITH THE 4TH TAGLINE RANKING.
5TH
THEIRS WAS A FATEFUL MEETING. LIKE THE MEETING OF WIND AND RAIN THAT PAINT THE SKY WITH A STORM.
(CHAPTER 33, TITLE PAGE)
THIS ONE DOESN'T HAVE ANYTHING IN IT DIRECTED AT CHATEAU TO HARASS HER WITH, BUT IT'S STILL AN INTENSE TAGLINE.
PALLOR LEVEL: 1
4TH
TO THE OTHER SIDE OF THIS HELL.
(CHAPTER 34, TITLE PAGE)
PALLOR LEVEL: 2
SONG WENT THROUGH A HARD TIME WHEN HE WAS A CHILD...

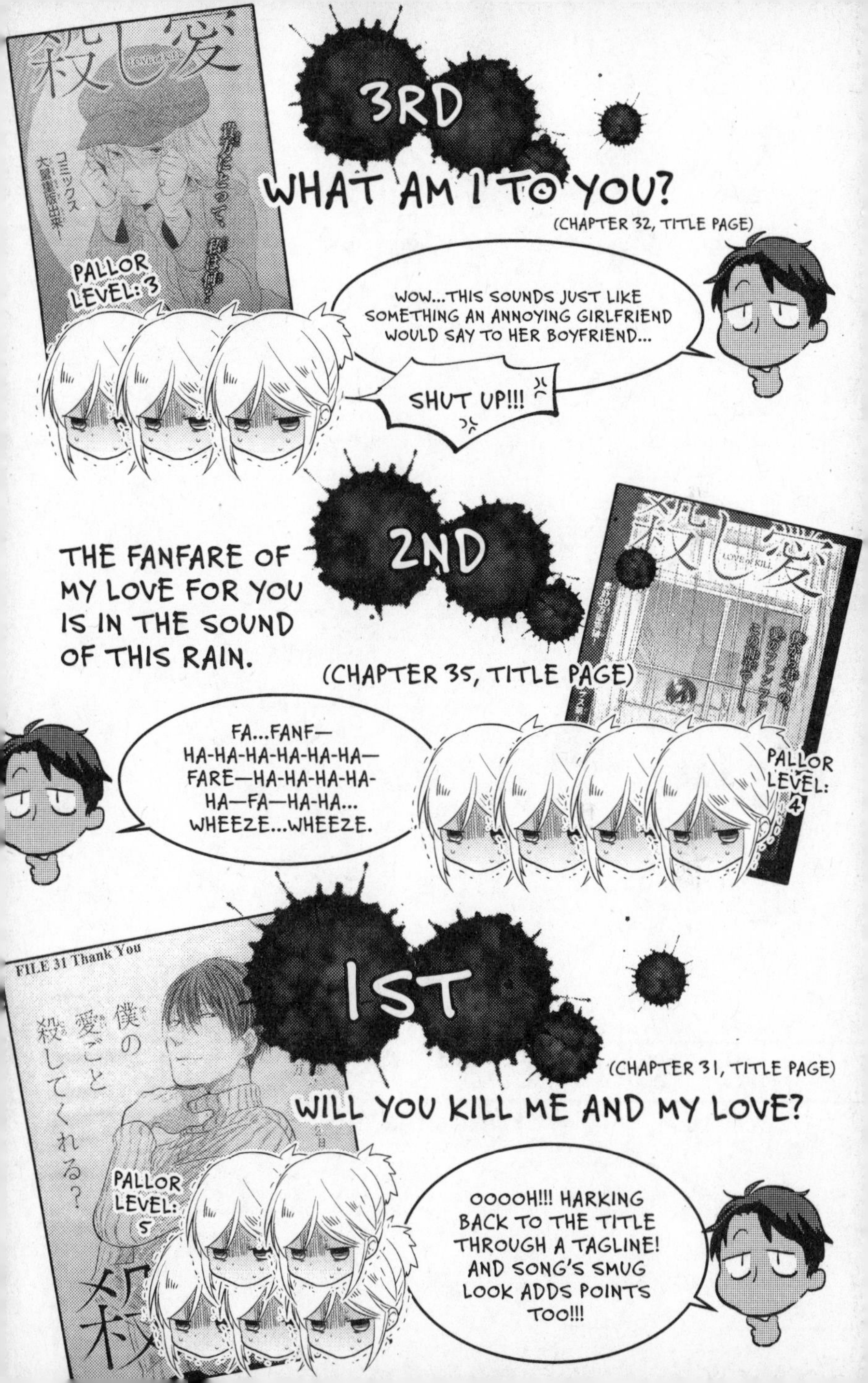

殺し愛
3RD
WHAT AM I TO YOU?
(CHAPTER 32, TITLE PAGE)
PALLOR LEVEL: 3
WOW...THIS SOUNDS JUST LIKE SOMETHING AN ANNOYING GIRLFRIEND WOULD SAY TO HER BOYFRIEND...
SHUT UP!!!
殺し愛
LOVE of KILL
2ND
THE FANFARE OF MY LOVE FOR YOU IS IN THE SOUND OF THIS RAIN.
(CHAPTER 35, TITLE PAGE)
PALLOR LEVEL: 4
FA...FANF— HA-HA-HA-HA-HA-HA— FARE—HA-HA-HA-HA-HA—FA—HA-HA... WHEEZE...WHEEZE.
FILE 31 Thank You
1ST
僕の愛ごと殺してくれる？
(CHAPTER 31, TITLE PAGE)
WILL YOU KILL ME AND MY LOVE?
PALLOR LEVEL: 5
OOOOH!!! HARKING BACK TO THE TITLE THROUGH A TAGLINE! AND SONG'S SMUG LOOK ADDS POINTS TOO!!!

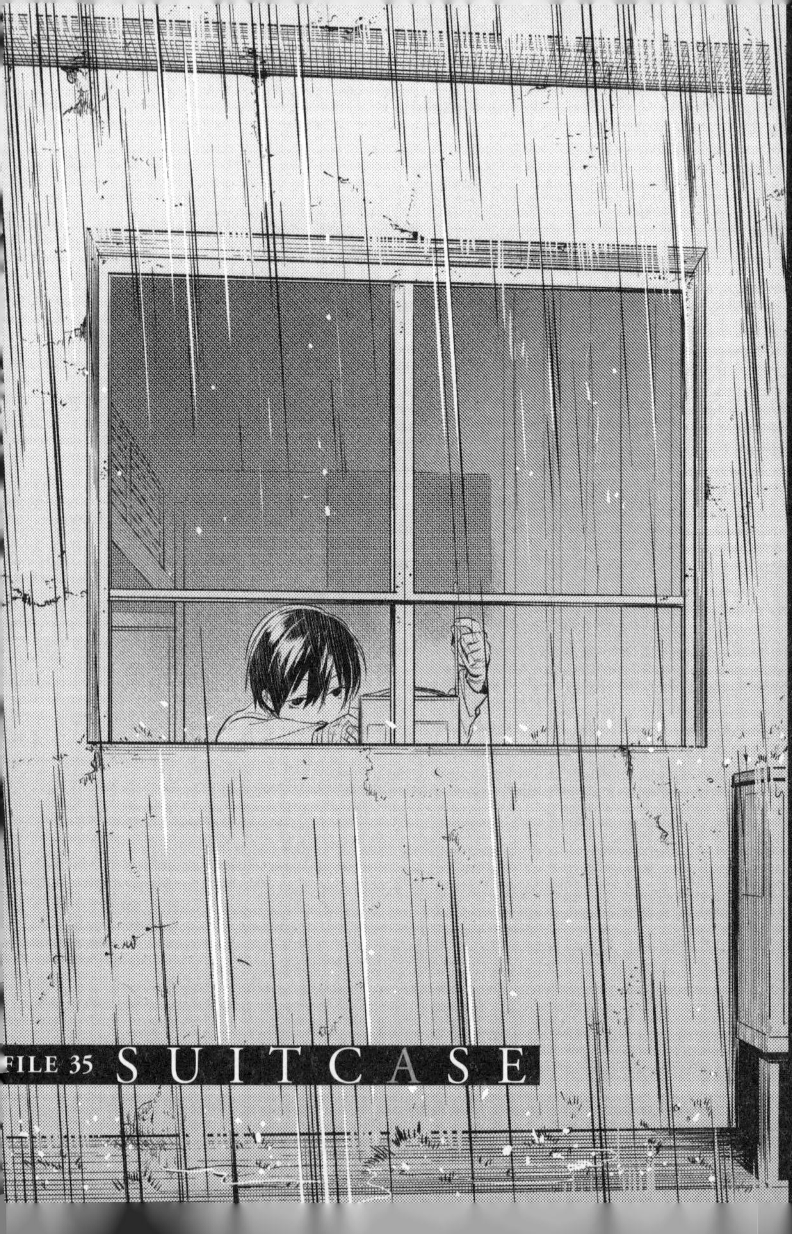
FILE 35 SUITCASE

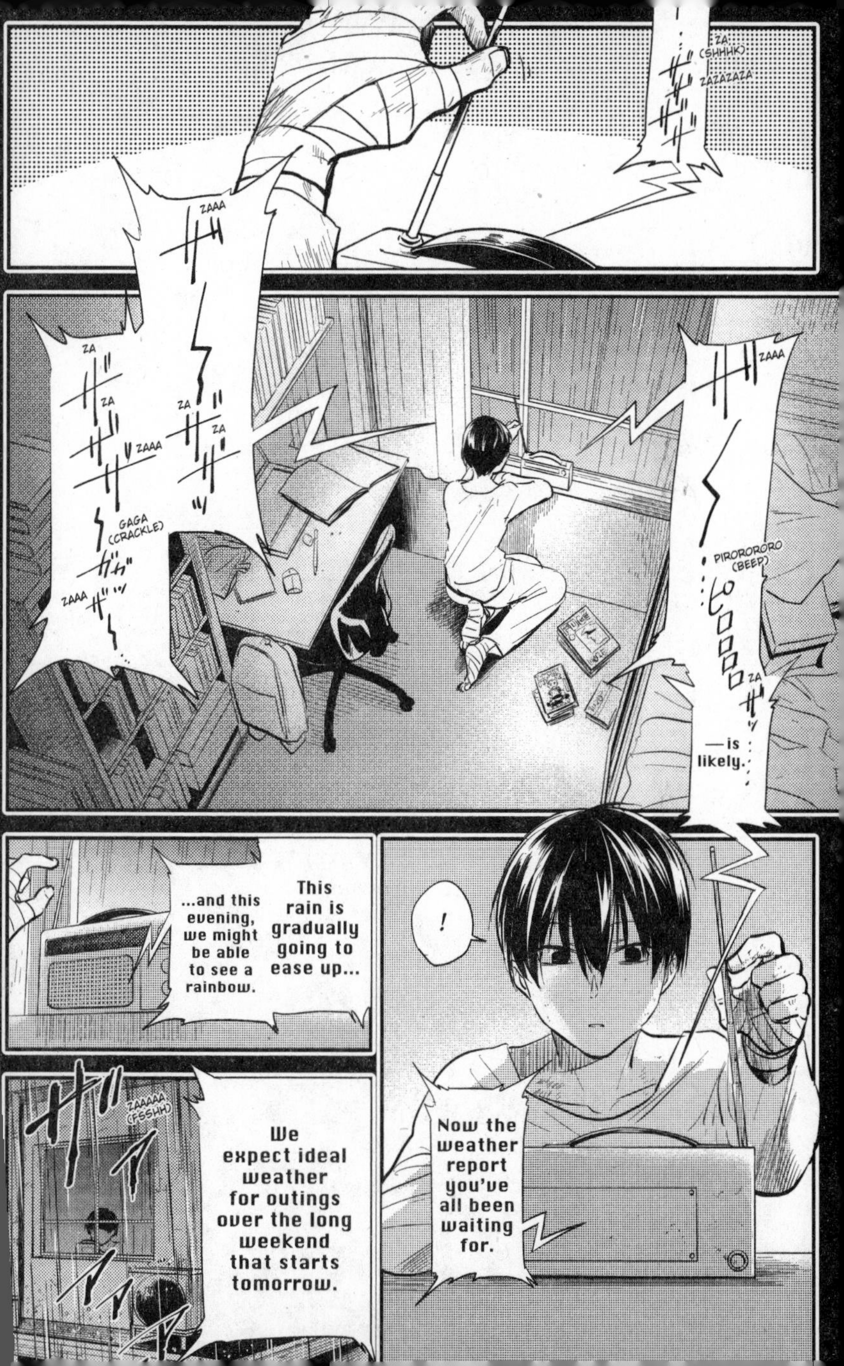
ZA (SHHHK)
ZAZAZAZA
ZAAA
ZAAA
PIROROROR (BEEP)
ZA
—is likely.
ZA
ZA
ZAAA
ZA
ZA
GAGA (CRACKLE)
ZAAA
!
Now the weather report you've all been waiting for.
This rain is gradually going to ease up...
...and this evening, we might be able to see a rainbow.
ZAAAAA (FSSHH)
We expect ideal weather for outings over the long weekend that starts tomorrow.

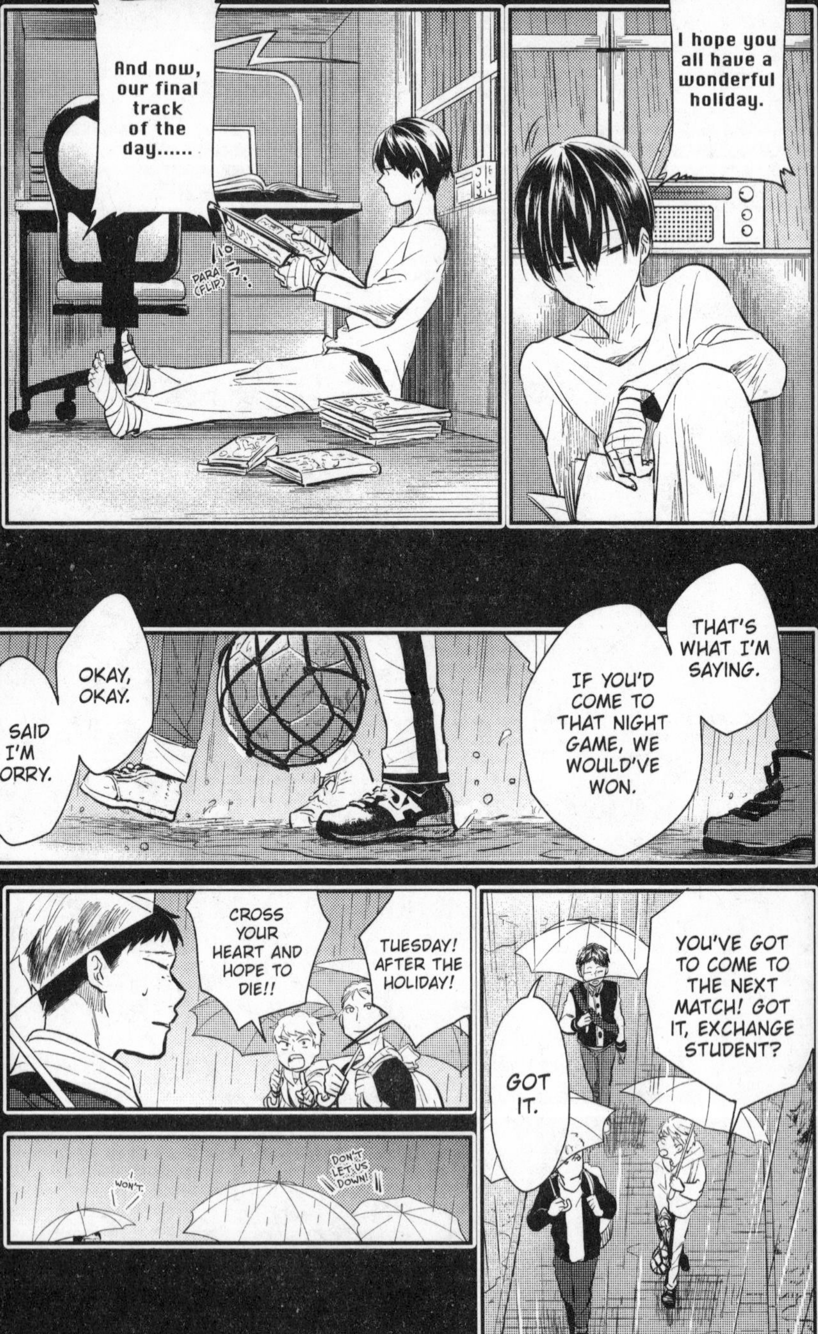
I hope you all have a wonderful holiday.
And now, our final track of the day......
PARA (FLIP)
THAT'S WHAT I'M SAYING.
IF YOU'D COME TO THAT NIGHT GAME, WE WOULD'VE WON.
OKAY, OKAY.
I SAID I'M SORRY.
YOU'VE GOT TO COME TO THE NEXT MATCH! GOT IT, EXCHANGE STUDENT?
GOT IT.
TUESDAY! AFTER THE HOLIDAY!
CROSS YOUR HEART AND HOPE TO DIE!!
DON'T LET US DOWN!
I WON'T.

KON
コン

KON
(CLANG)
コン

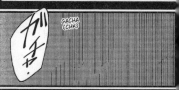

GACHA
(CHK)
ガチャ

♪♬♫♪

♪♪♫

GISHI
(CREAK)
ギッ…

BATAN
(SHUT)
バタン

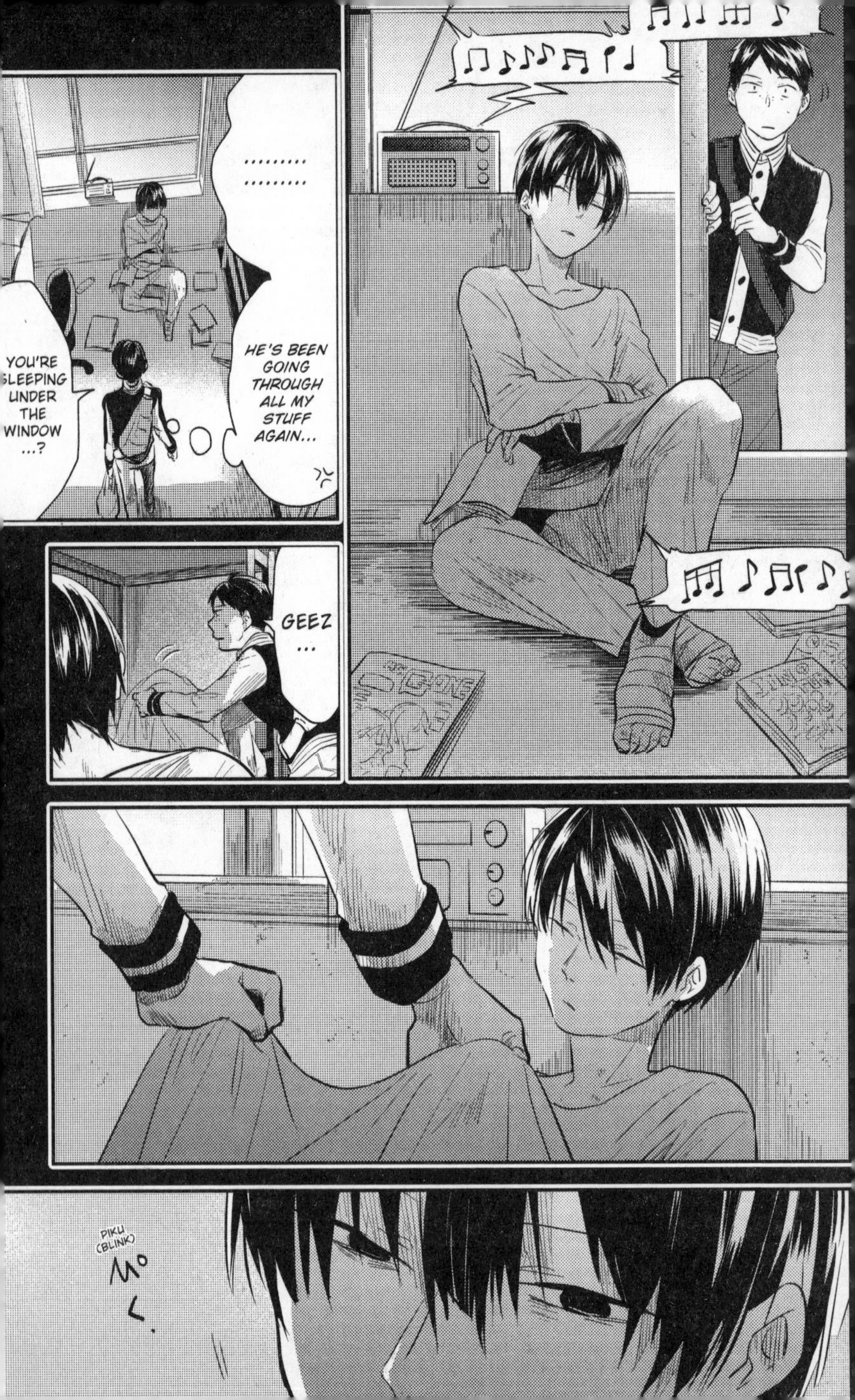
..........
..........
HE'S BEEN GOING THROUGH ALL MY STUFF AGAIN...
YOU'RE SLEEPING UNDER THE WINDOW ...?
GEEZ ...
PIKU (BLINK)

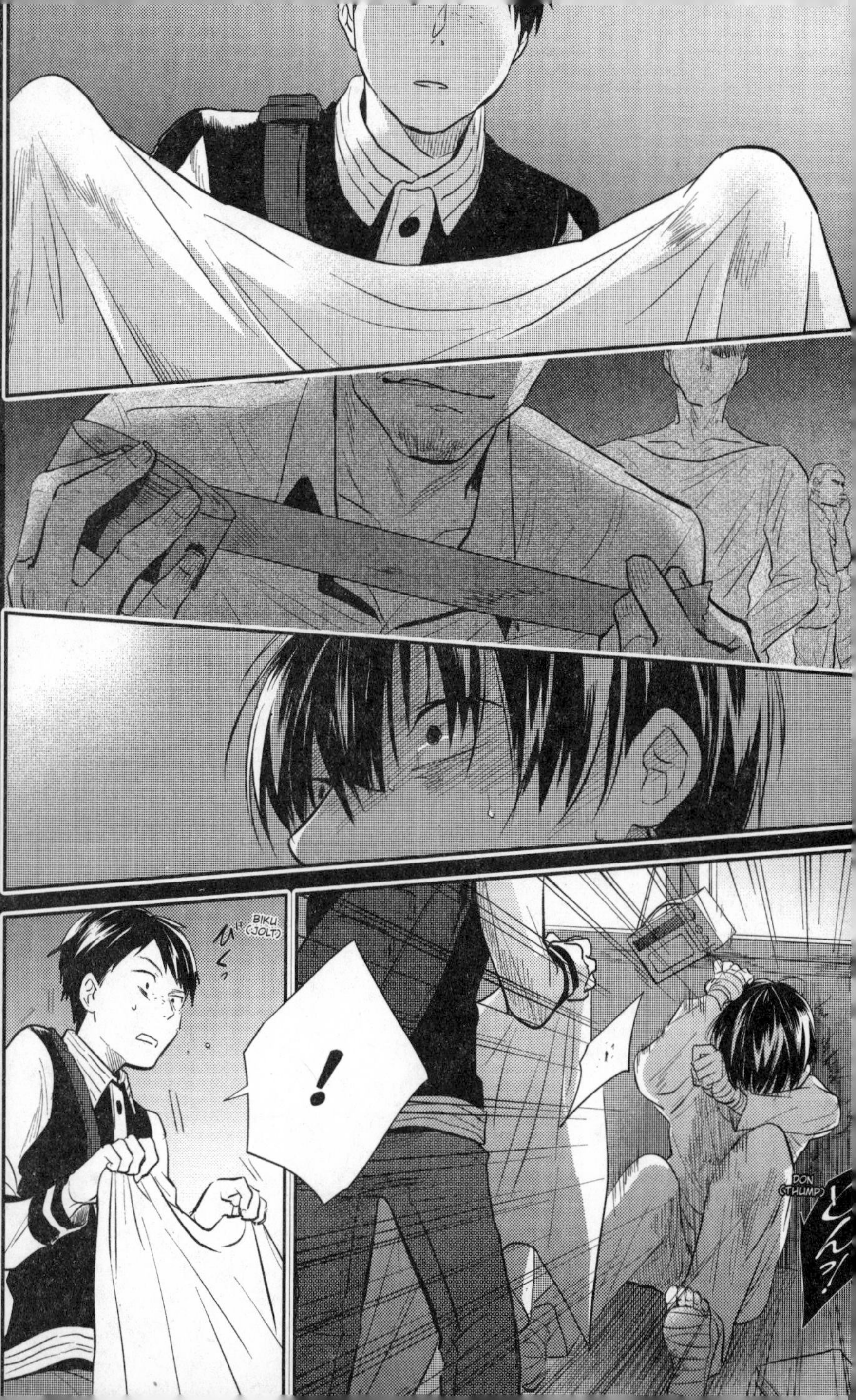
!
どんっ!
DON (THUMP)
びくっ
BIKU (JOLT)
!

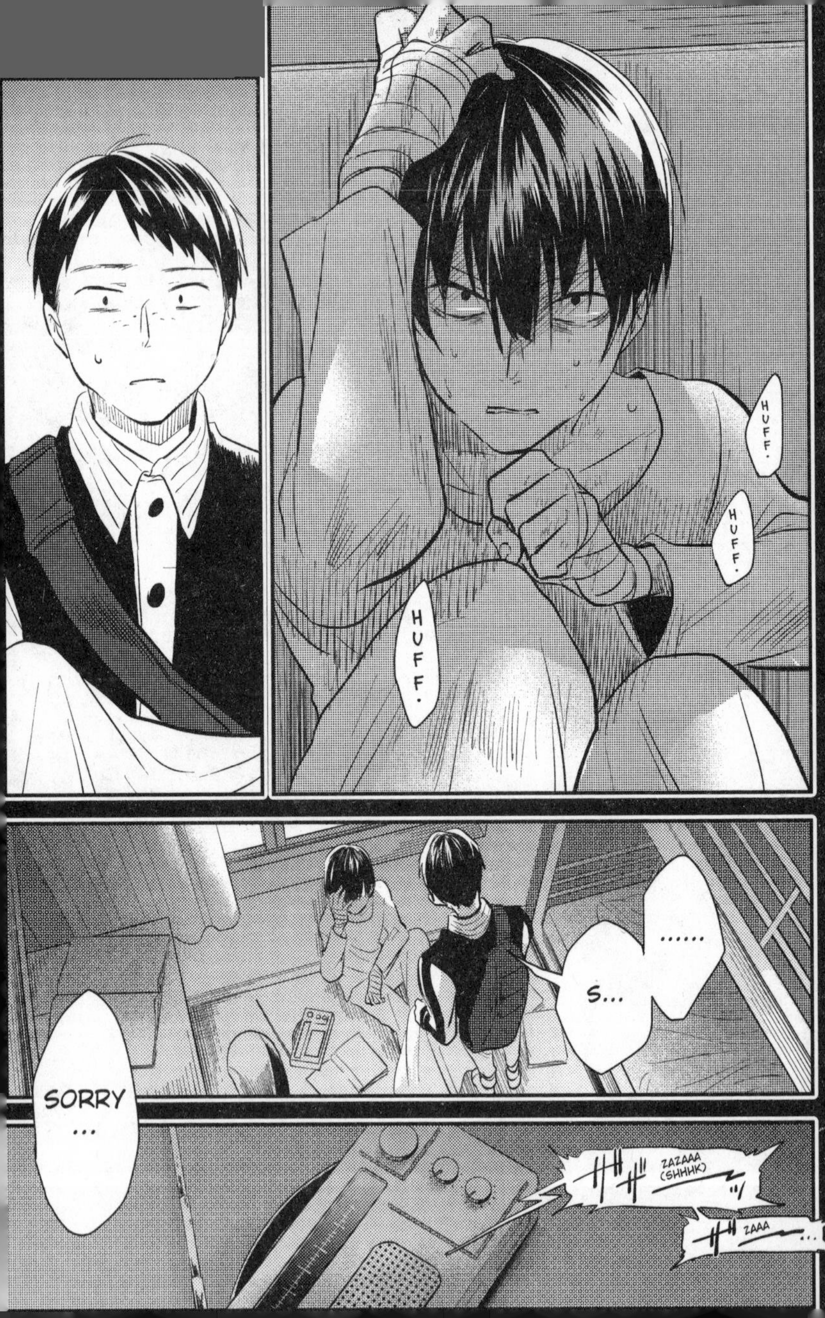
HUFF.
HUFF.
HUFF.
......
S...
SORRY ...
ZAZAAA (SHHHK)
ZAAA...

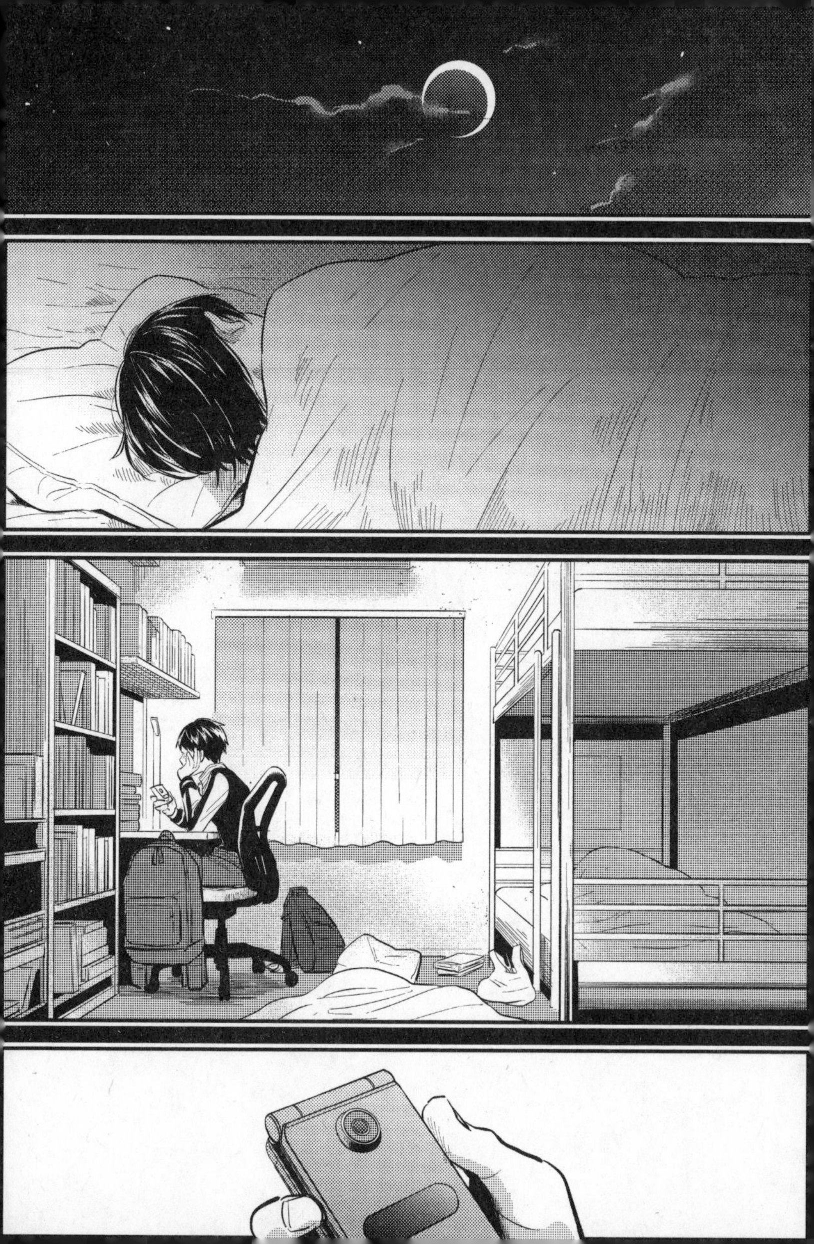

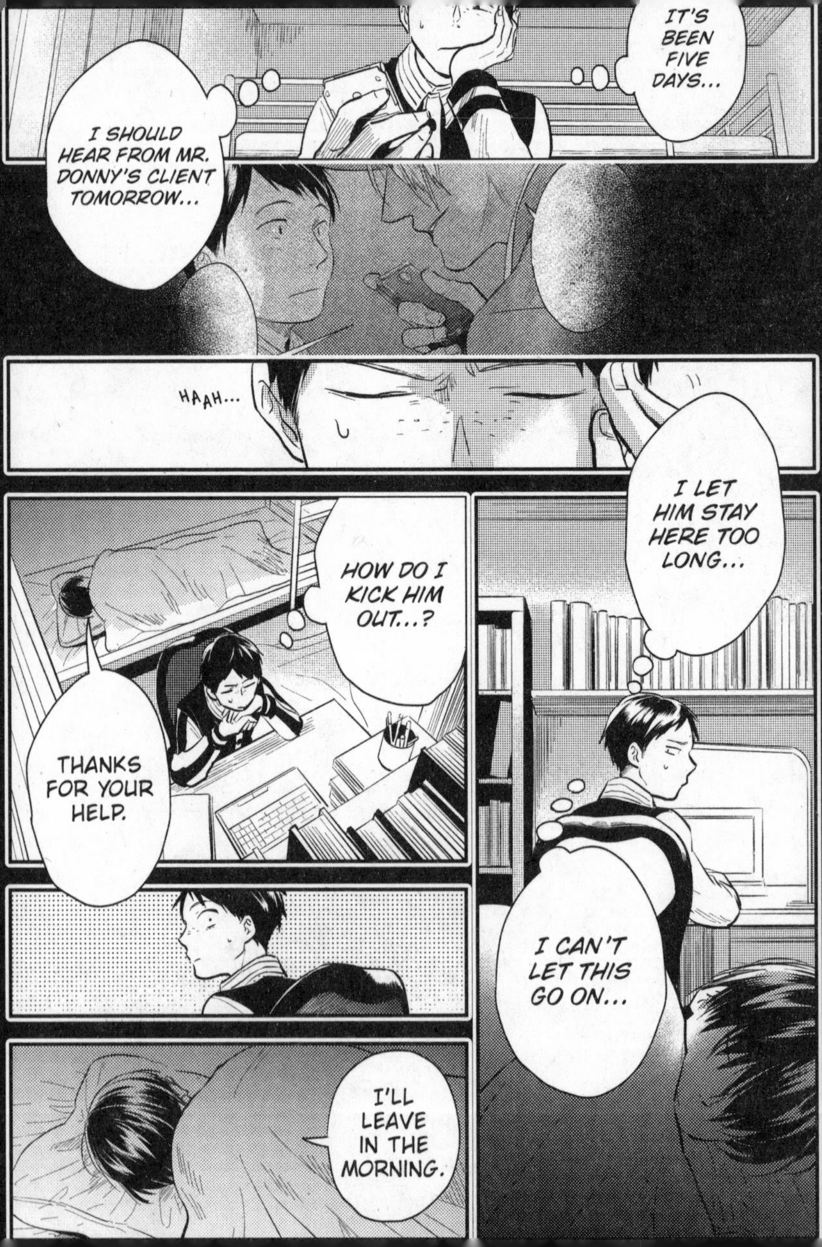
IT'S BEEN FIVE DAYS...
I SHOULD HEAR FROM MR. DONNY'S CLIENT TOMORROW...
HAAH...
I LET HIM STAY HERE TOO LONG...
I CAN'T LET THIS GO ON...
HOW DO I KICK HIM OUT...?
THANKS FOR YOUR HELP.
I'LL LEAVE IN THE MORNING.

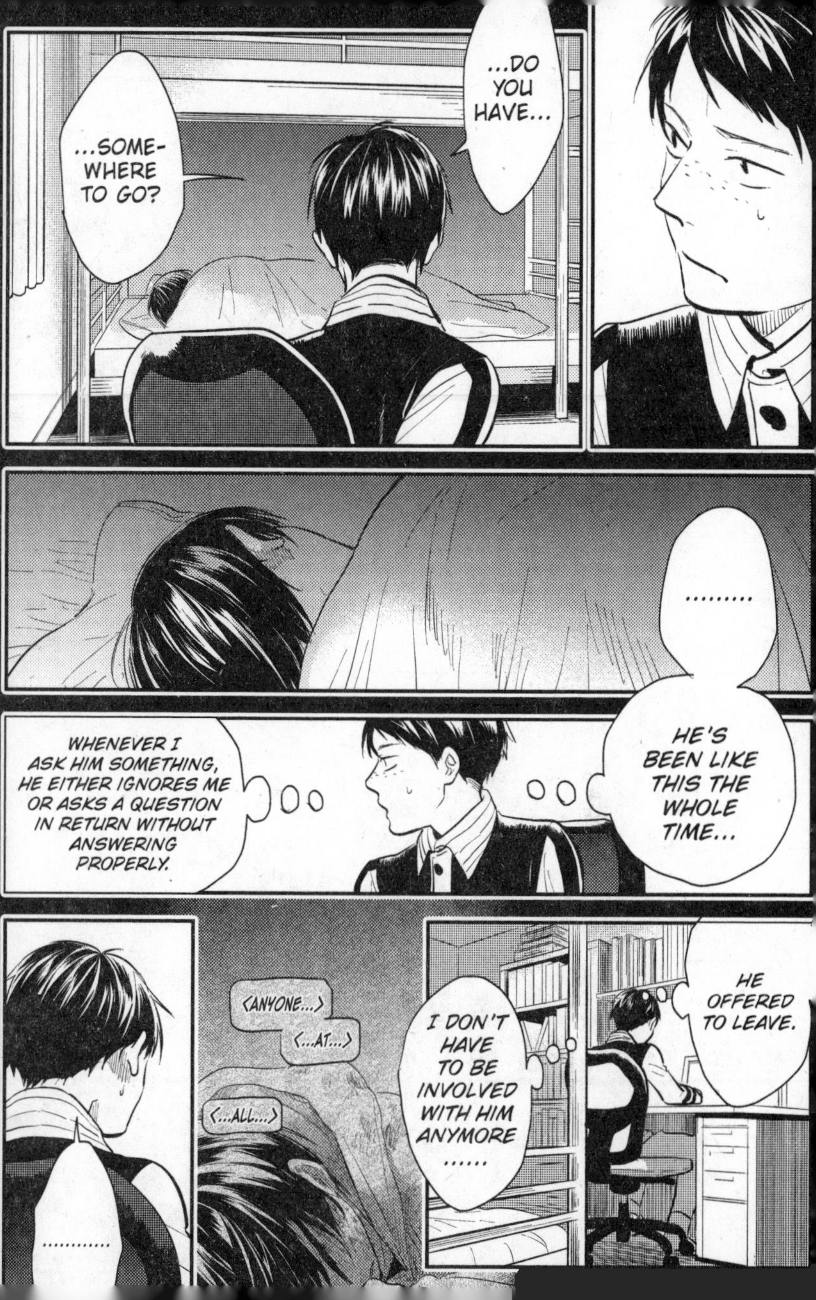
...DO YOU HAVE...
...SOME-WHERE TO GO?
.........
HE'S BEEN LIKE THIS THE WHOLE TIME...
WHENEVER I ASK HIM SOMETHING, HE EITHER IGNORES ME OR ASKS A QUESTION IN RETURN WITHOUT ANSWERING PROPERLY.
HE OFFERED TO LEAVE.
I DON'T HAVE TO BE INVOLVED WITH HIM ANYMORE ......
<ANYONE...>
<...AT...>
<...ALL...>
...........

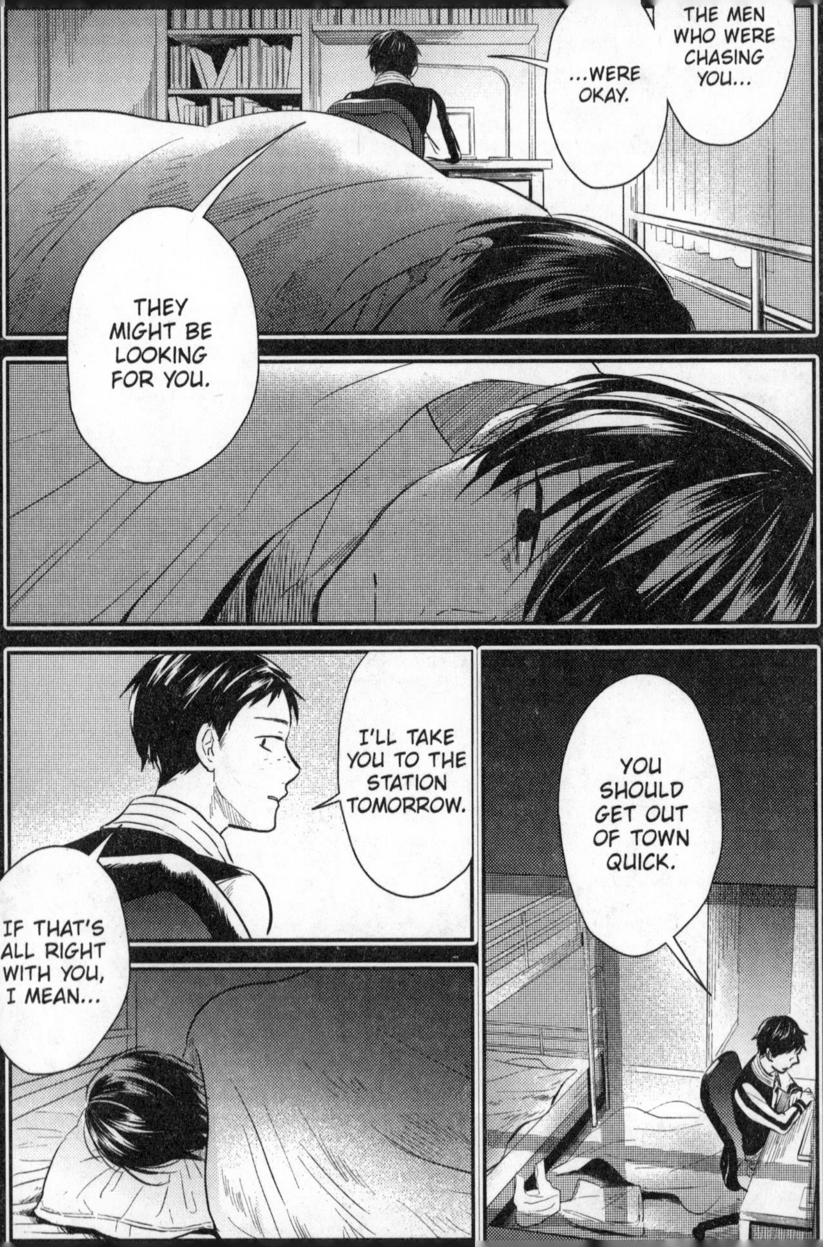
THE MEN WHO WERE CHASING YOU...
...WERE OKAY.
THEY MIGHT BE LOOKING FOR YOU.
YOU SHOULD GET OUT OF TOWN QUICK.
I'LL TAKE YOU TO THE STATION TOMORROW.
IF THAT'S ALL RIGHT WITH YOU, I MEAN...

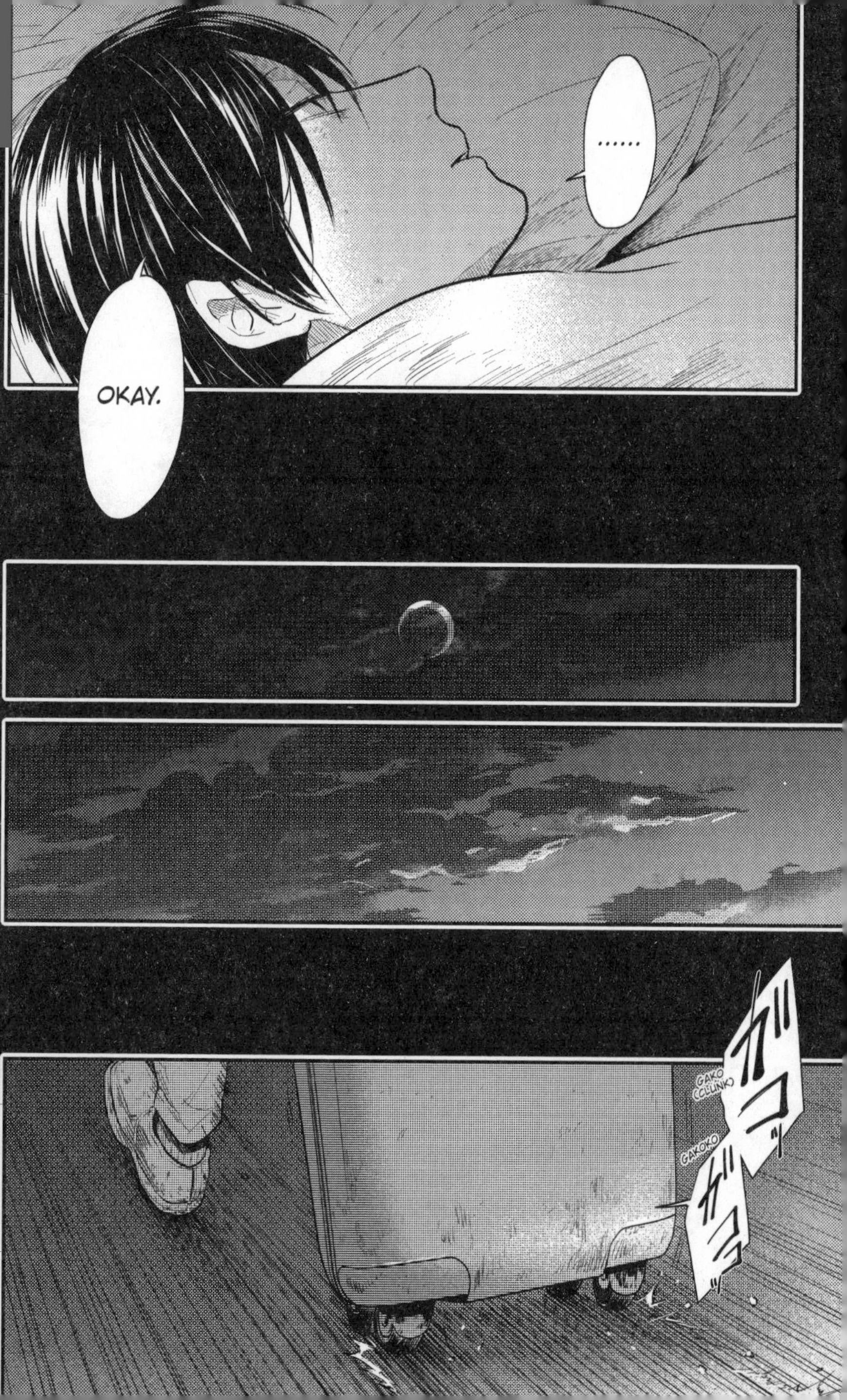
......
OKAY.
GAKO (CLUNK)
GAKOKO

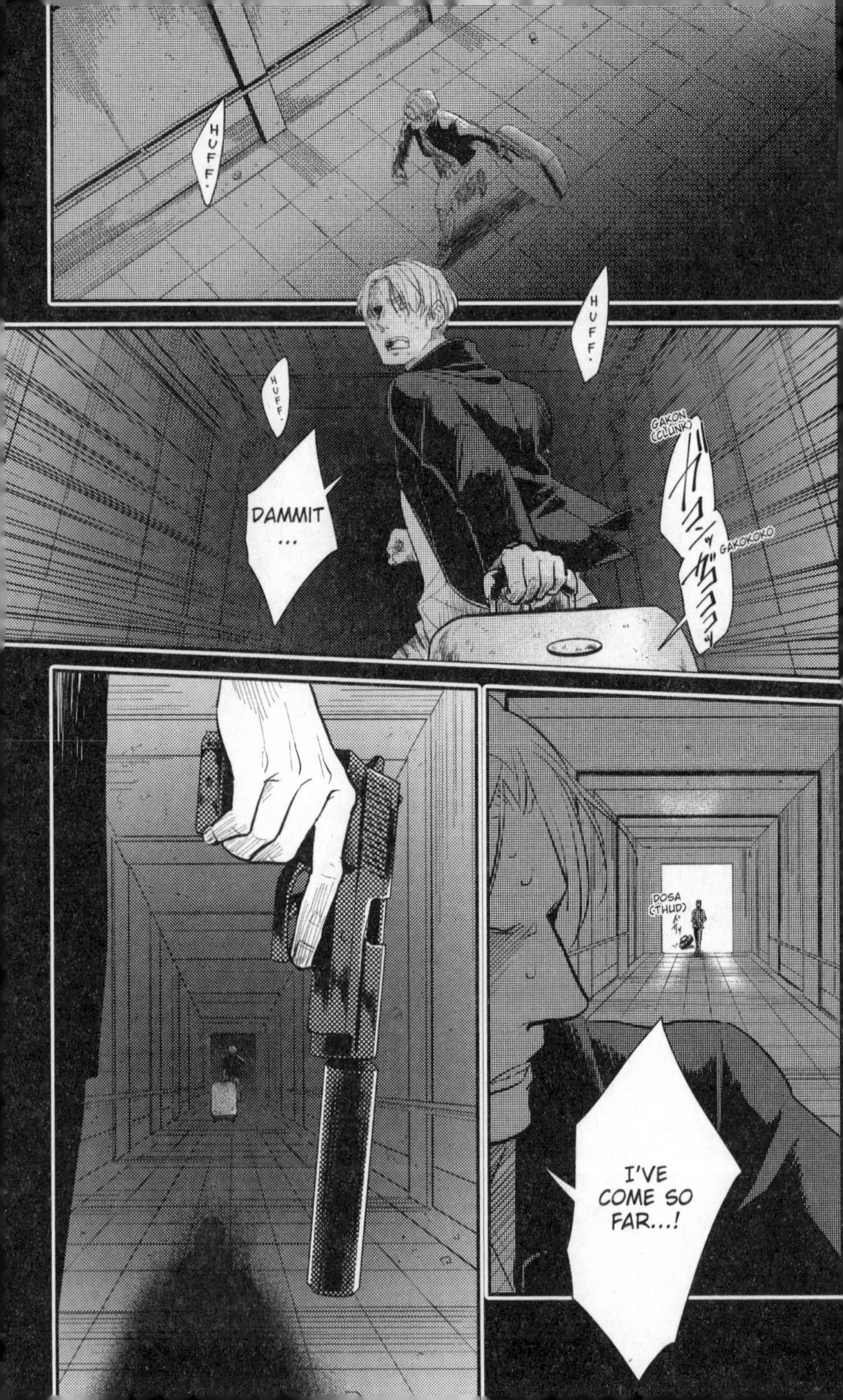
HUFF.
HUFF.
GAKON (CLUNK)
GAKOKOKO
HUFF.
DAMMIT...
DOSA (THUD)
I'VE COME SO FAR...!

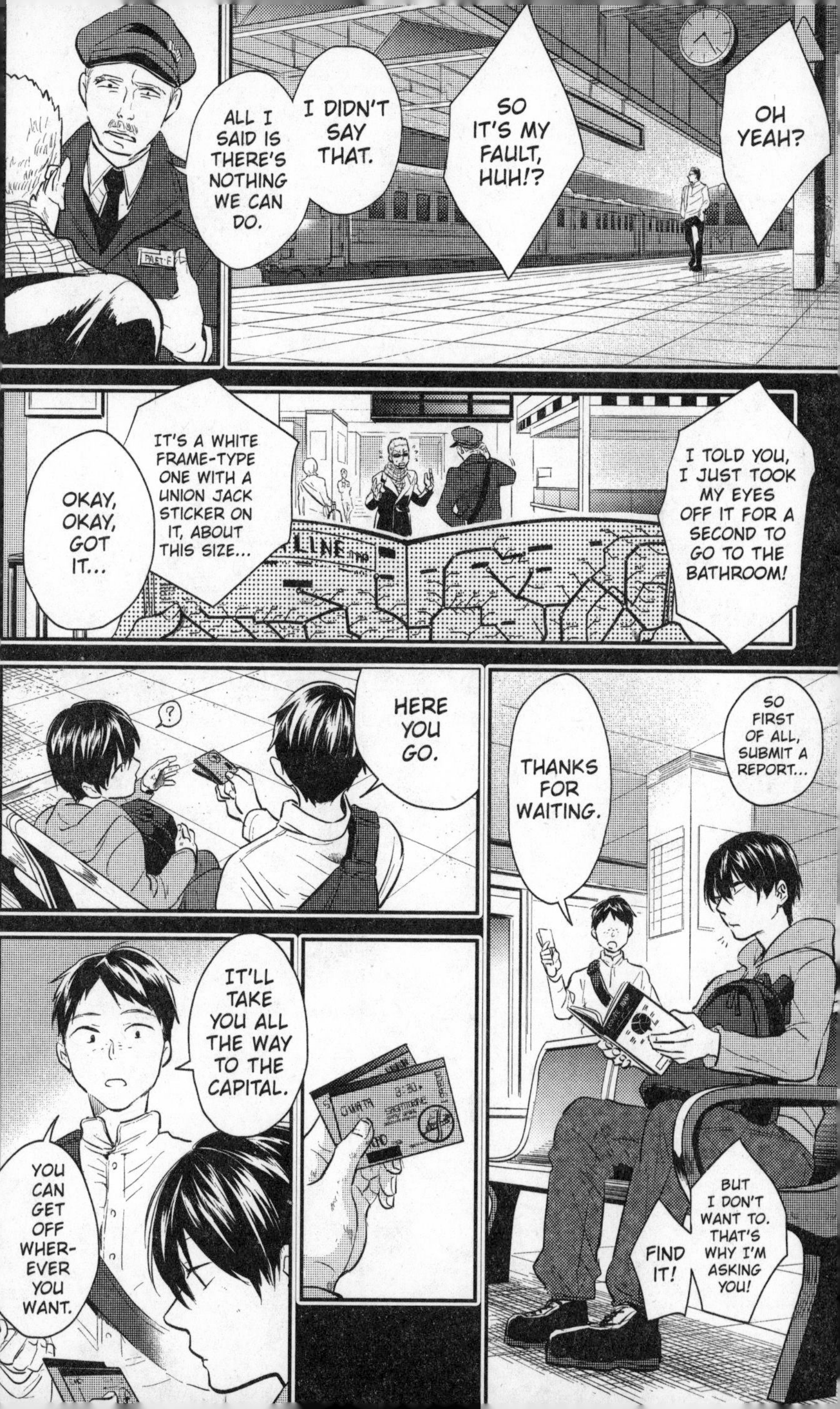
OH YEAH?
SO IT'S MY FAULT, HUH!?
I DIDN'T SAY THAT.
ALL I SAID IS THERE'S NOTHING WE CAN DO.
I TOLD YOU, I JUST TOOK MY EYES OFF IT FOR A SECOND TO GO TO THE BATHROOM!
IT'S A WHITE FRAME-TYPE ONE WITH A UNION JACK STICKER ON IT, ABOUT THIS SIZE...
OKAY, OKAY, GOT IT...
SO FIRST OF ALL, SUBMIT A REPORT...
THANKS FOR WAITING.
BUT I DON'T WANT TO. THAT'S WHY I'M ASKING YOU!
FIND IT!
HERE YOU GO.
IT'LL TAKE YOU ALL THE WAY TO THE CAPITAL.
YOU CAN GET OFF WHER-EVER YOU WANT.

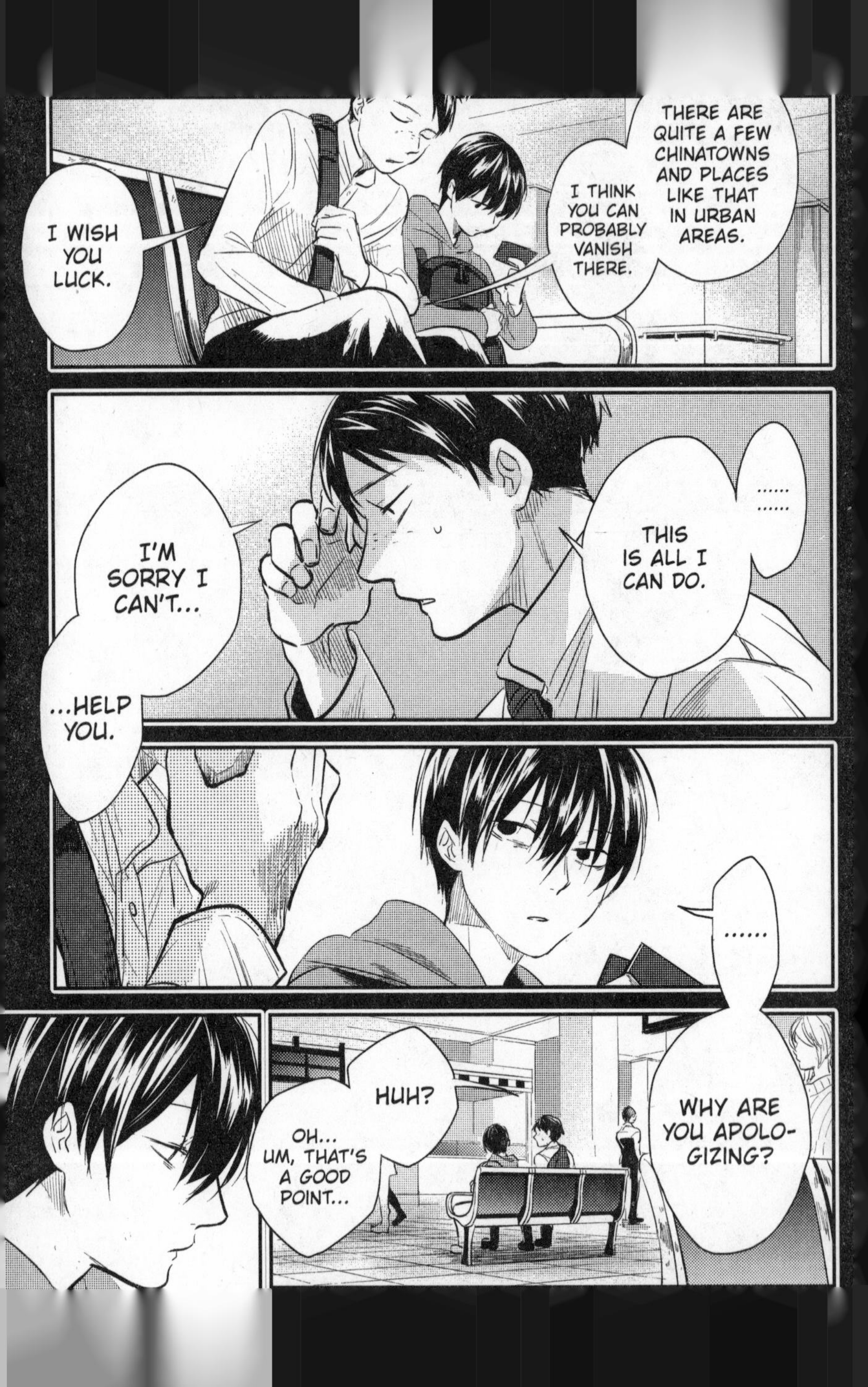
THERE ARE QUITE A FEW CHINATOWNS AND PLACES LIKE THAT IN URBAN AREAS.
I THINK YOU CAN PROBABLY VANISH THERE.
I WISH YOU LUCK.
...... ......
THIS IS ALL I CAN DO.
I'M SORRY I CAN'T...
...HELP YOU.
......
WHY ARE YOU APOLO-GIZING?
HUH?
OH... UM, THAT'S A GOOD POINT...

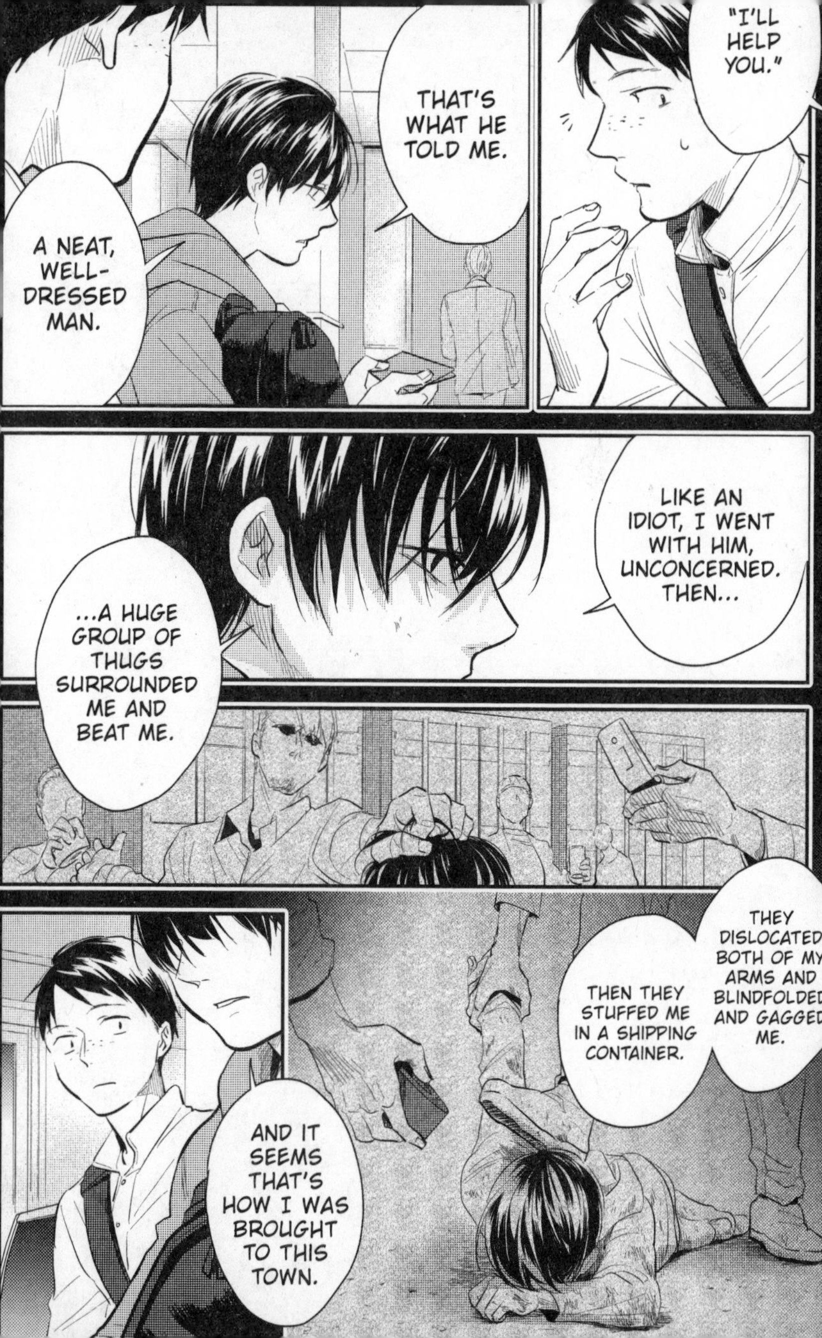
"I'LL HELP YOU."
THAT'S WHAT HE TOLD ME.
A NEAT, WELL-DRESSED MAN.
LIKE AN IDIOT, I WENT WITH HIM, UNCONCERNED. THEN...
...A HUGE GROUP OF THUGS SURROUNDED ME AND BEAT ME.
THEY DISLOCATED BOTH OF MY ARMS AND BLINDFOLDED AND GAGGED ME.
THEN THEY STUFFED ME IN A SHIPPING CONTAINER.
AND IT SEEMS THAT'S HOW I WAS BROUGHT TO THIS TOWN.

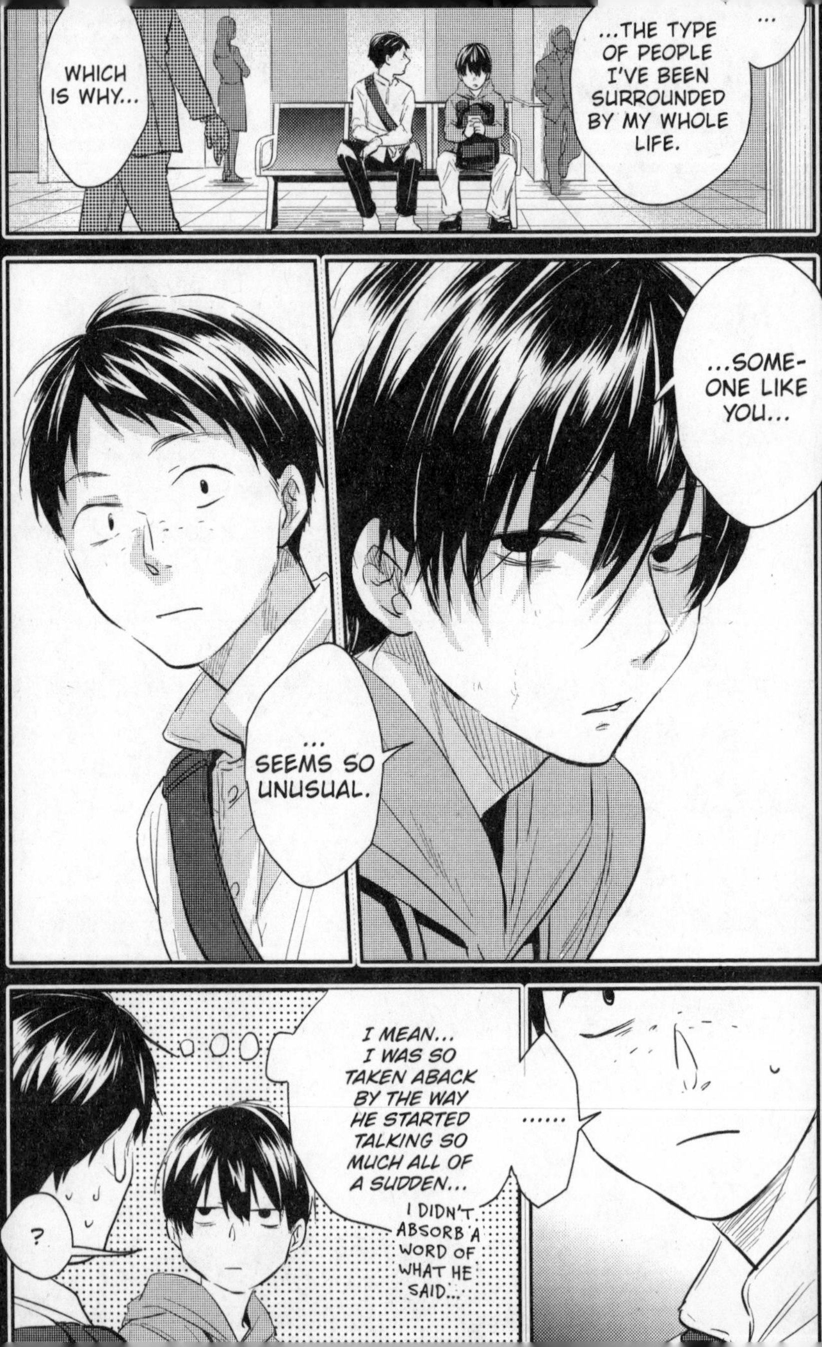
...
...THE TYPE OF PEOPLE I'VE BEEN SURROUNDED BY MY WHOLE LIFE.
WHICH IS WHY...
...SOME-ONE LIKE YOU...
... SEEMS SO UNUSUAL.
......
I MEAN... I WAS SO TAKEN ABACK BY THE WAY HE STARTED TALKING SO MUCH ALL OF A SUDDEN...
I DIDN'T ABSORB A WORD OF WHAT HE SAID...
?

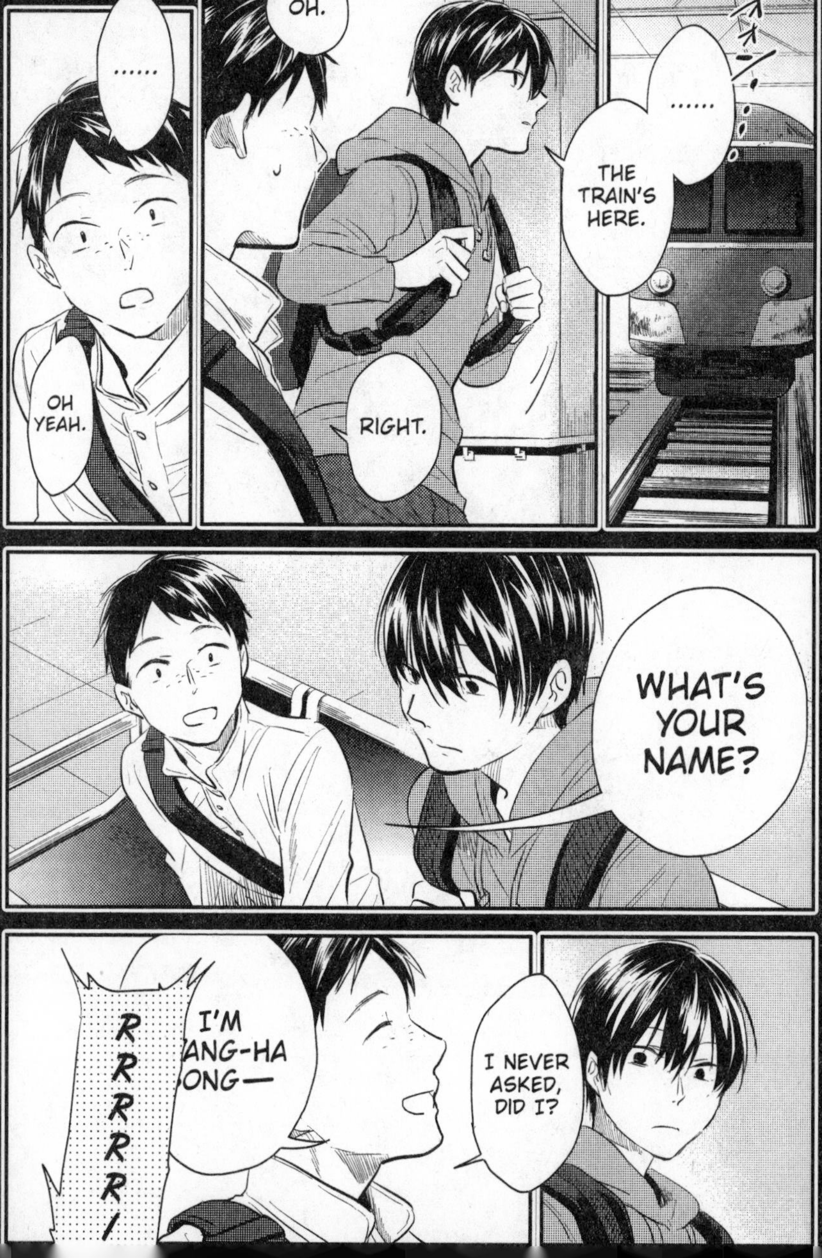
FUOOON (HONK)
......
THE TRAIN'S HERE.
OH.
RIGHT.
......
OH YEAH.
WHAT'S YOUR NAME?
I NEVER ASKED, DID I?
I'M
ANG-HA
ONG—
RRRRRI

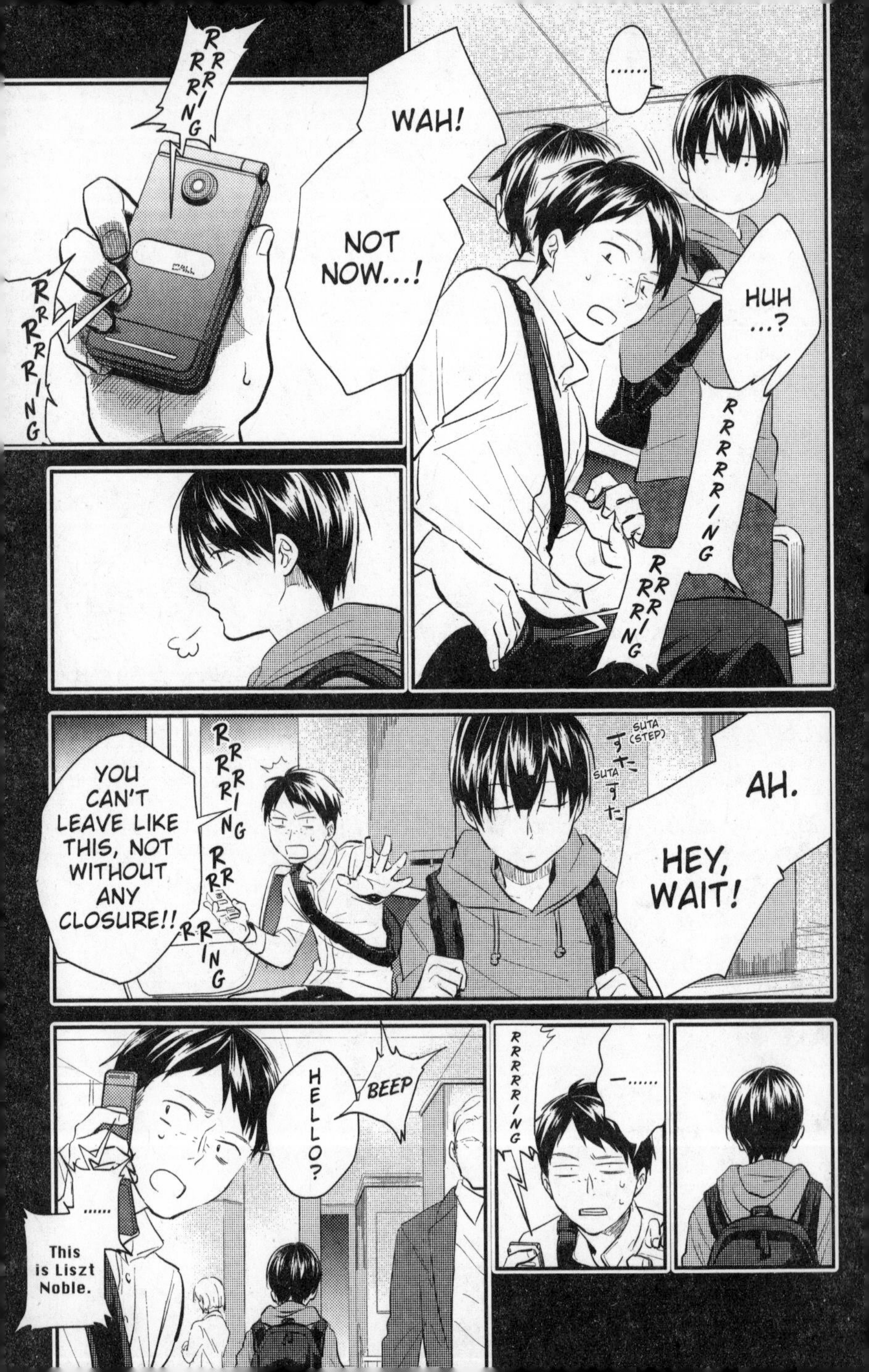
......
WAH!
NOT NOW...!
HUH ...?
RRRRRING
RRRRING
RRRRING
RRRRRING
SUTA (STEP) すた
SUTA すた
AH.
HEY, WAIT!
YOU CAN'T LEAVE LIKE THIS, NOT WITHOUT ANY CLOSURE!!
RRRRRING
RRRRING
RRRRRING
—......
BEEP
HELLO?
......
This is Liszt Noble.

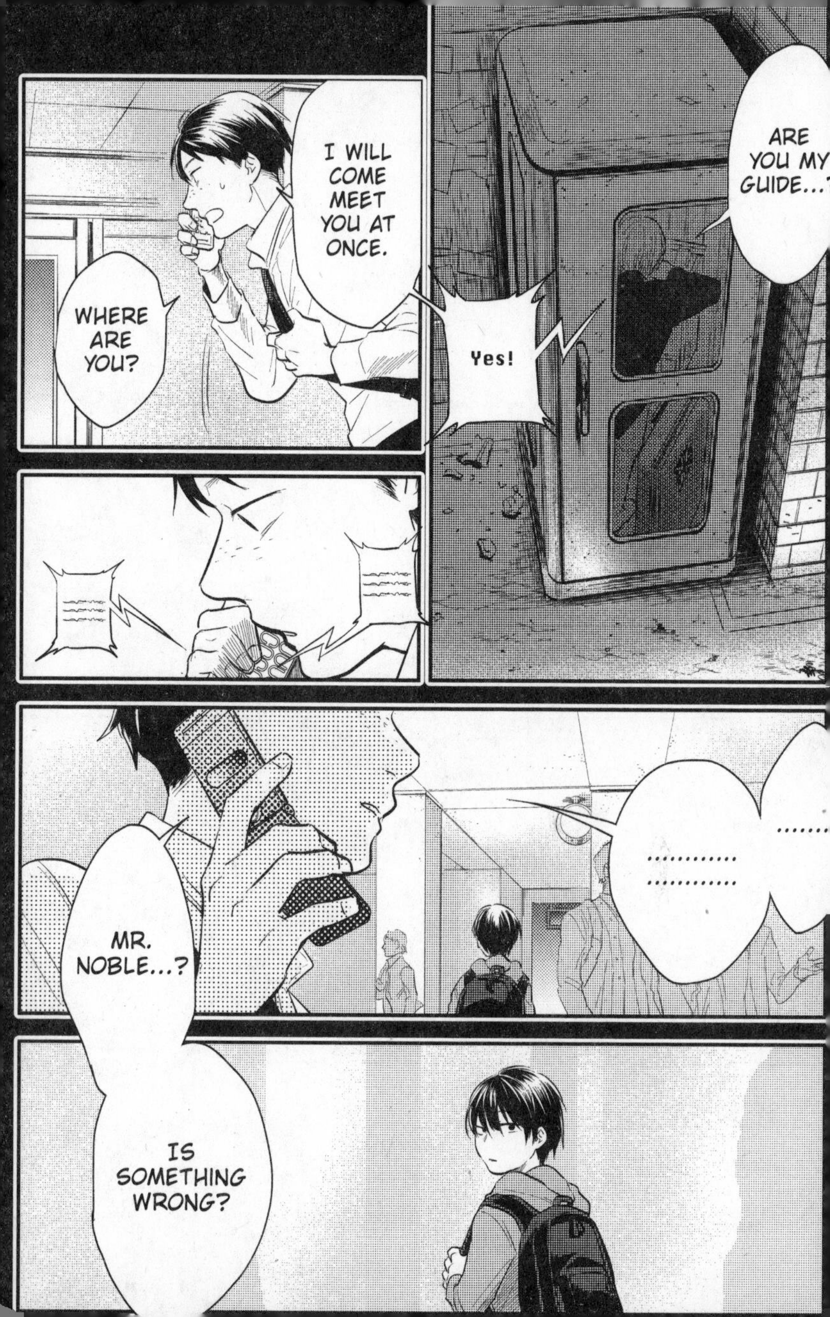
ARE YOU MY GUIDE...?
Yes!
I WILL COME MEET YOU AT ONCE.
WHERE ARE YOU?
.......
............
............
MR. NOBLE...?
IS SOMETHING WRONG?

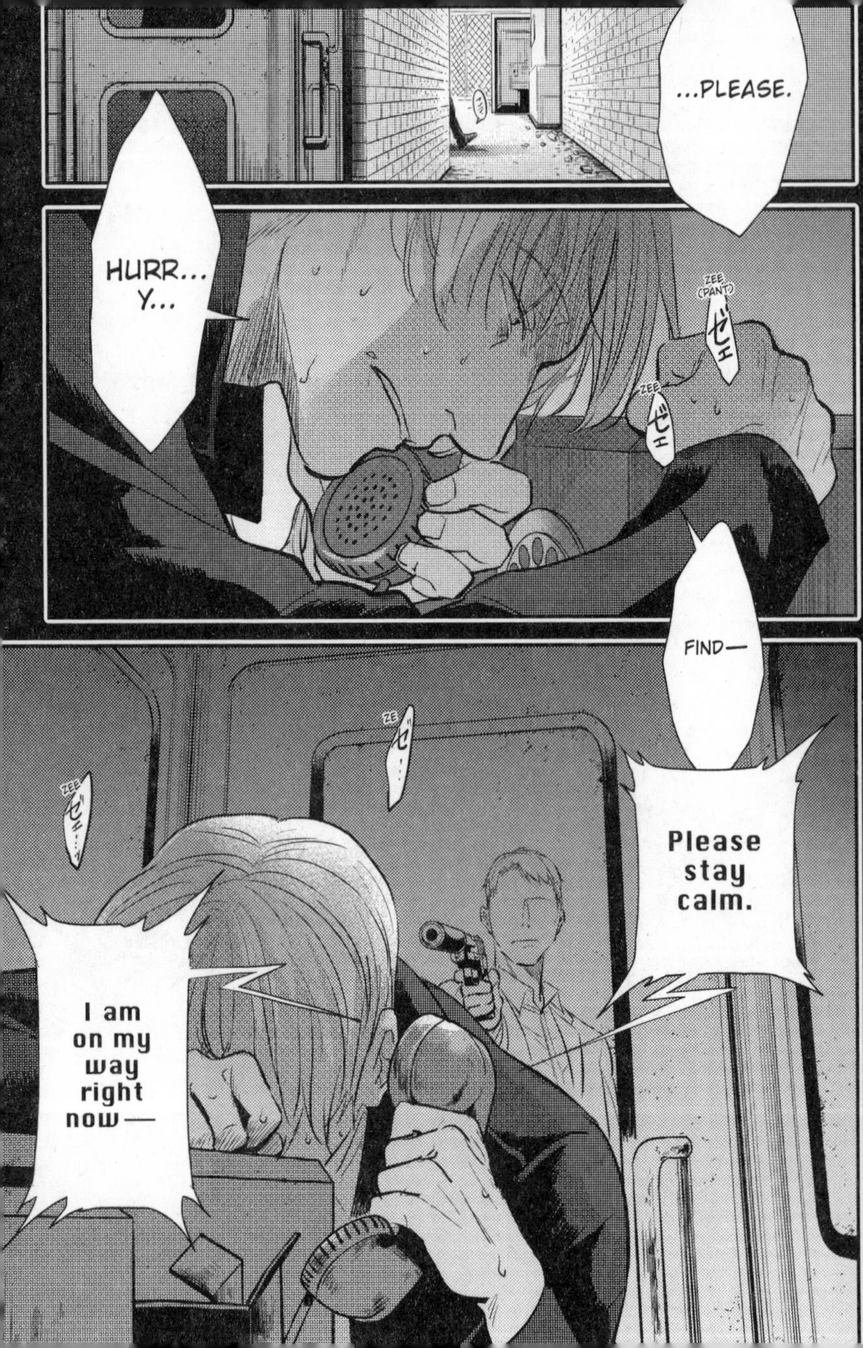
...PLEASE.
HURR... Y...
ZEE (PANT)
ゼェ
ZEE
ゼェ
FIND—
Please stay calm.
ZE
ゼ…
ZEE
ゼェ…
I am on my way right now—

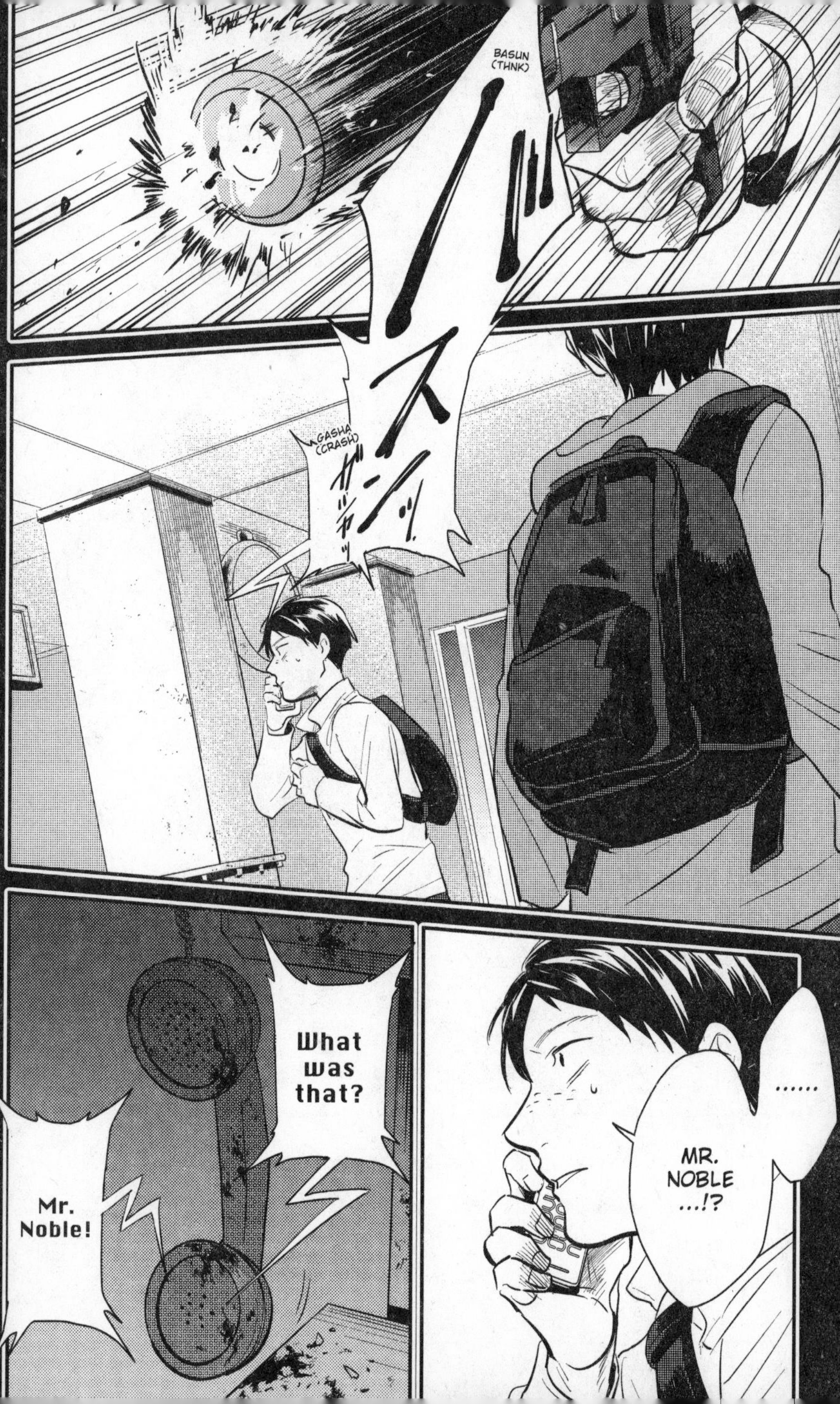
BASUN (THNK)
GASHA (CRASH)
......
MR. NOBLE ...!?
What was that?
Mr. Noble!

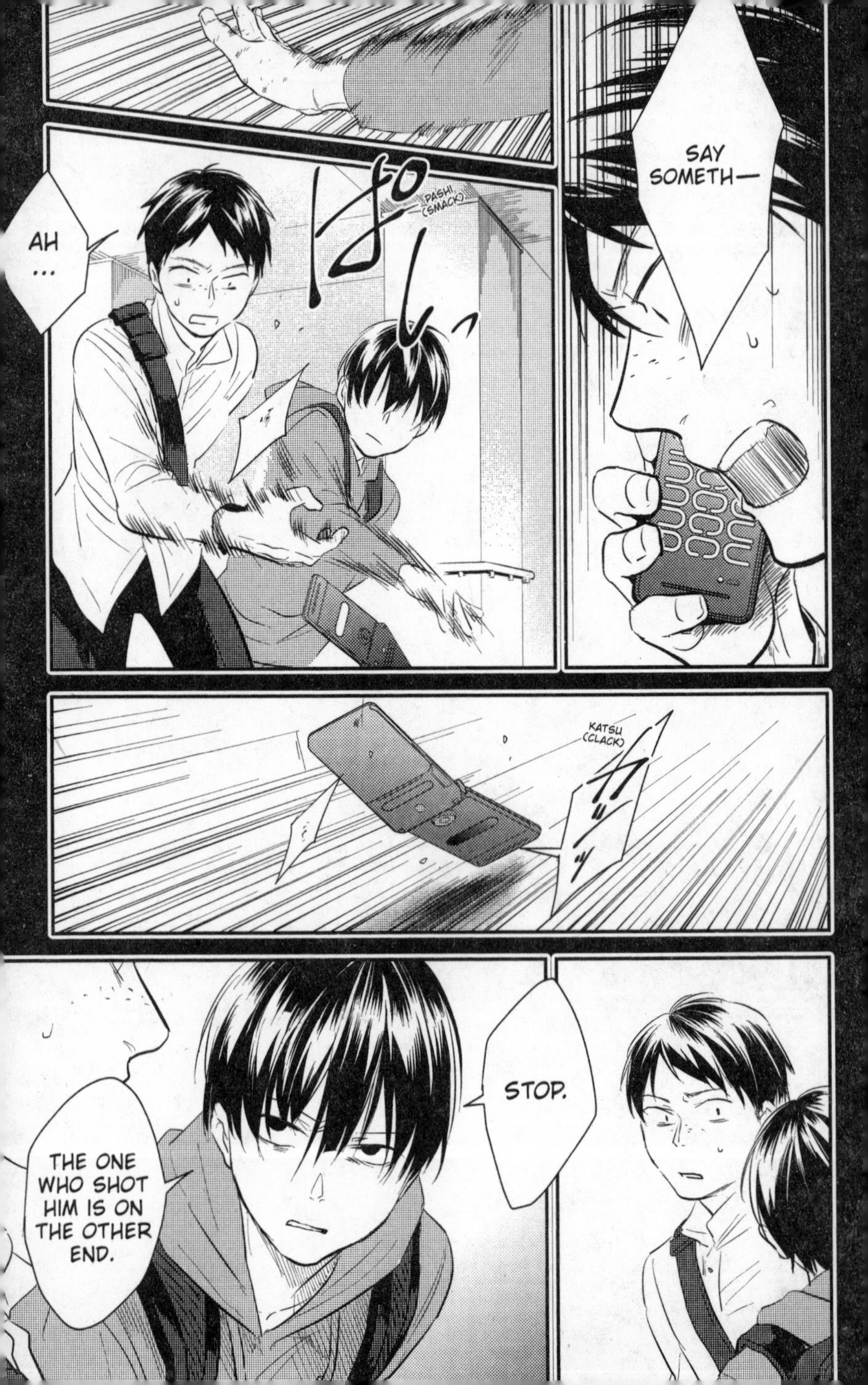
SAY SOMETH—
AH ...
PASHI (SMACK)
KATSU (CLACK)
STOP.
THE ONE WHO SHOT HIM IS ON THE OTHER END.

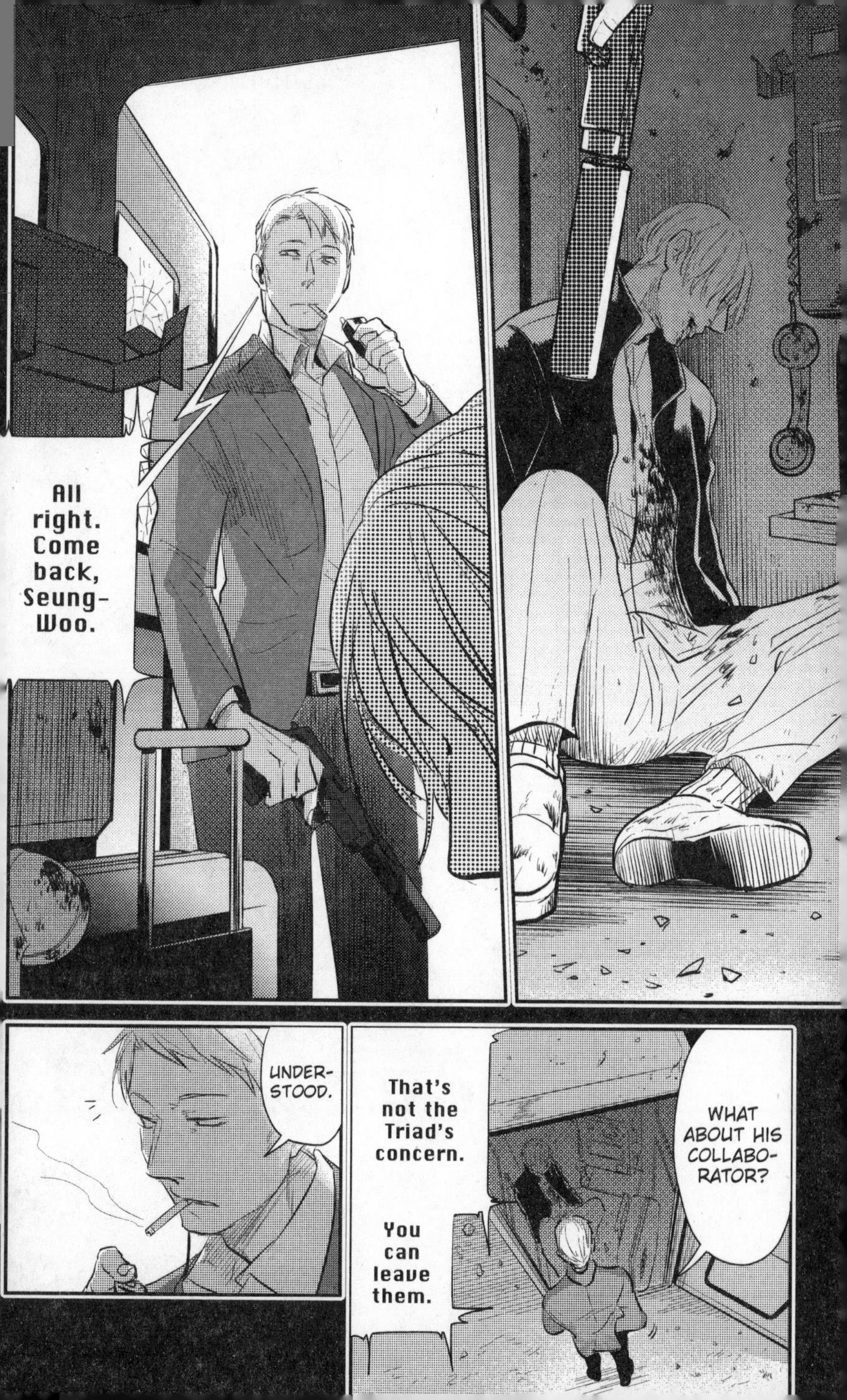
All right. Come back, Seung-Woo.
WHAT ABOUT HIS COLLABO-RATOR?
That's not the Triad's concern.
You can leave them.
UNDER-STOOD.

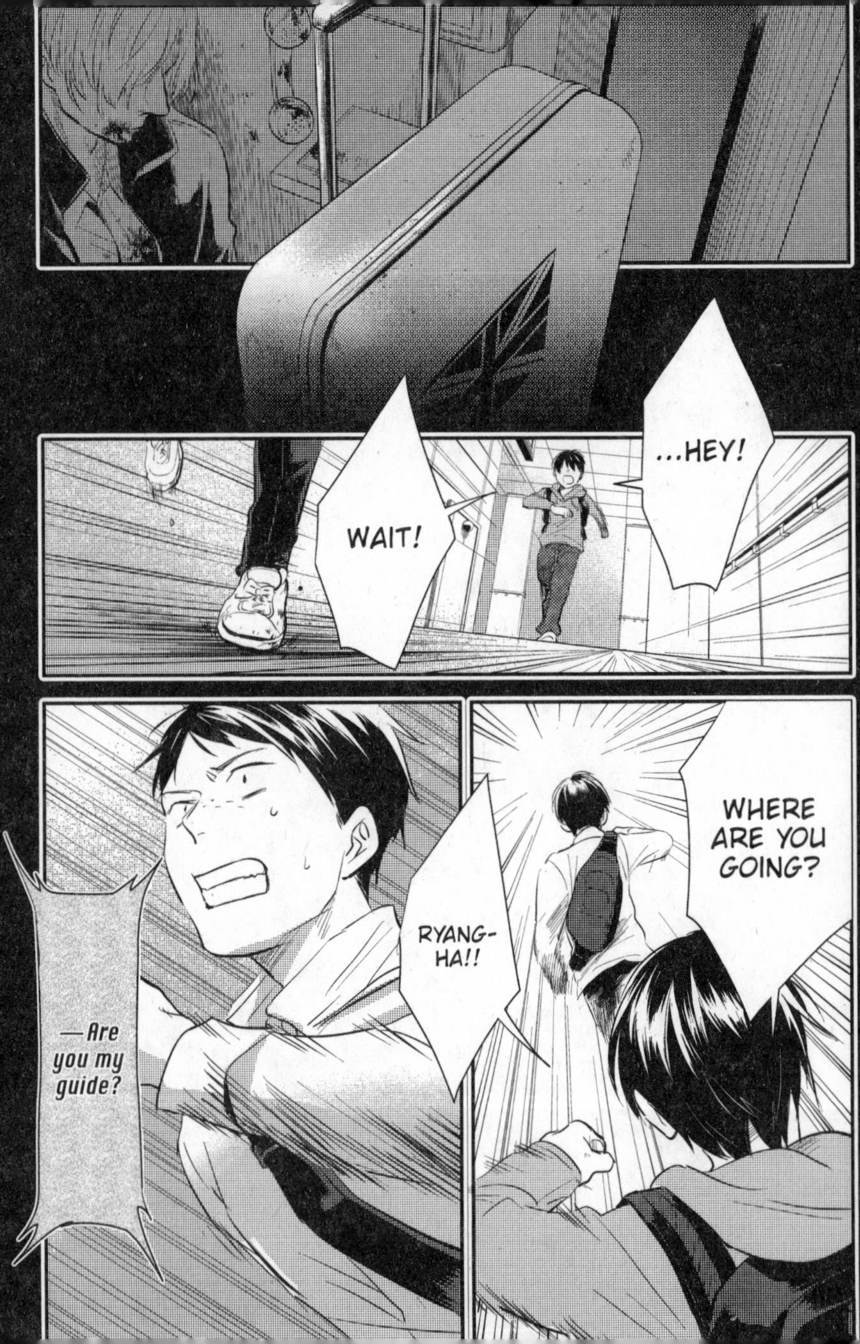
...HEY!
WAIT!
WHERE ARE YOU GOING?
RYANG-HA!!
—Are you my guide?

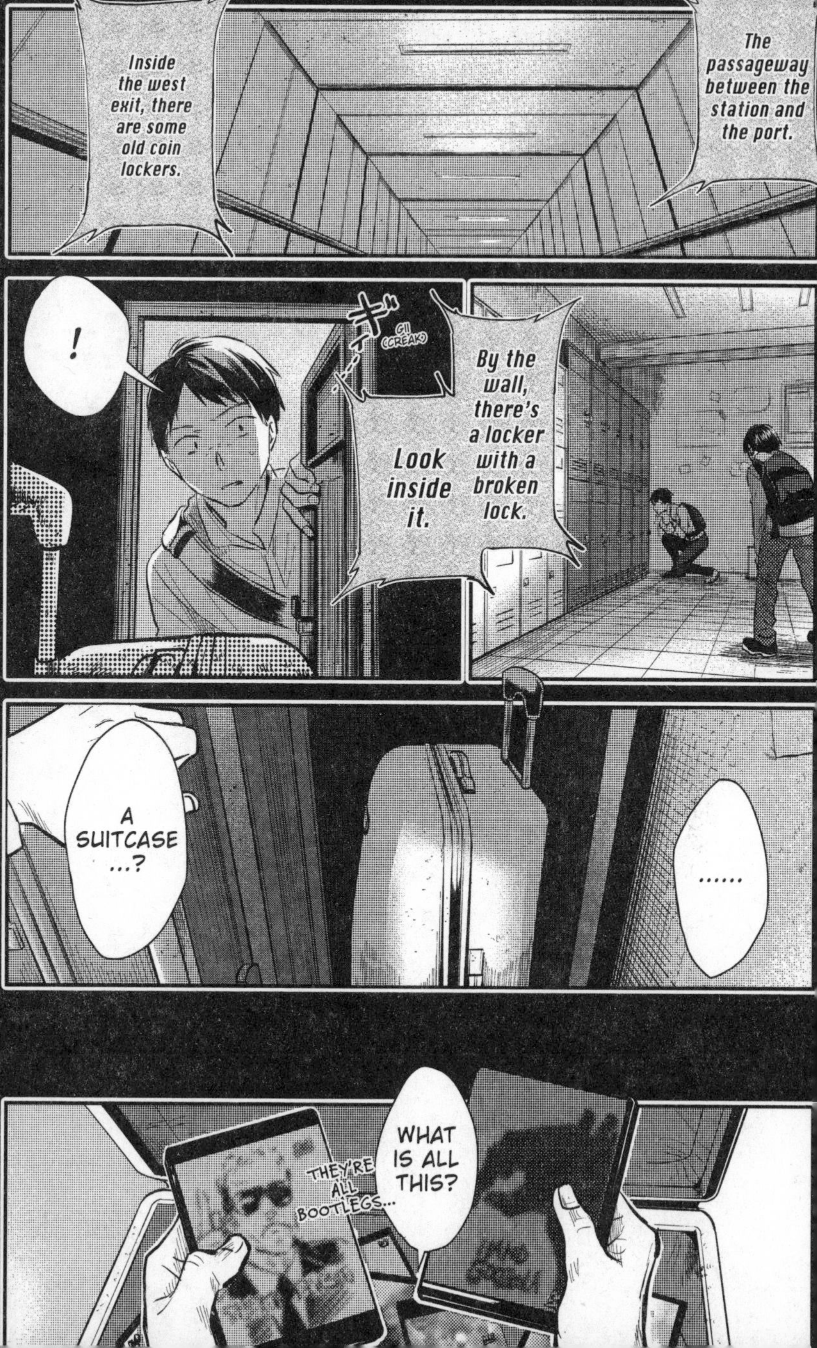

The passageway between the station and the port.
Inside the west exit, there are some old coin lockers.
By the wall, there's a locker with a broken lock.
Look inside it.
GII (CREAK)
!
......
A SUITCASE ...?
WHAT IS ALL THIS?
THEY'RE ALL BOOTLEGS...

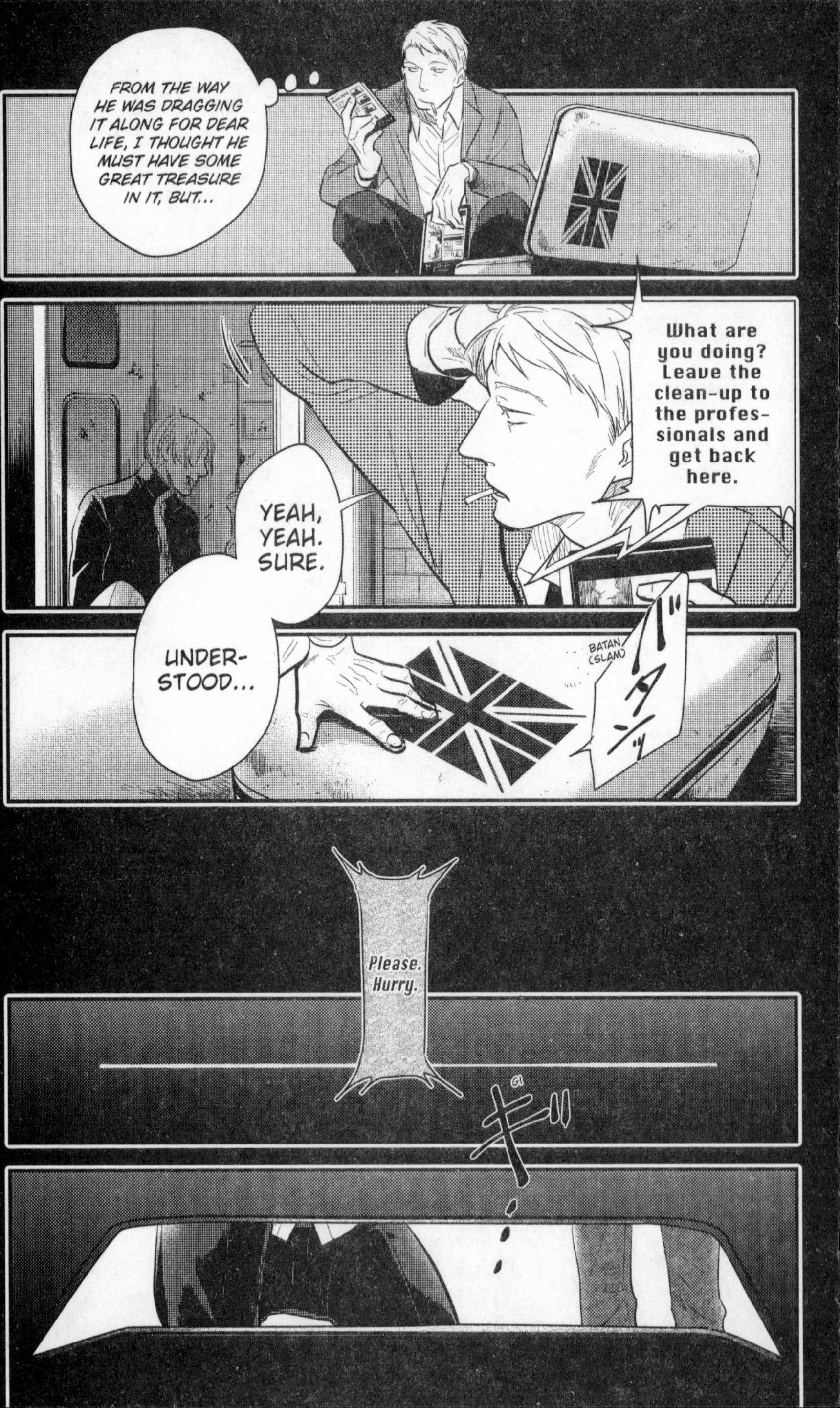
FROM THE WAY HE WAS DRAGGING IT ALONG FOR DEAR LIFE, I THOUGHT HE MUST HAVE SOME GREAT TREASURE IN IT, BUT...
What are you doing? Leave the clean-up to the profes-sionals and get back here.
YEAH, YEAH. SURE.
BATAN (SLAM)
UNDER-STOOD...
Please. Hurry.

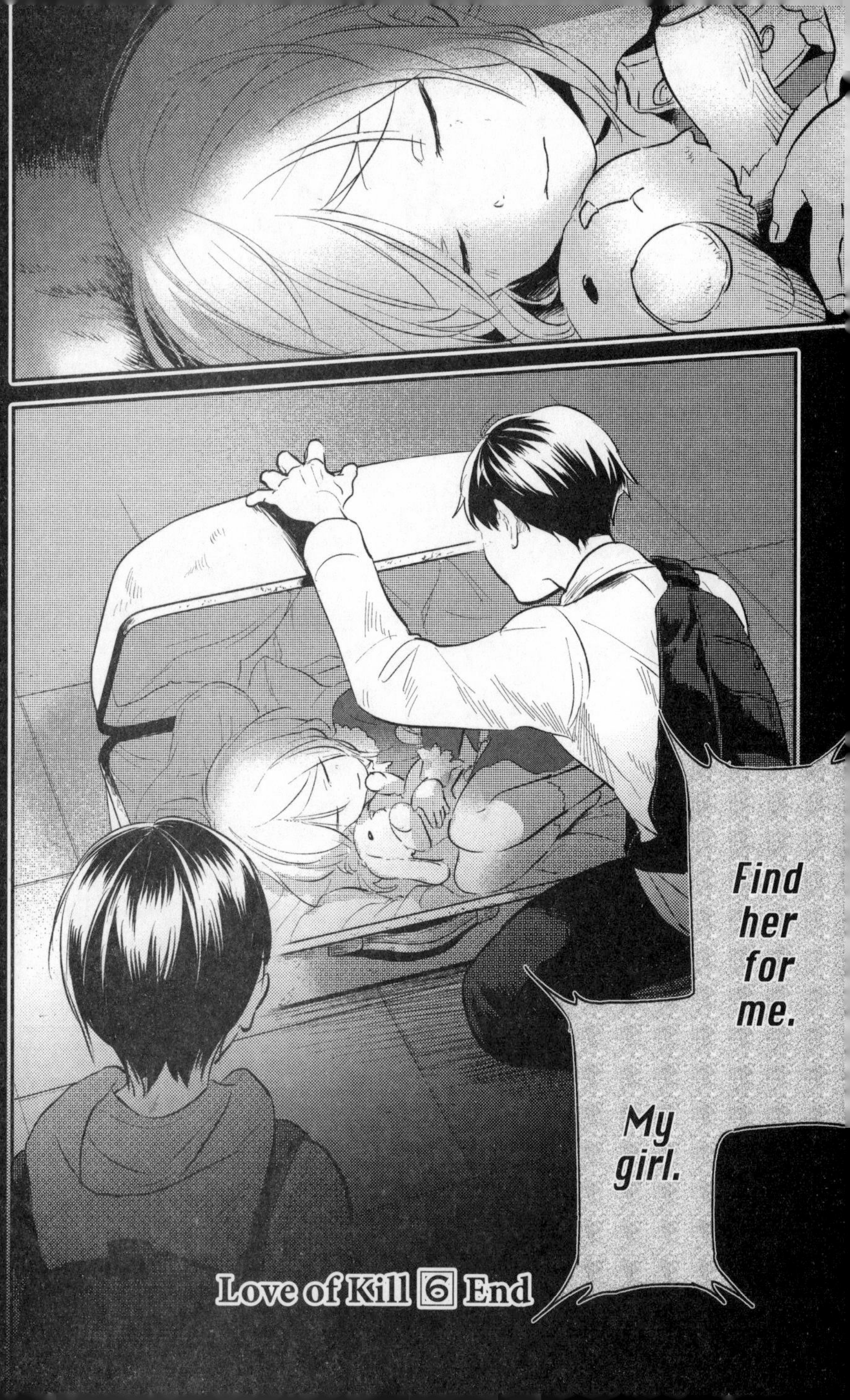
Find her for me.
My girl.
Love of Kill 6 End

# FILE 34: HELP

INCIDENTALLY, IT APPEARS THAT THE PRESENT-DAY MAIN CHARACTER AND THE ORIGINAL RYANG-HA HAVE AN AGE GAP OF AROUND TWO OR THREE YEARS. THE ORIGINAL RYANG-HA IS ABOUT SIXTEEN AT THIS POINT. THE CURRENT RYANG-HA IS THIRTEEN OR FOURTEEN HERE.
HE GREW A WHOLE LOT TALLER LATER.

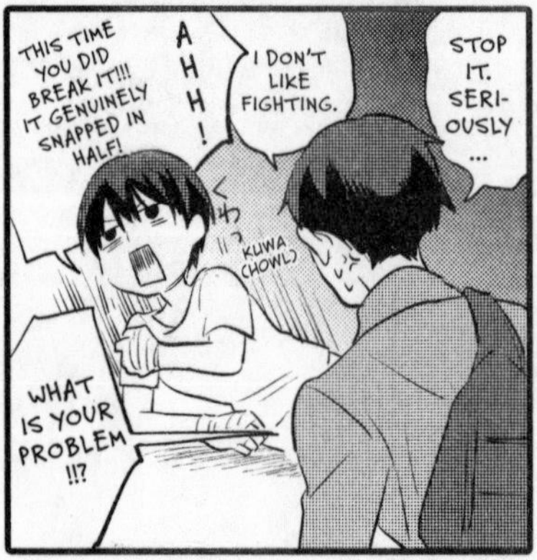
STOP IT. SERIOUSLY...
I DON'T LIKE FIGHTING.
AHH!
THIS TIME YOU DID BREAK IT!!! IT GENUINELY SNAPPED IN HALF!
KUWA (HOWL)
WHAT IS YOUR PROBLEM!!?

# FILE 35: SUITCASE

AN UNEXPECTED REAPPEARANCE.
(ALTHOUGH I DOUBT MANY PEOPLE WERE LOOKING FORWARD TO SEEING HIM AGAIN THAT BADLY, LOL...)
SEUNG-WOO WILL GO ON TO PICK UP HOU A FEW YEARS AFTER THIS INCIDENT.
BY THE WAY, WHEN THEY WERE IN THE TRIAD, HOU HAD A HIGHER POSITION THAN RYANG-HA, BUT HOU WAS ACTUALLY THE YOUNGER OF THE TWO. LENGTH OF MEMBERSHIP = PECKING ORDER.

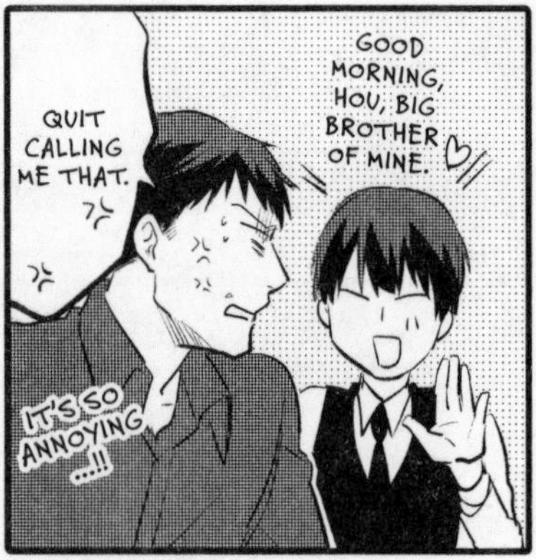
GOOD MORNING, HOU, BIG BROTHER OF MINE.
QUIT CALLING ME THAT.
IT'S SO ANNOYING...!!

THIS VOLUME CONTAINS ONE LESS CHAPTER OF THE STORY THAN USUAL. THIS IS BECAUSE I TOOK MY FIRST BREAK FROM PUBLICATION...
(NOTE: WITH PRIOR PERMISSION.)
HOWEVER, THERE WAS NO WAY TO DELAY THE RELEASE OF THE COLLECTED VOLUME BY A MONTH, LOL...
IT MAY BE ONE CHAPTER SHORT, BUT I WORKED HARD ON THE SPECIAL COMIC TO MAKE UP THE PAGE COUNT, SO PLEASE FORGIVE ME...

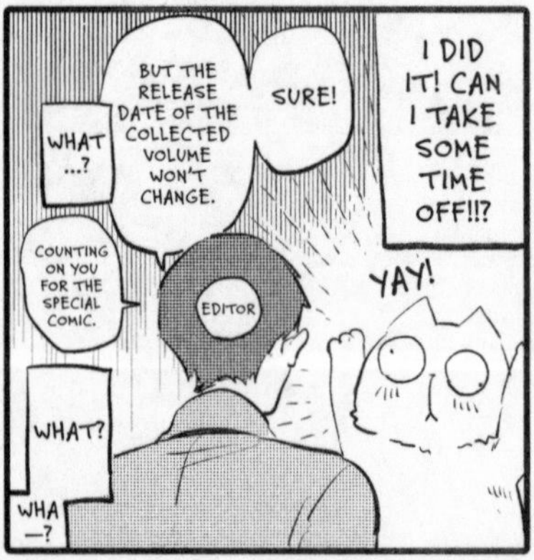
I DID IT! CAN I TAKE SOME TIME OFF!!?
SURE!
BUT THE RELEASE DATE OF THE COLLECTED VOLUME WON'T CHANGE.
WHAT...?
YAY!
COUNTING ON YOU FOR THE SPECIAL COMIC.
EDITOR
WHAT?
WHA—?

THE FOLLOWING IS A SPECIAL COMIC FOR THE COLLECTED VOLUME.

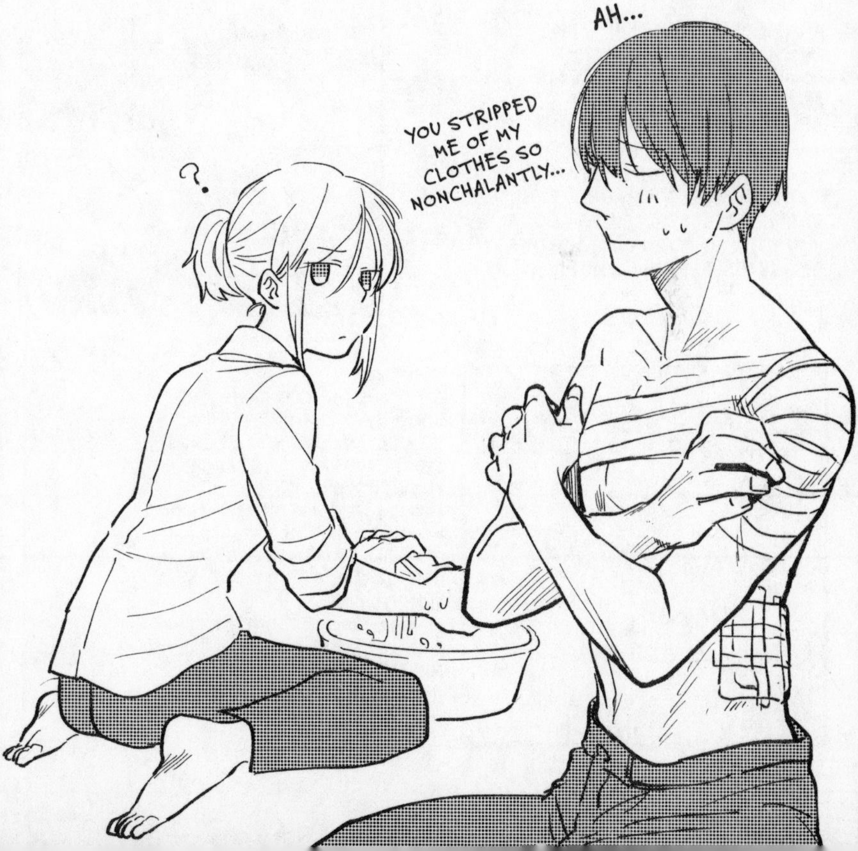
AH...
YOU STRIPPED ME OF MY CLOTHES SO NONCHALANTLY...

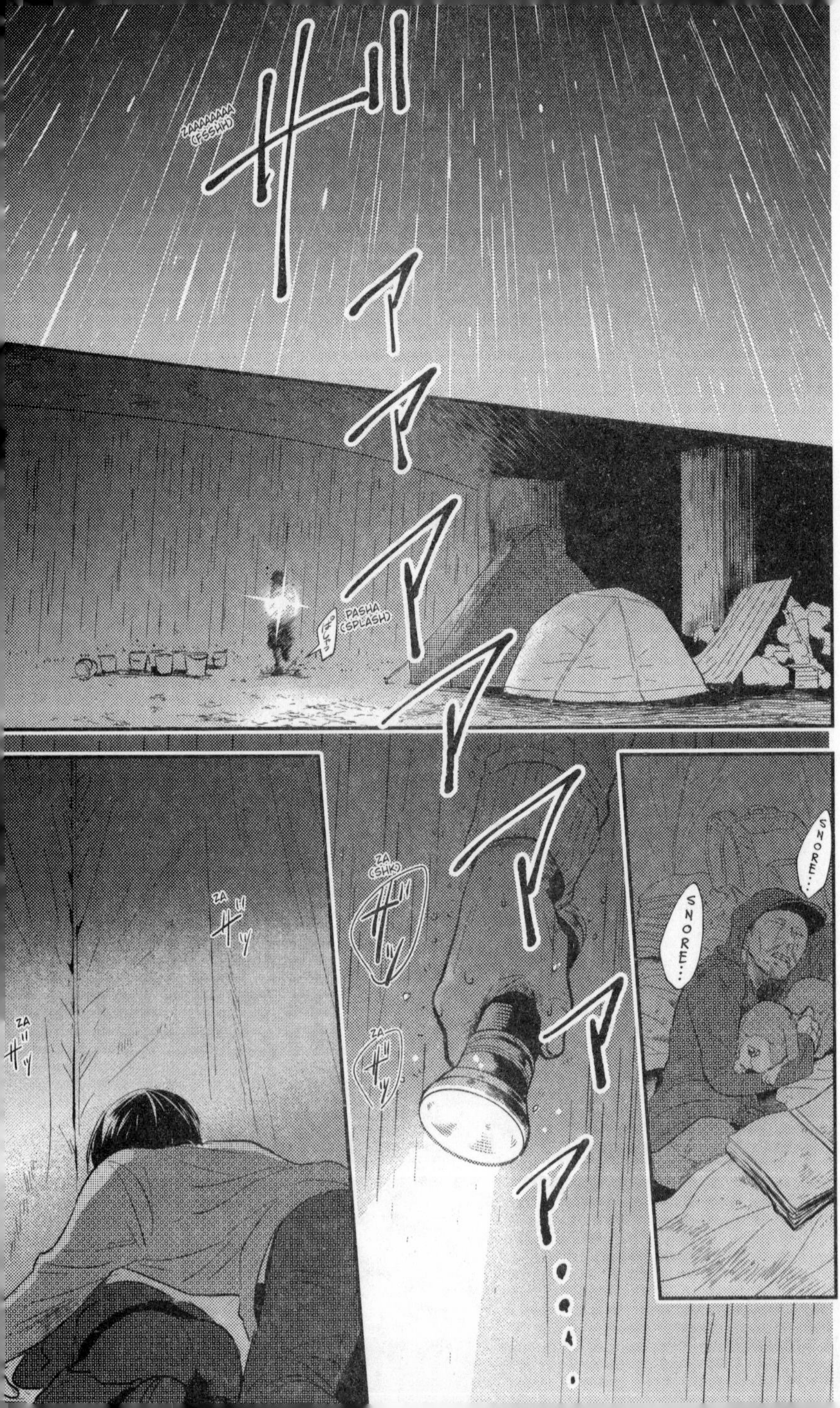
ザァァァァァァァ…
ZAAAAAAAAA (FSSHH)
パシャ
PASHA (SPLASH)
SNORE...
SNORE...
ザッ
ZA (SHK)
ザッ
ZA
ザッ
ZA
ザッ
ZA

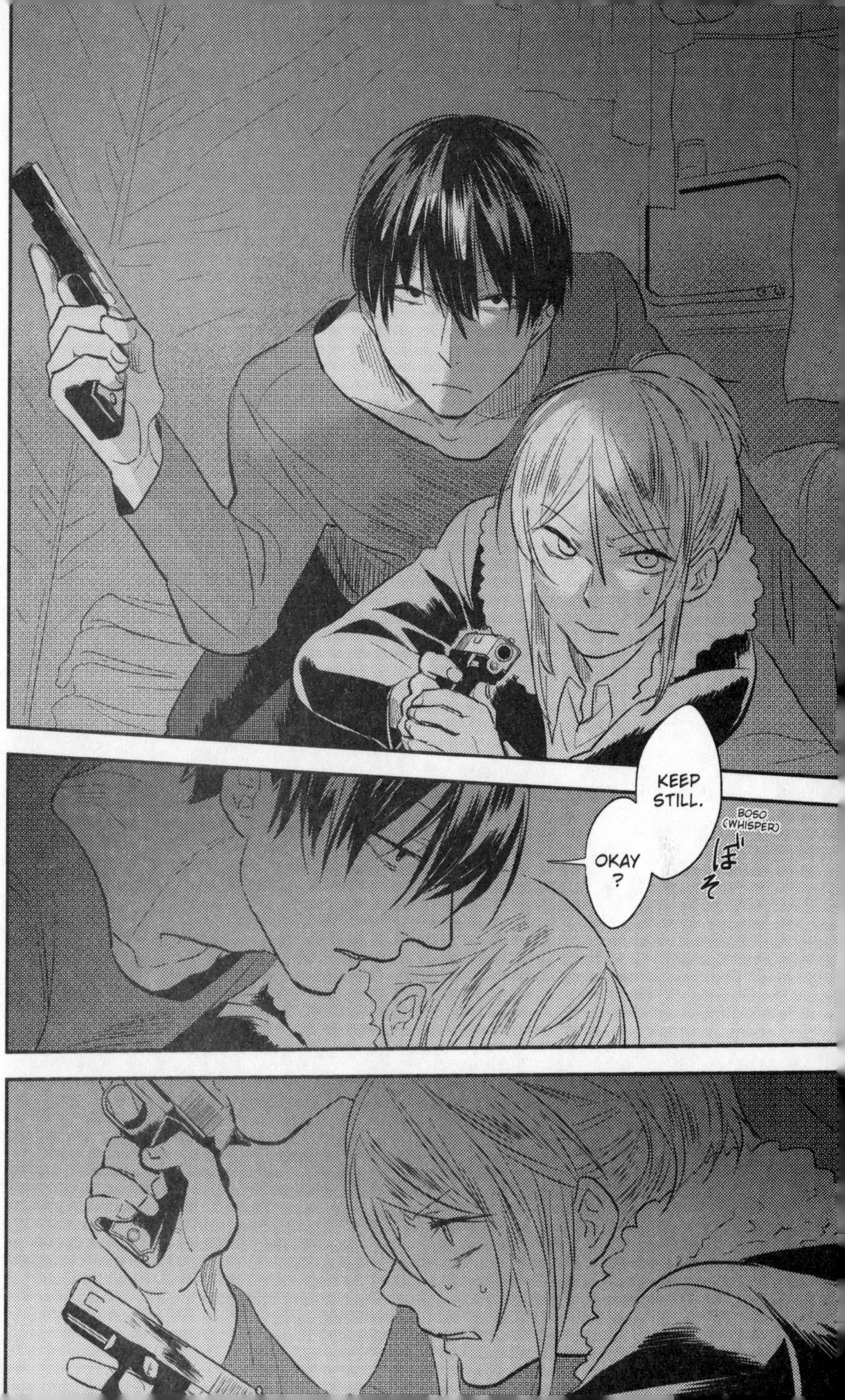
KEEP STILL.
OKAY ?
BOSO (WHISPER)
ぼそ

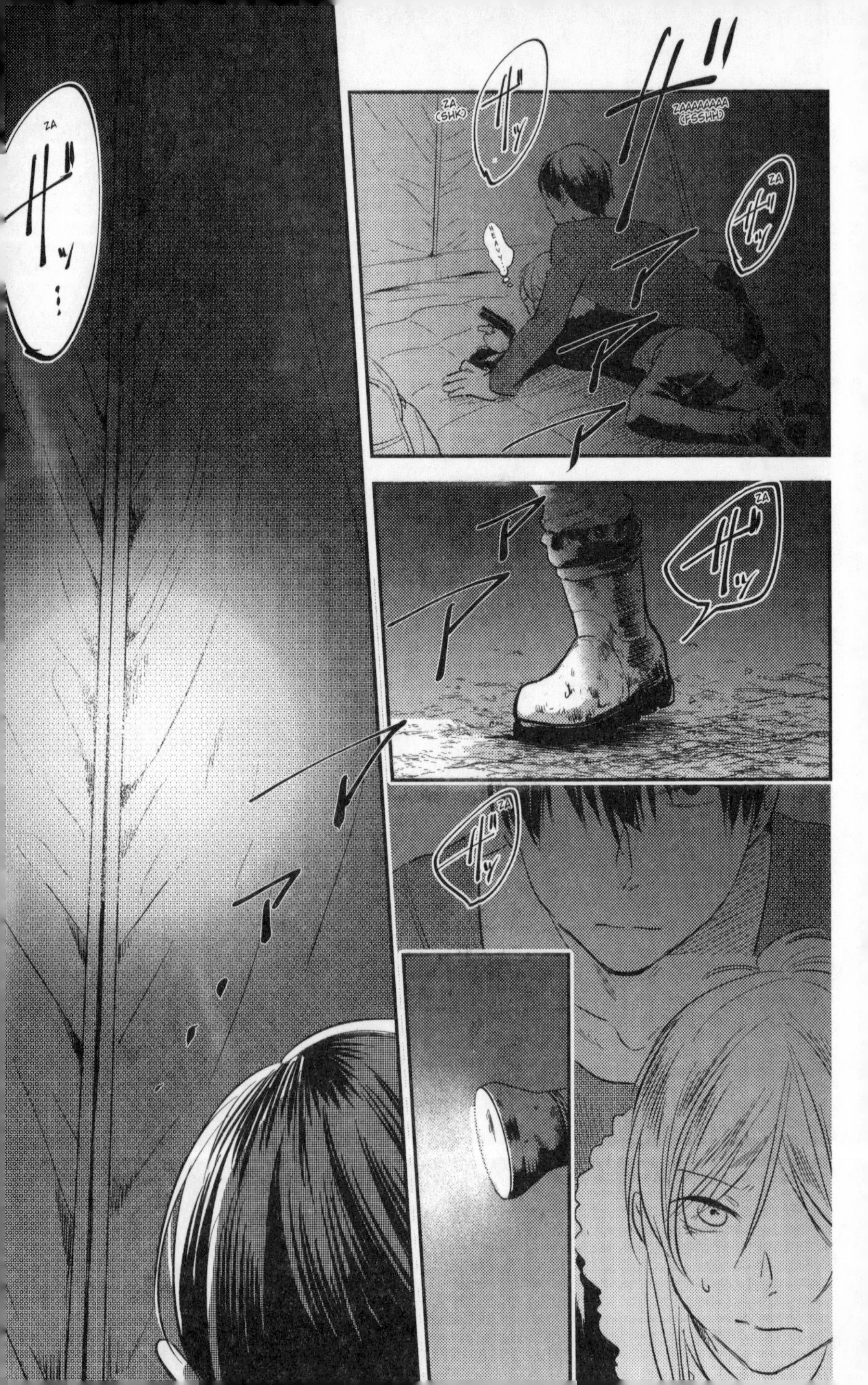
ZA
ZAAAAAAAA (FSSHH)
ZA (SHK)
HEAVY...
ZA
ZA
ZA

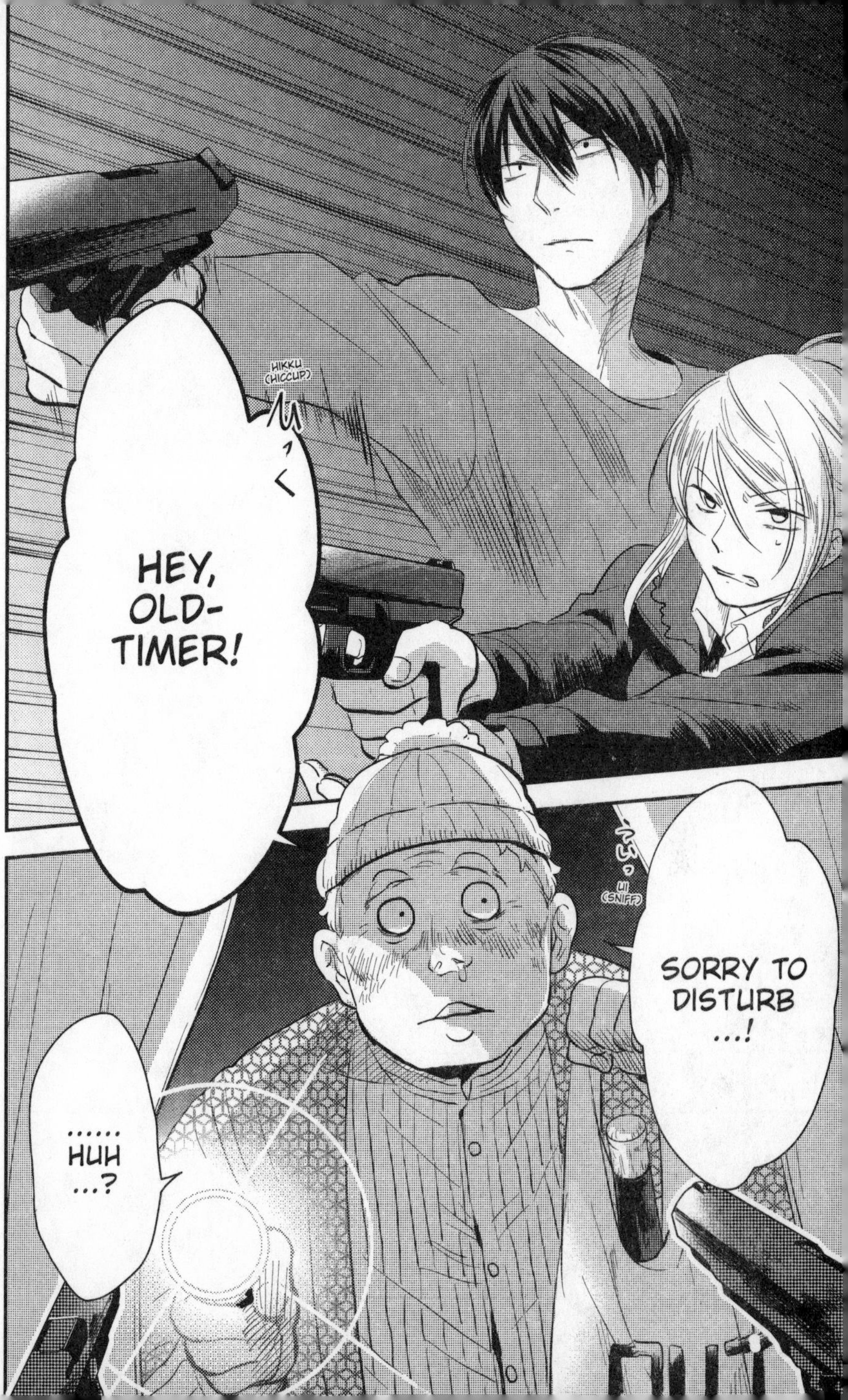
HIKKU (HICCUP)
HEY, OLD-TIMER!
UI (SNIFF)
SORRY TO DISTURB ...!
...... HUH ...?

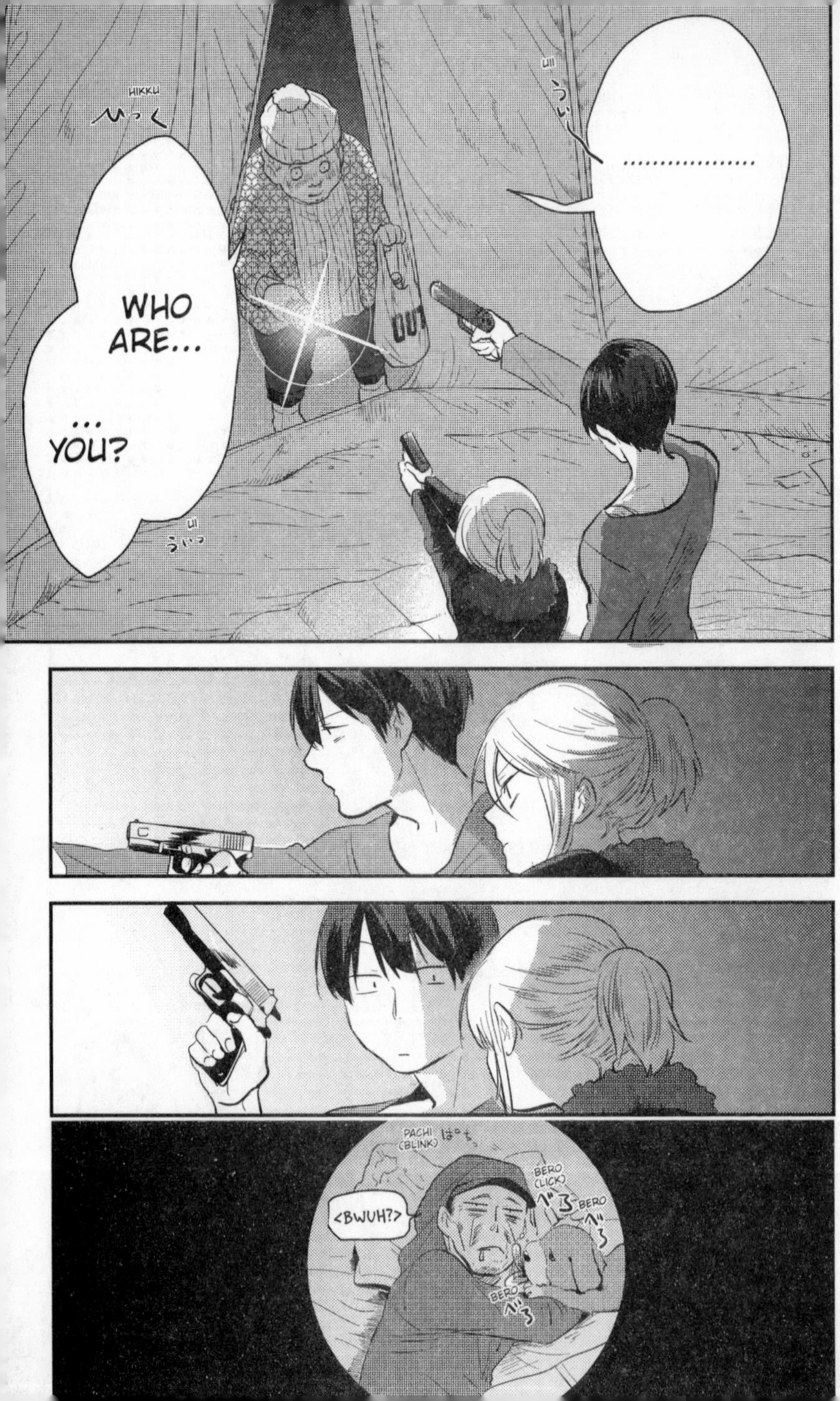

UI
...................
HIKKU
ひっく
WHO ARE...
...YOU?
UI
PACHI (BLINK)
ぱちっ
BERO (LICK)
べろ
BERO
べろ
<BWUH?>
BERO
べろ

## Special File

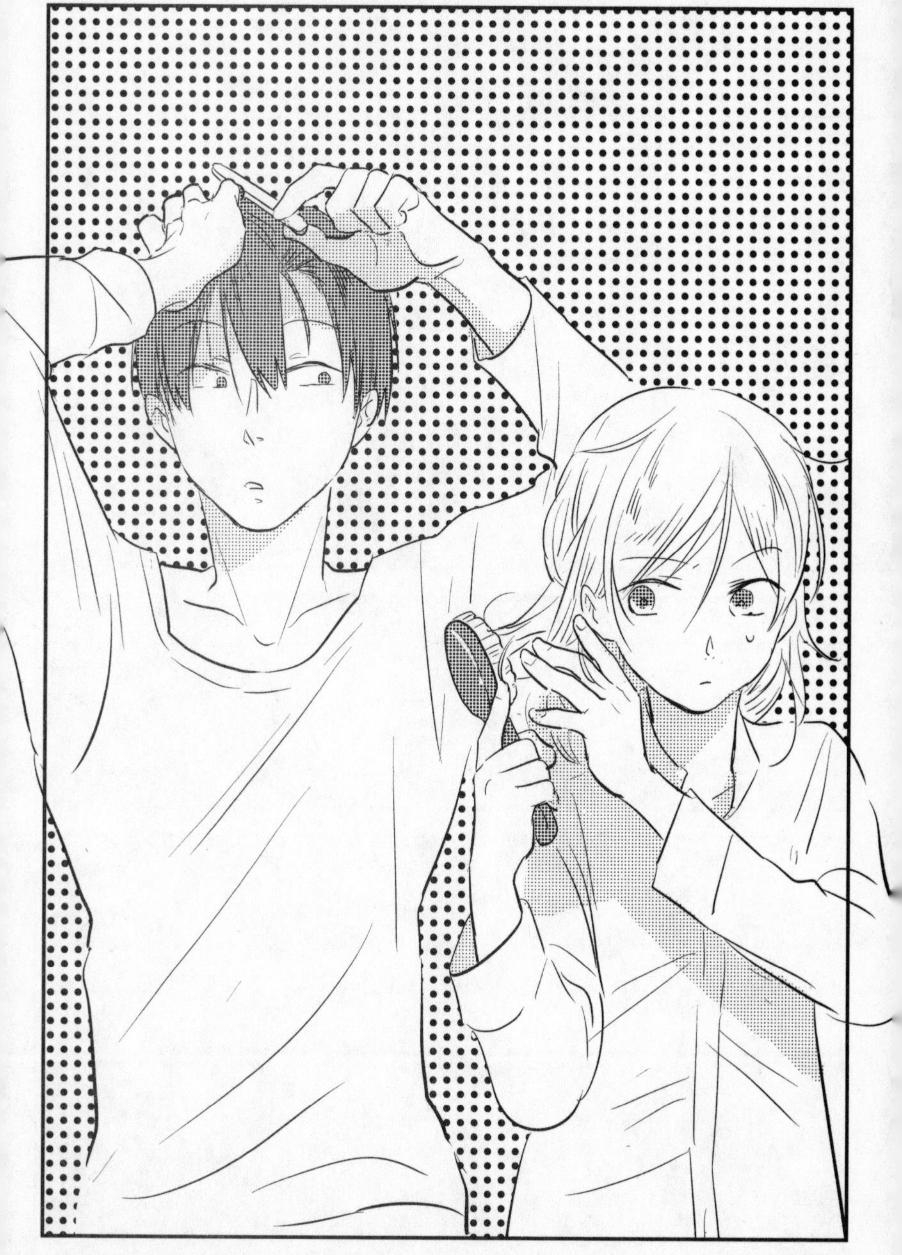

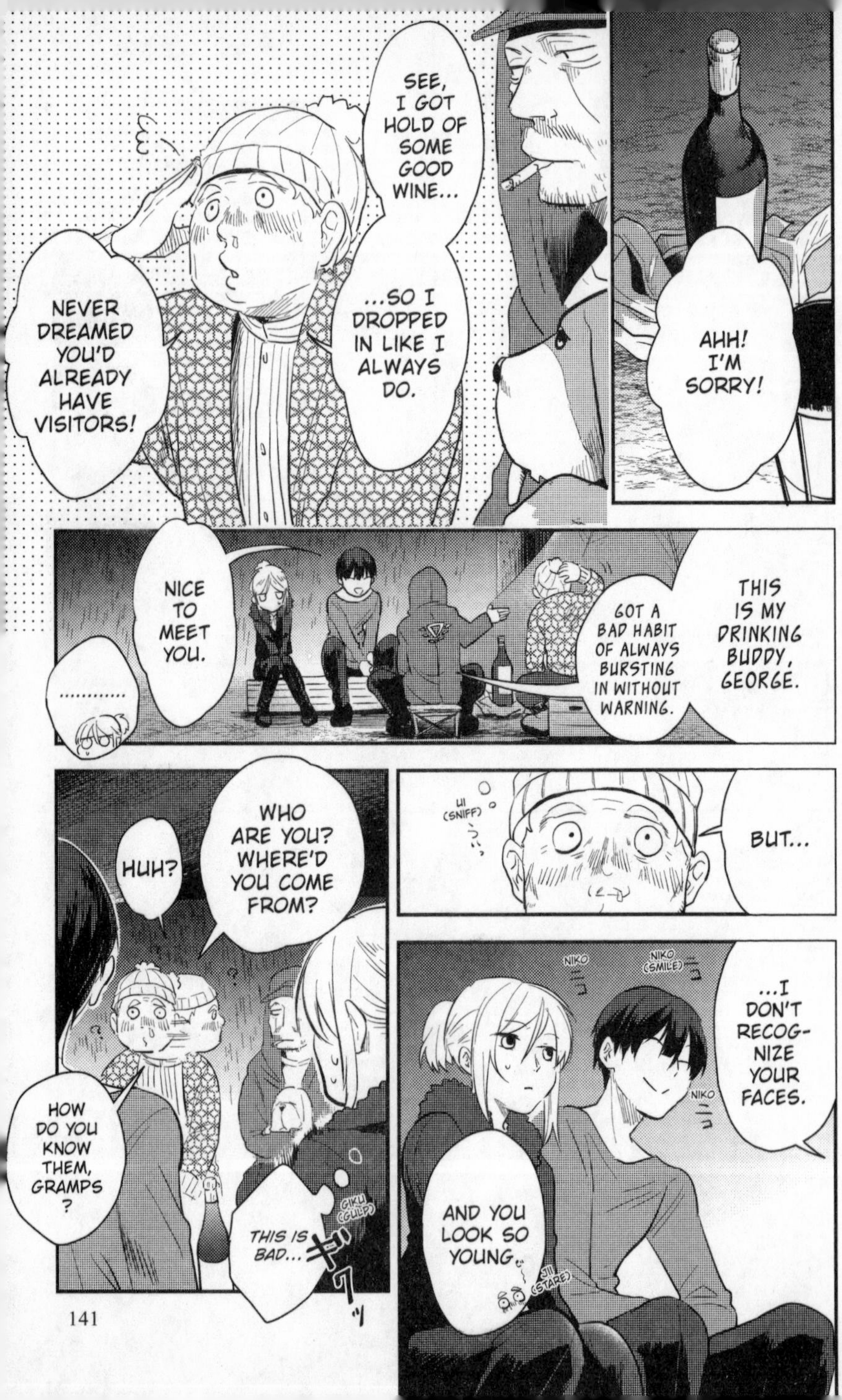

AHH! I'M SORRY!
SEE, I GOT HOLD OF SOME GOOD WINE...
...SO I DROPPED IN LIKE I ALWAYS DO.
NEVER DREAMED YOU'D ALREADY HAVE VISITORS!
THIS IS MY DRINKING BUDDY, GEORGE.
GOT A BAD HABIT OF ALWAYS BURSTING IN WITHOUT WARNING.
NICE TO MEET YOU.
............
BUT...
UI (SNIFF)
...I DON'T RECOG-NIZE YOUR FACES.
NIKO (SMILE)
NIKO
NIKO
AND YOU LOOK SO YOUNG...
JII (STARE)
WHO ARE YOU? WHERE'D YOU COME FROM?
HUH?
HOW DO YOU KNOW THEM, GRAMPS?
GIKU (GULP)
THIS IS BAD...

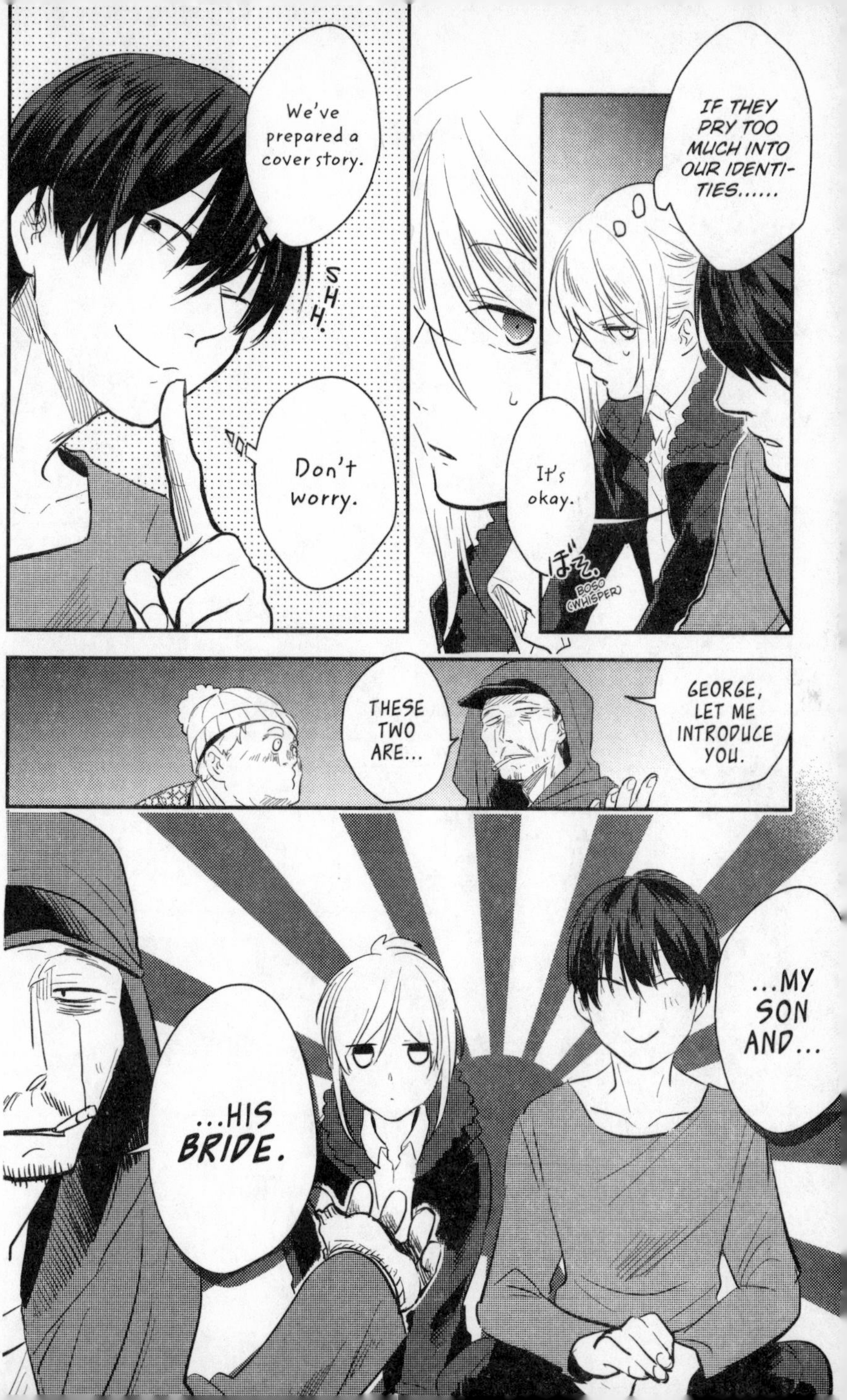
IF THEY PRY TOO MUCH INTO OUR IDENTITIES......
It's okay.
ぼそ.
BOSO (WHISPER)
We've prepared a cover story.
SHH.
Don't worry.
GEORGE, LET ME INTRODUCE YOU.
THESE TWO ARE...
...MY SON AND...
...HIS BRIDE.

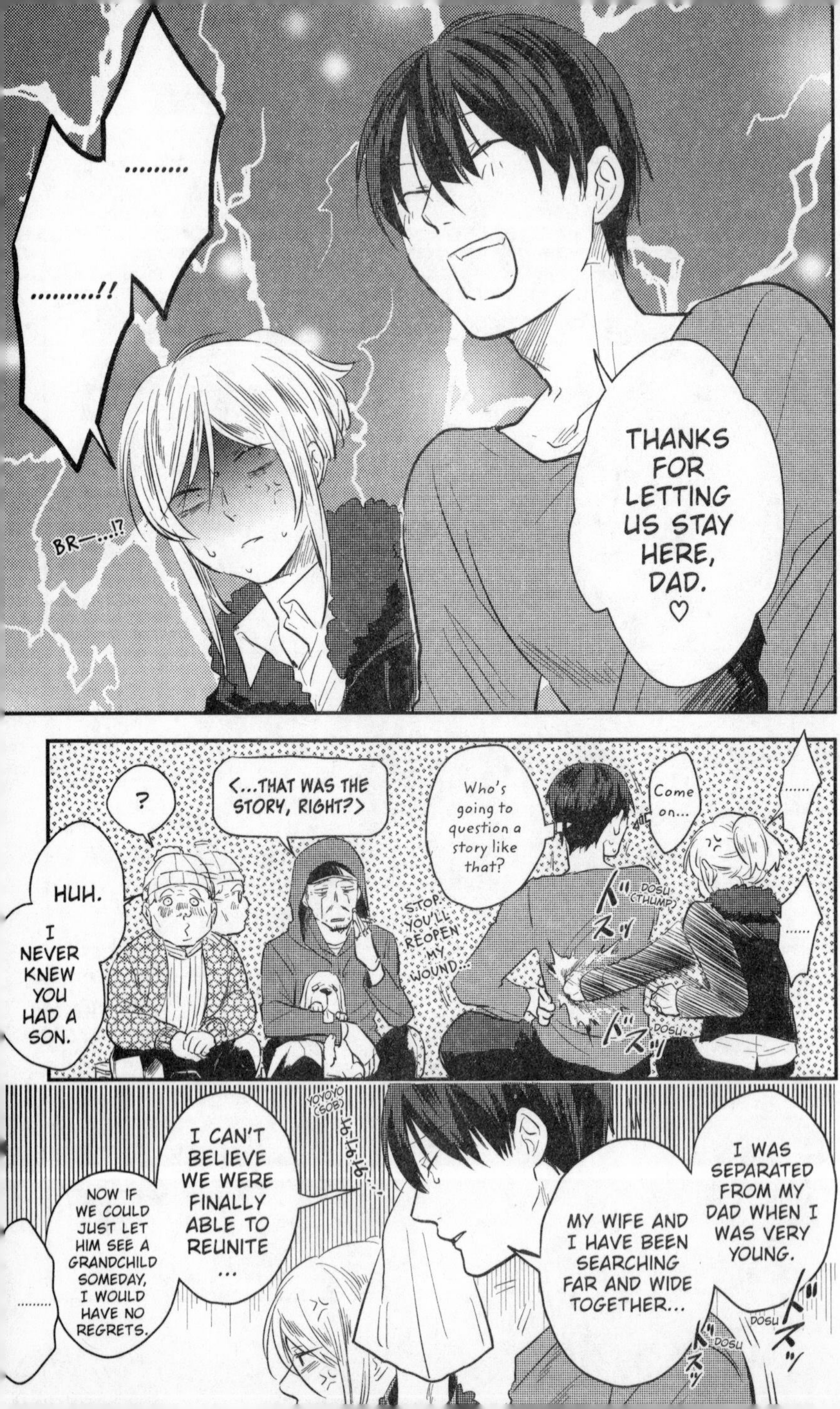
THANKS FOR LETTING US STAY HERE, DAD. ♡
.........
..........!!
BR—...!?
......
......
Come on...
Who's going to question a story like that?
DOSU (THUMP)
DOSU
STOP, YOU'LL REOPEN MY WOUND...
<...THAT WAS THE STORY, RIGHT?>
?
HUH.
I NEVER KNEW YOU HAD A SON.
I WAS SEPARATED FROM MY DAD WHEN I WAS VERY YOUNG.
DOSU
DOSU
MY WIFE AND I HAVE BEEN SEARCHING FAR AND WIDE TOGETHER...
YOYOYO (SOB)
I CAN'T BELIEVE WE WERE FINALLY ABLE TO REUNITE ...
NOW IF WE COULD JUST LET HIM SEE A GRANDCHILD SOMEDAY, I WOULD HAVE NO REGRETS.
.........

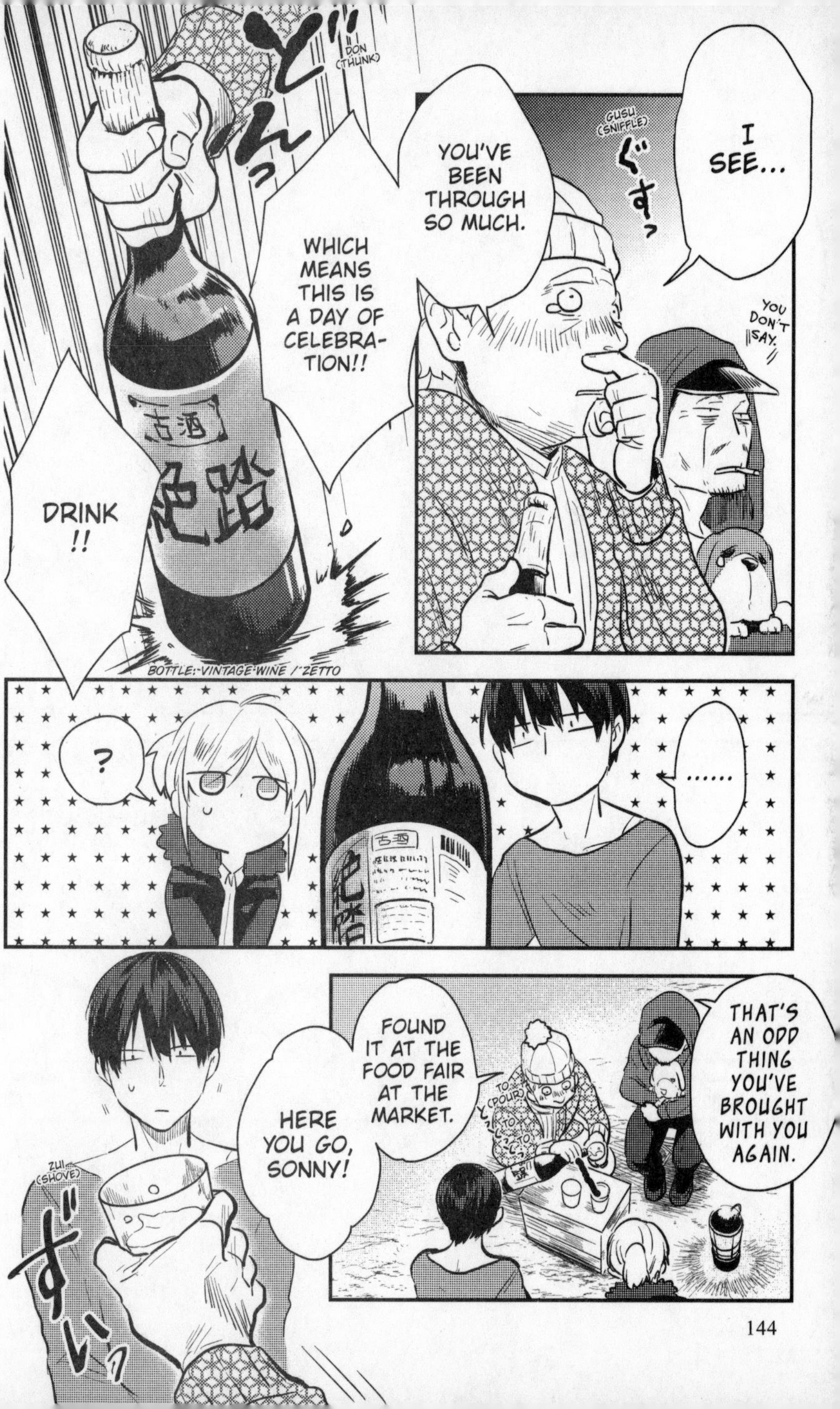
I SEE...
GUSU (SNIFFLE)
YOU'VE BEEN THROUGH SO MUCH.
YOU DON'T SAY.
DON (THUNK)
WHICH MEANS THIS IS A DAY OF CELEBRATION!!
DRINK!!
BOTTLE: VINTAGE WINE / ZETTO
......
?
THAT'S AN ODD THING YOU'VE BROUGHT WITH YOU AGAIN.
FOUND IT AT THE FOOD FAIR AT THE MARKET.
TO (POUR) TO
HERE YOU GO, SONNY!
ZUI... (SHOVE)

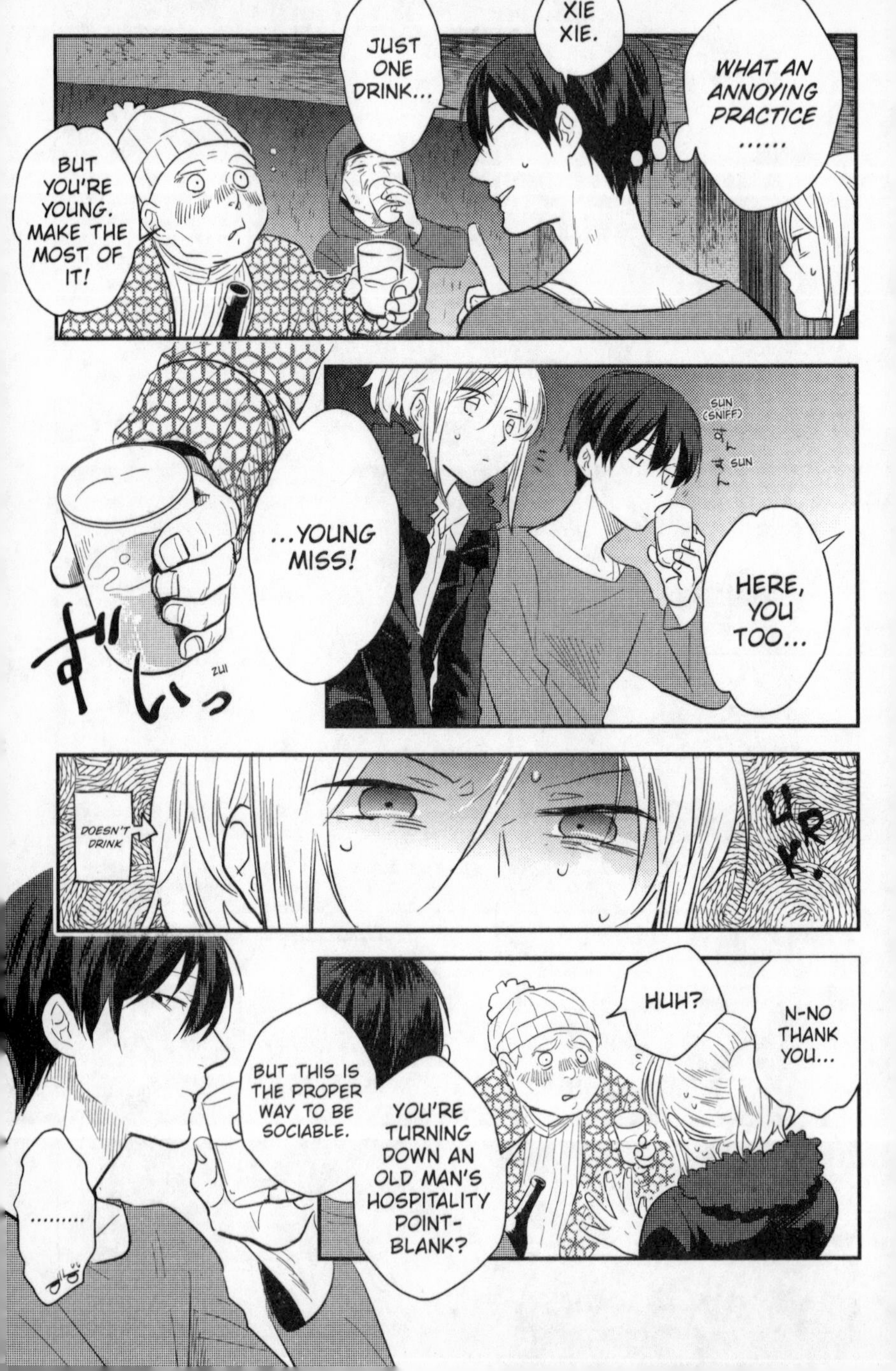
WHAT AN ANNOYING PRACTICE ......
XIE XIE.
JUST ONE DRINK...
BUT YOU'RE YOUNG. MAKE THE MOST OF IT!
HERE, YOU TOO...
SUN (SNIFF)
すん
SUN
...YOUNG MISS!
ずいっ
ZUI
URKK
DOESN'T DRINK
N-NO THANK YOU...
HUH?
YOU'RE TURNING DOWN AN OLD MAN'S HOSPITALITY POINT-BLANK?
BUT THIS IS THE PROPER WAY TO BE SOCIABLE.
........

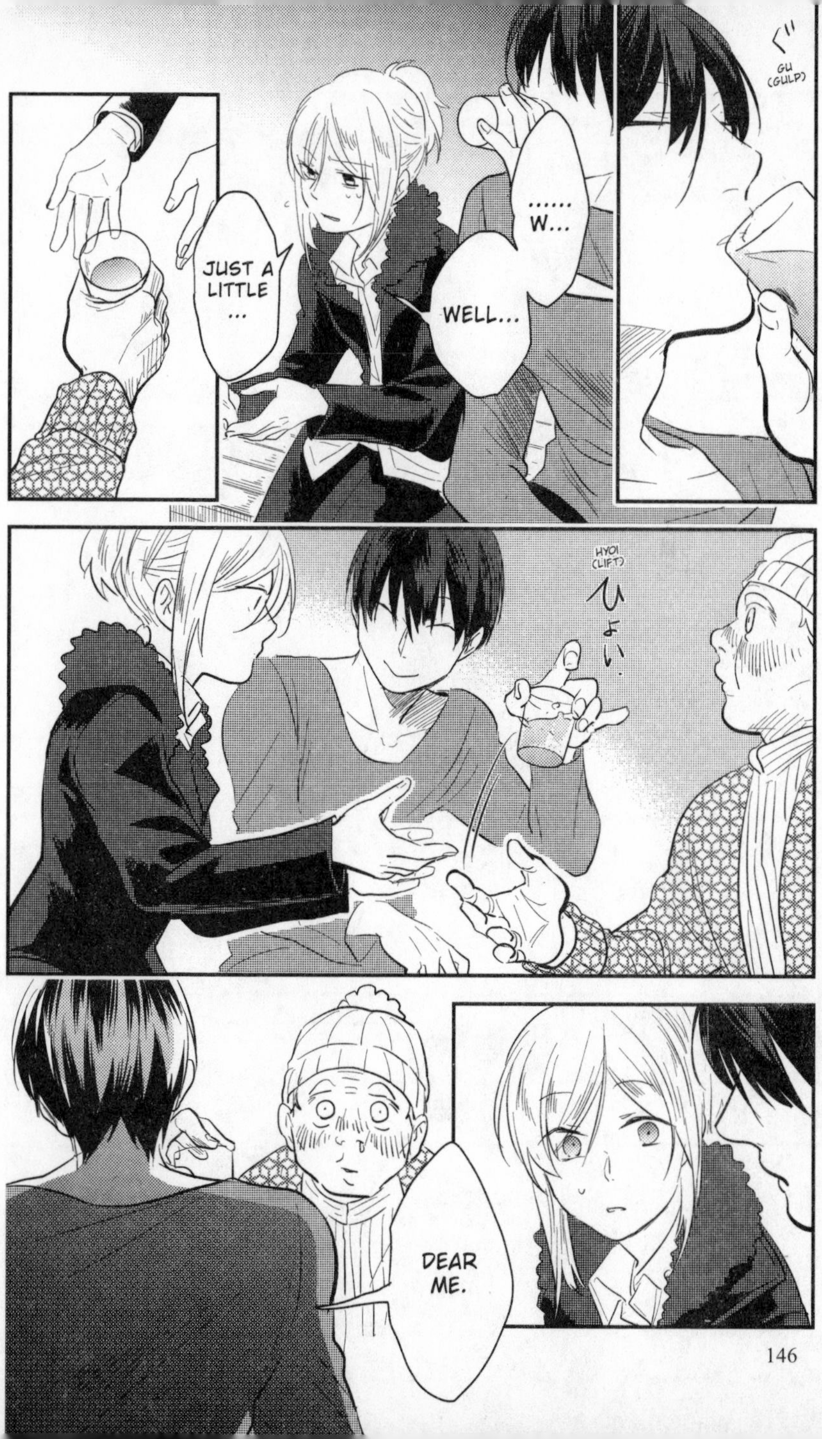
ぐ
GU (GULP)
......W...
WELL...
JUST A LITTLE ...
ひょい
HYOI (LIFT)
DEAR ME.

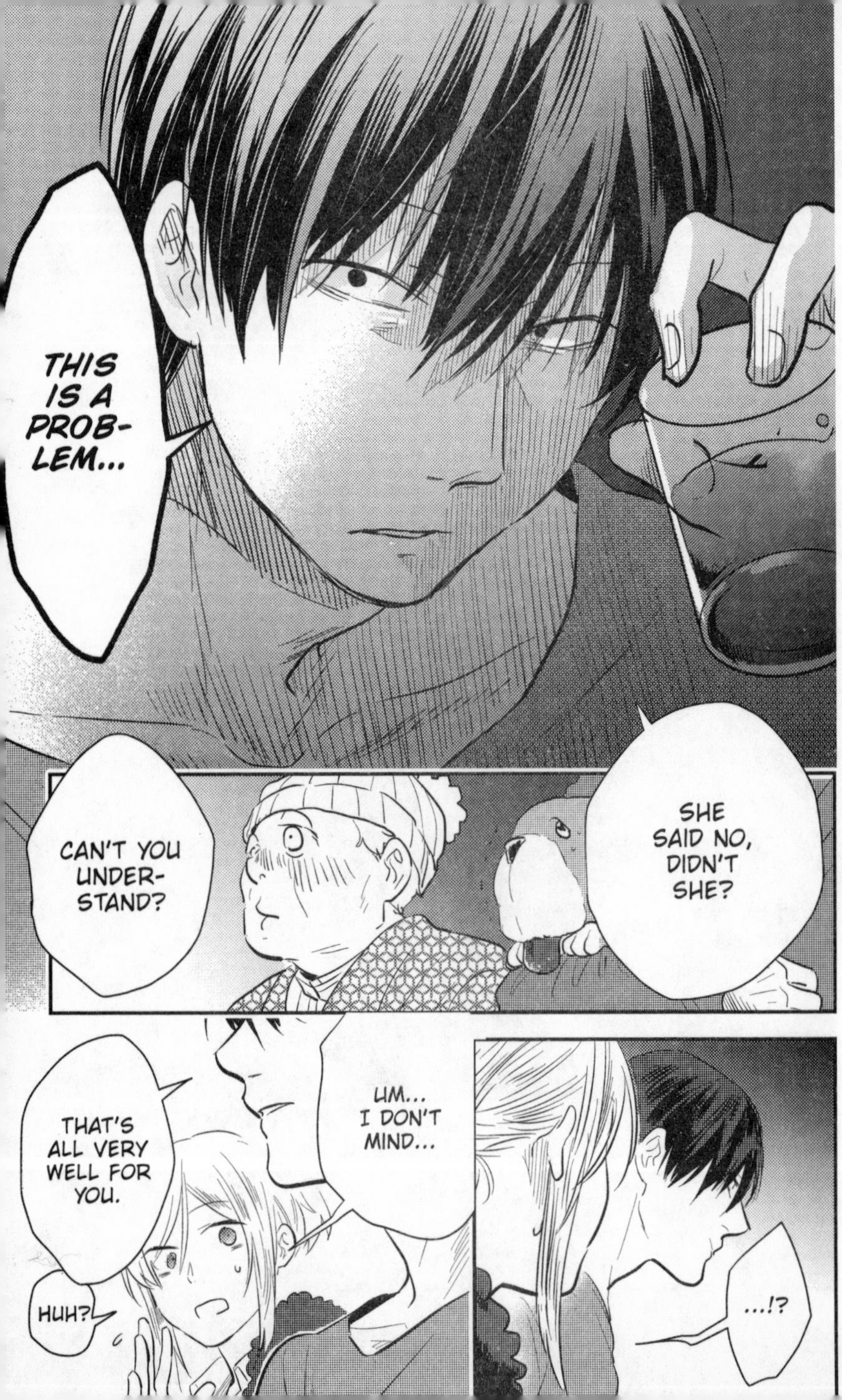
THIS IS A PROBLEM...
SHE SAID NO, DIDN'T SHE?
CAN'T YOU UNDERSTAND?
...!?
UM... I DON'T MIND...
THAT'S ALL VERY WELL FOR YOU.
HUH?

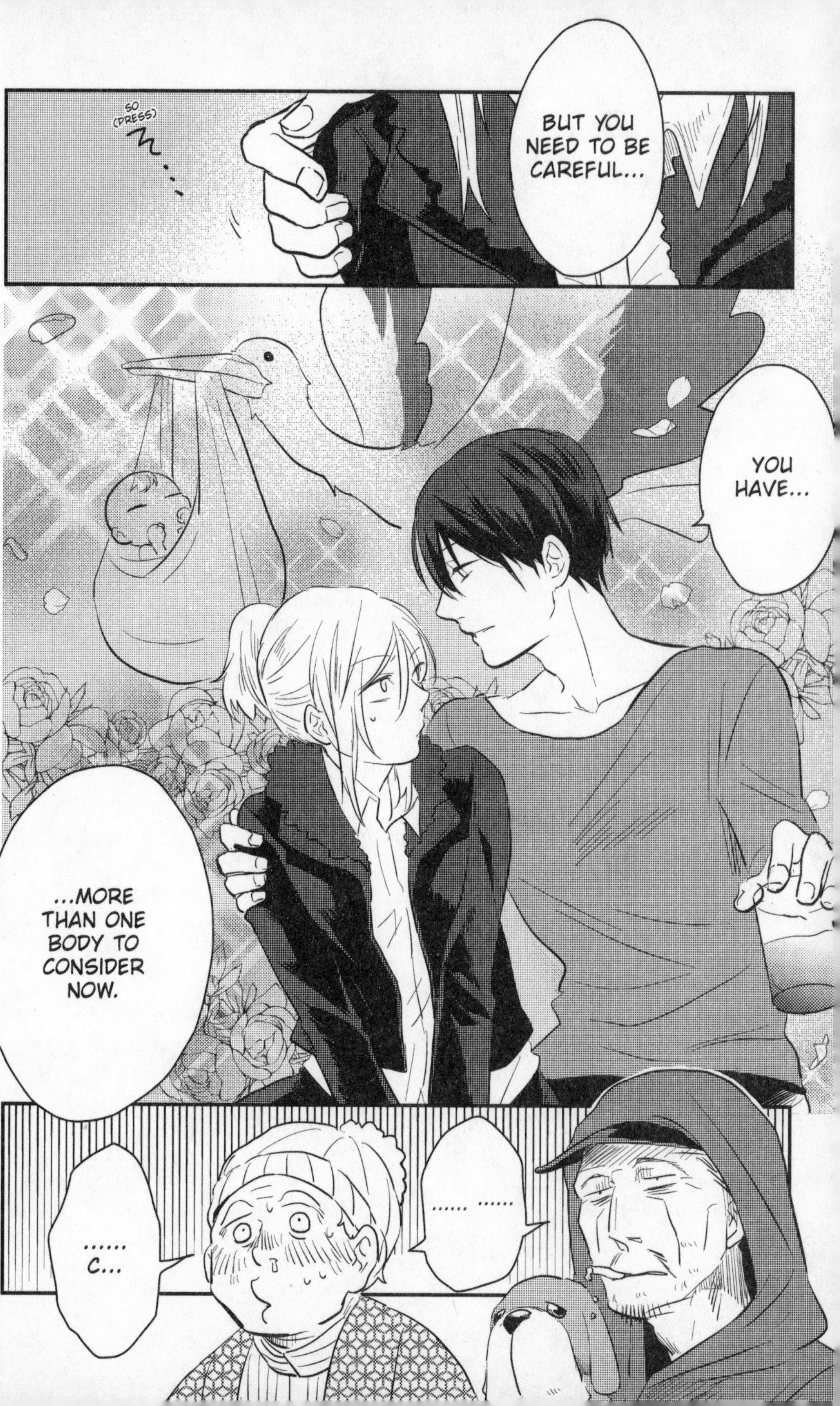
BUT YOU NEED TO BE CAREFUL...
SO (PRESS)
YOU HAVE...
...MORE THAN ONE BODY TO CONSIDER NOW.
...... ......
...... C...

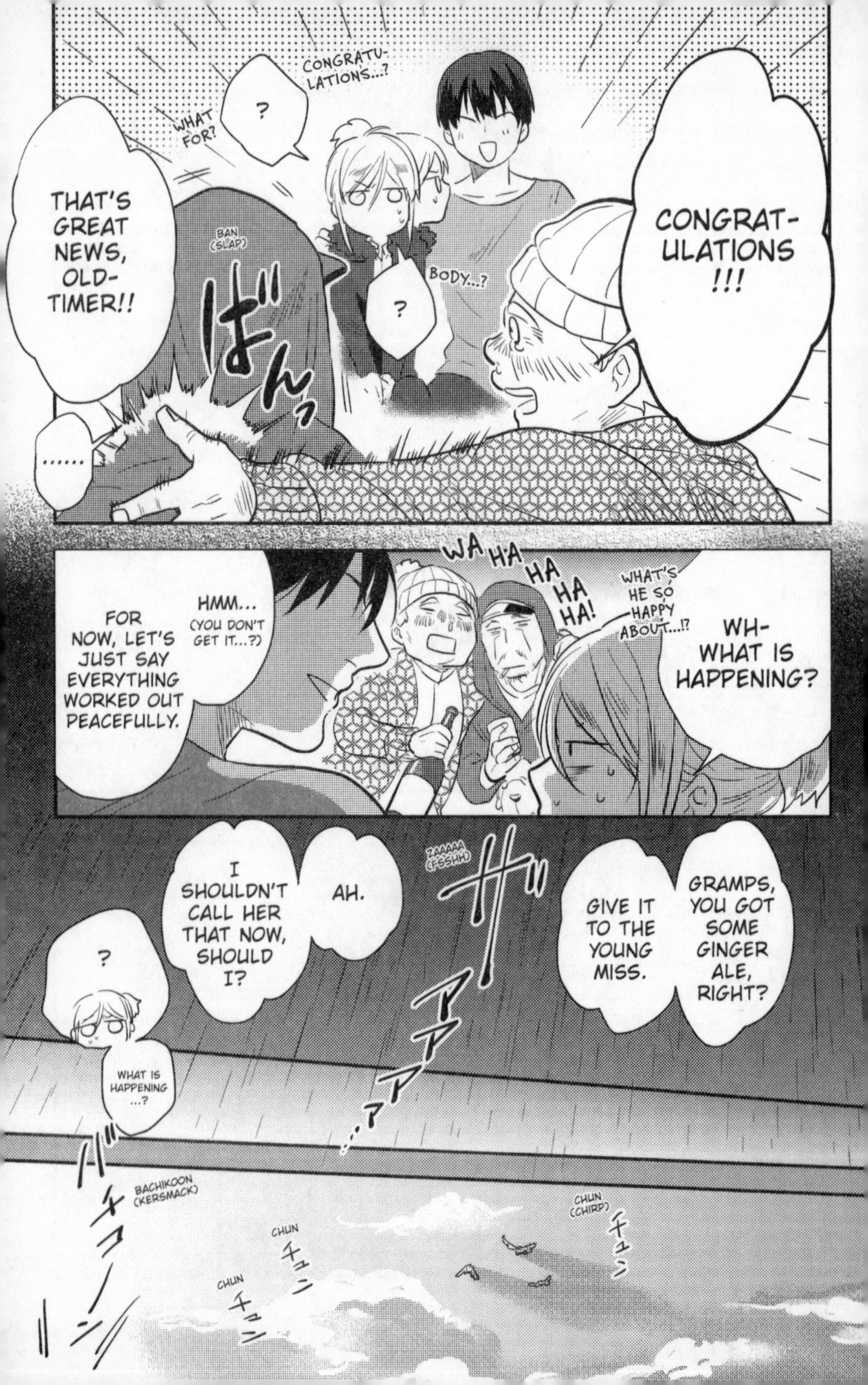
CONGRAT-ULATIONS!!!
CONGRATU-LATIONS...?
?
WHAT FOR?
BODY...?
?
BAN (SLAP)
ばんっ
THAT'S GREAT NEWS, OLD-TIMER!!
......
WH-WHAT IS HAPPENING?
WHAT'S HE SO HAPPY ABOUT...!?
WA HA HA HA HA!
HMM... (YOU DON'T GET IT...?)
FOR NOW, LET'S JUST SAY EVERYTHING WORKED OUT PEACEFULLY.
GRAMPS, YOU GOT SOME GINGER ALE, RIGHT?
GIVE IT TO THE YOUNG MISS.
ZAAAAA (FSSHH)
AH.
I SHOULDN'T CALL HER THAT NOW, SHOULD I?
?
WHAT IS HAPPENING ...?
BACHIKOON (KERSMACK)
CHUN (CHIRP)
CHUN
CHUN

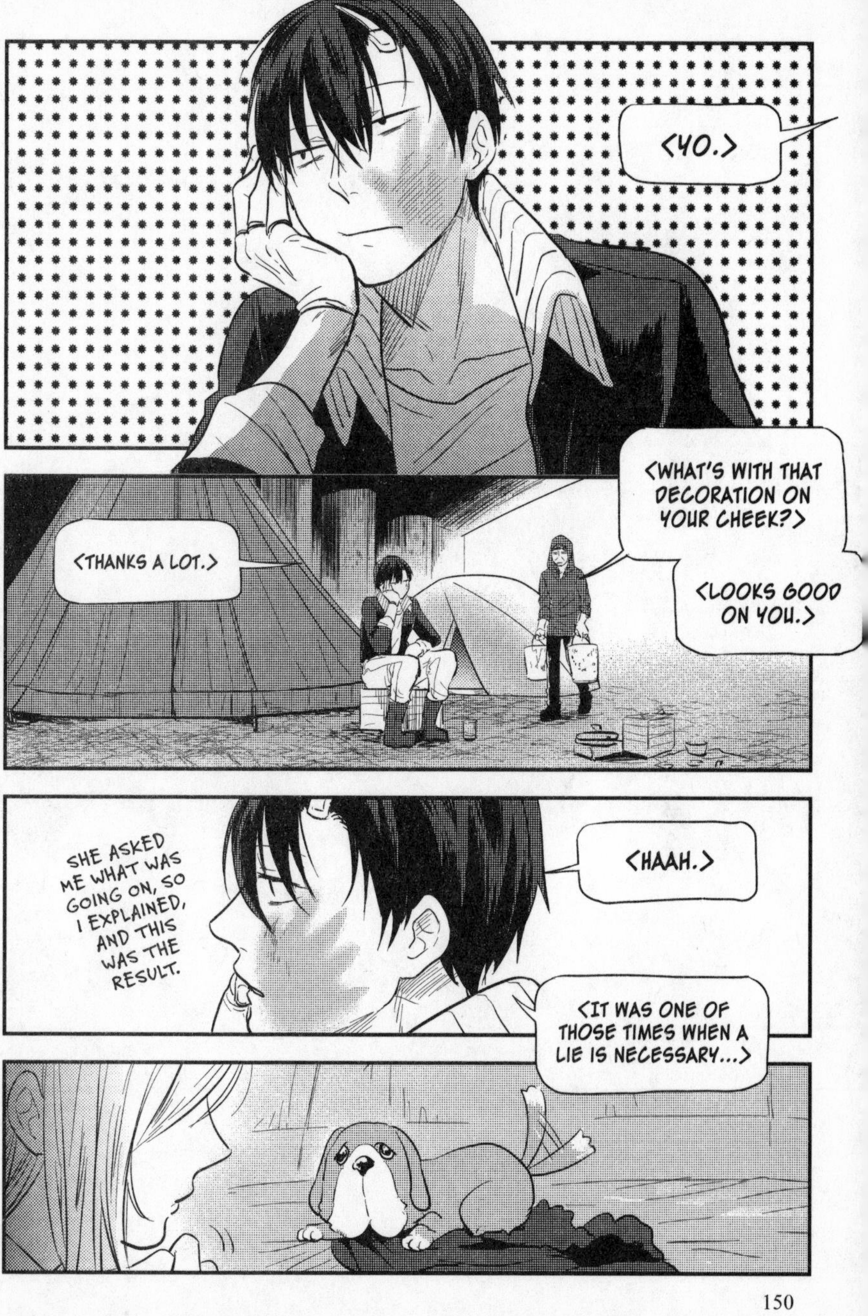
<YO.>
<WHAT'S WITH THAT DECORATION ON YOUR CHEEK?>
<LOOKS GOOD ON YOU.>
<THANKS A LOT.>
<HAAH.>
SHE ASKED ME WHAT WAS GOING ON, SO I EXPLAINED, AND THIS WAS THE RESULT.
<IT WAS ONE OF THOSE TIMES WHEN A LIE IS NECESSARY...>

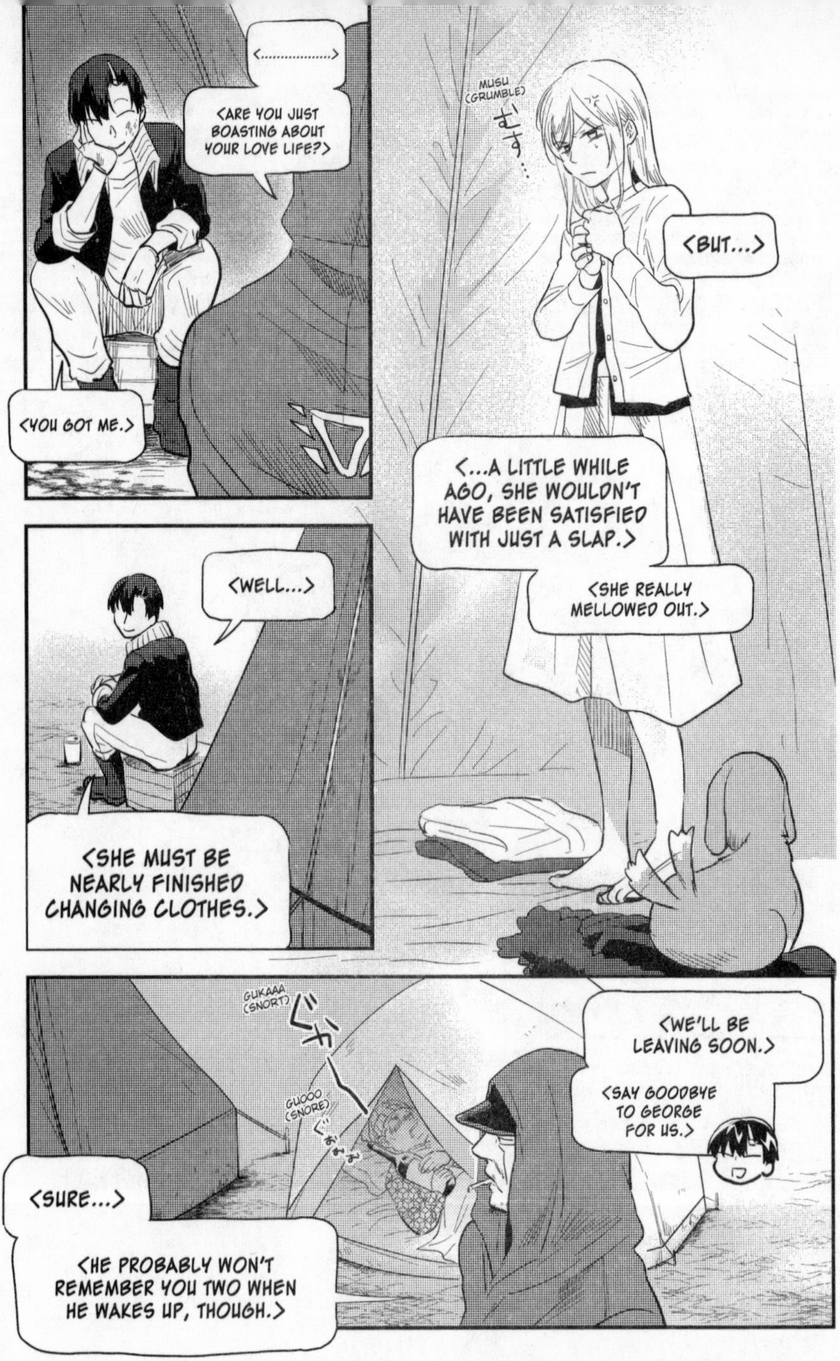

MUSU (GRUMBLE)
むす…
<BUT...>
<...A LITTLE WHILE AGO, SHE WOULDN'T HAVE BEEN SATISFIED WITH JUST A SLAP.>
<SHE REALLY MELLOWED OUT.>
<..................>
<ARE YOU JUST BOASTING ABOUT YOUR LOVE LIFE?>
<YOU GOT ME.>
<WELL...>
<SHE MUST BE NEARLY FINISHED CHANGING CLOTHES.>
GUKAAA (SNORT)
ぐかー
<WE'LL BE LEAVING SOON.>
<SAY GOODBYE TO GEORGE FOR US.>
GUOOO (SNORE)
ぐぉぉぉ
<SURE...>
<HE PROBABLY WON'T REMEMBER YOU TWO WHEN HE WAKES UP, THOUGH.>

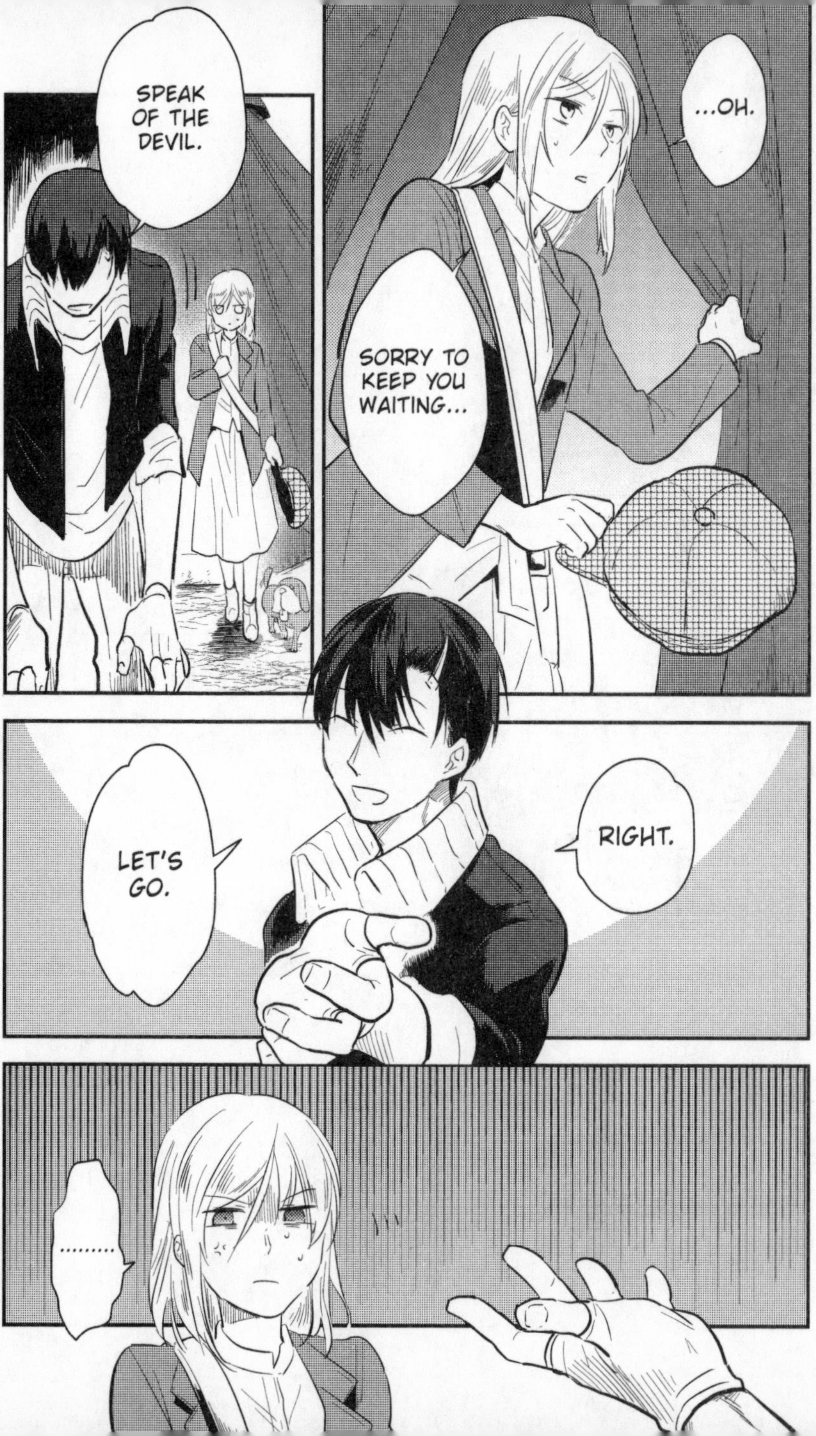
...OH.
SORRY TO KEEP YOU WAITING...
SPEAK OF THE DEVIL.
RIGHT.
LET'S GO.
.........

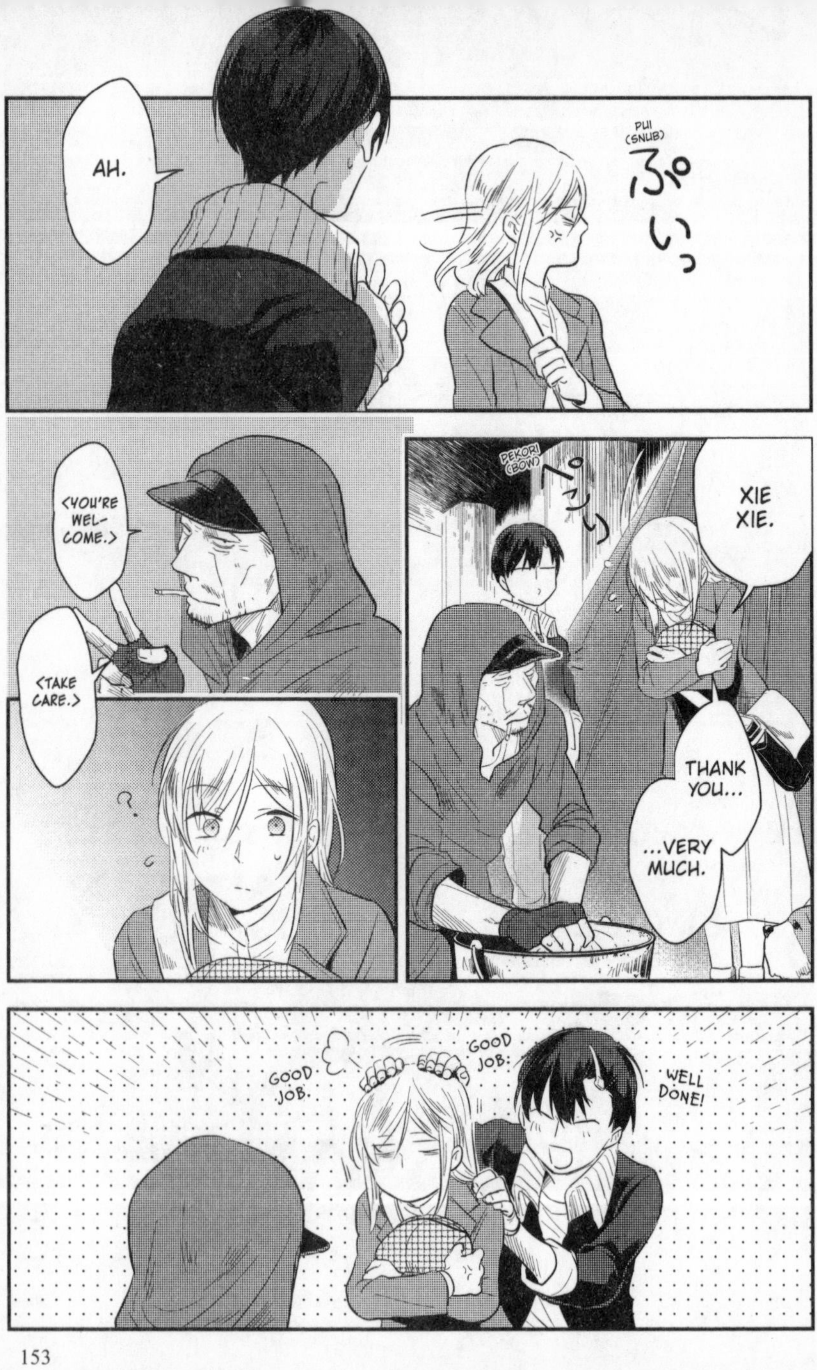
PUI (SNUB)
ぷいっ
AH.
XIE XIE.
PEKORI (BOW)
THANK YOU...
...VERY MUCH.
<YOU'RE WEL-COME.>
<TAKE CARE.>
WELL DONE!
GOOD JOB:
GOOD JOB.

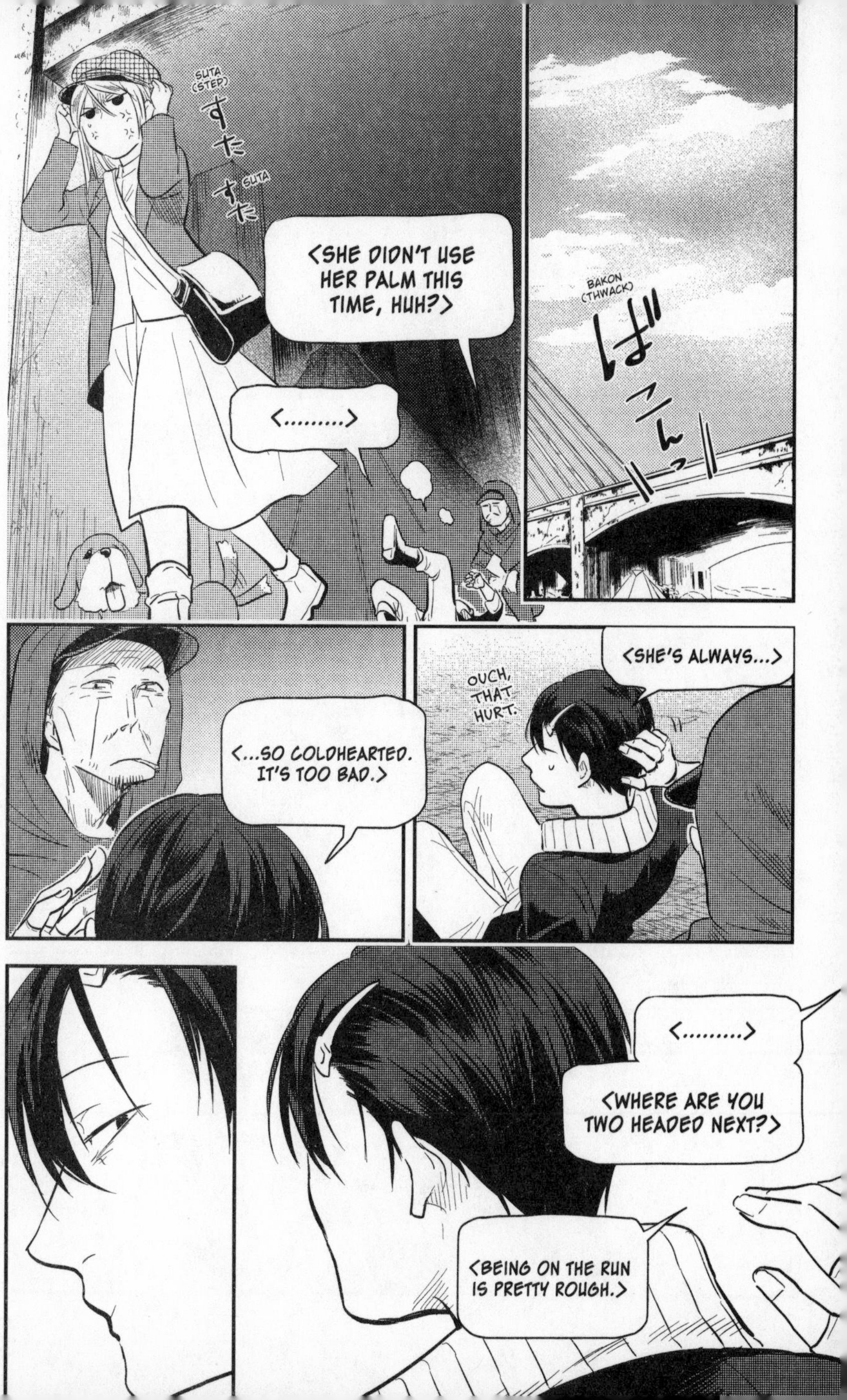
BAKON (THWACK)
ばこんっ
SUTA (STEP)
すた
SUTA
すた
<SHE DIDN'T USE HER PALM THIS TIME, HUH?>
<.........>
<SHE'S ALWAYS...>
OUCH, THAT HURT.
<...SO COLDHEARTED. IT'S TOO BAD.>
<.........>
<WHERE ARE YOU TWO HEADED NEXT?>
<BEING ON THE RUN IS PRETTY ROUGH.>

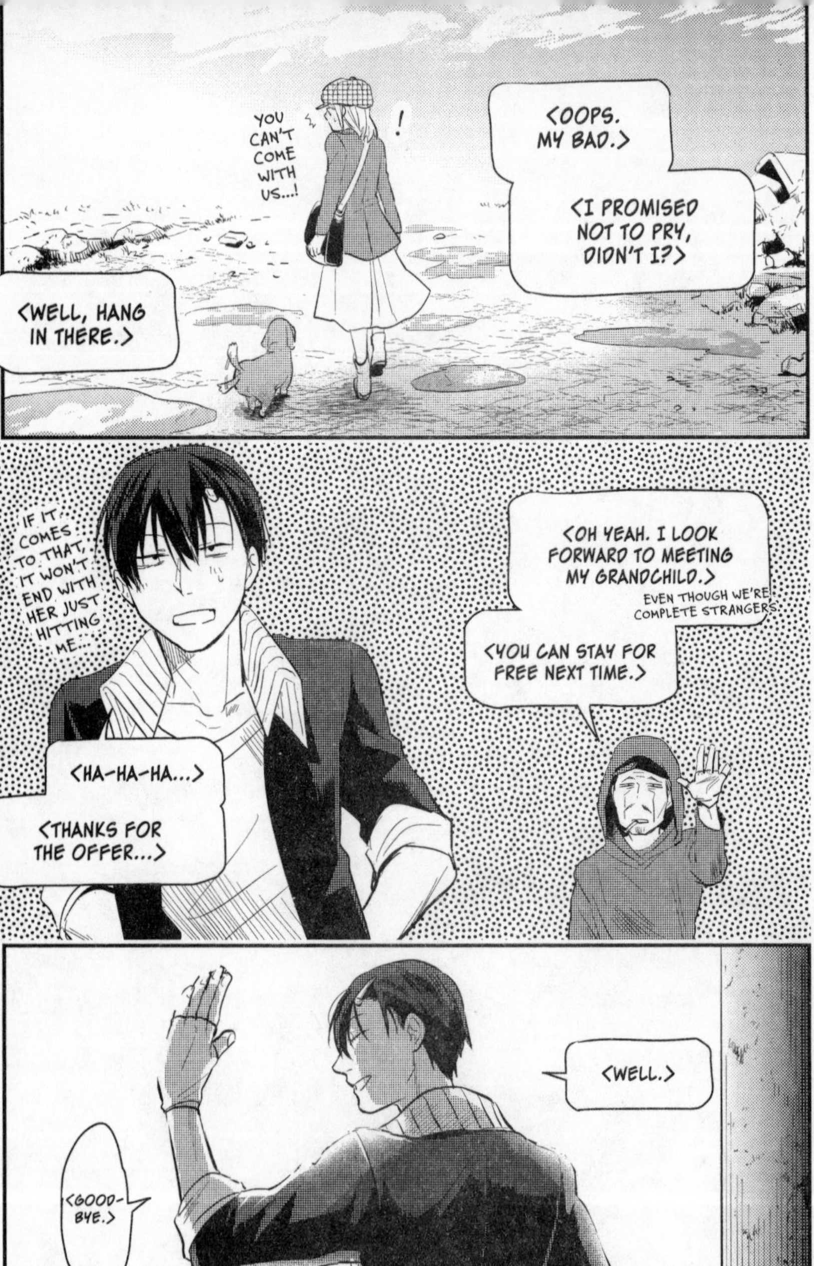
<OOPS. MY BAD.>
<I PROMISED NOT TO PRY, DIDN'T I?>
YOU CAN'T COME WITH US...!
!
<WELL, HANG IN THERE.>
<OH YEAH. I LOOK FORWARD TO MEETING MY GRANDCHILD.>
EVEN THOUGH WE'RE COMPLETE STRANGERS
<YOU CAN STAY FOR FREE NEXT TIME.>
IF IT COMES TO THAT, IT WON'T END WITH HER JUST HITTING ME...
<HA-HA-HA...>
<THANKS FOR THE OFFER...>
<WELL.>
<GOOD-BYE.>

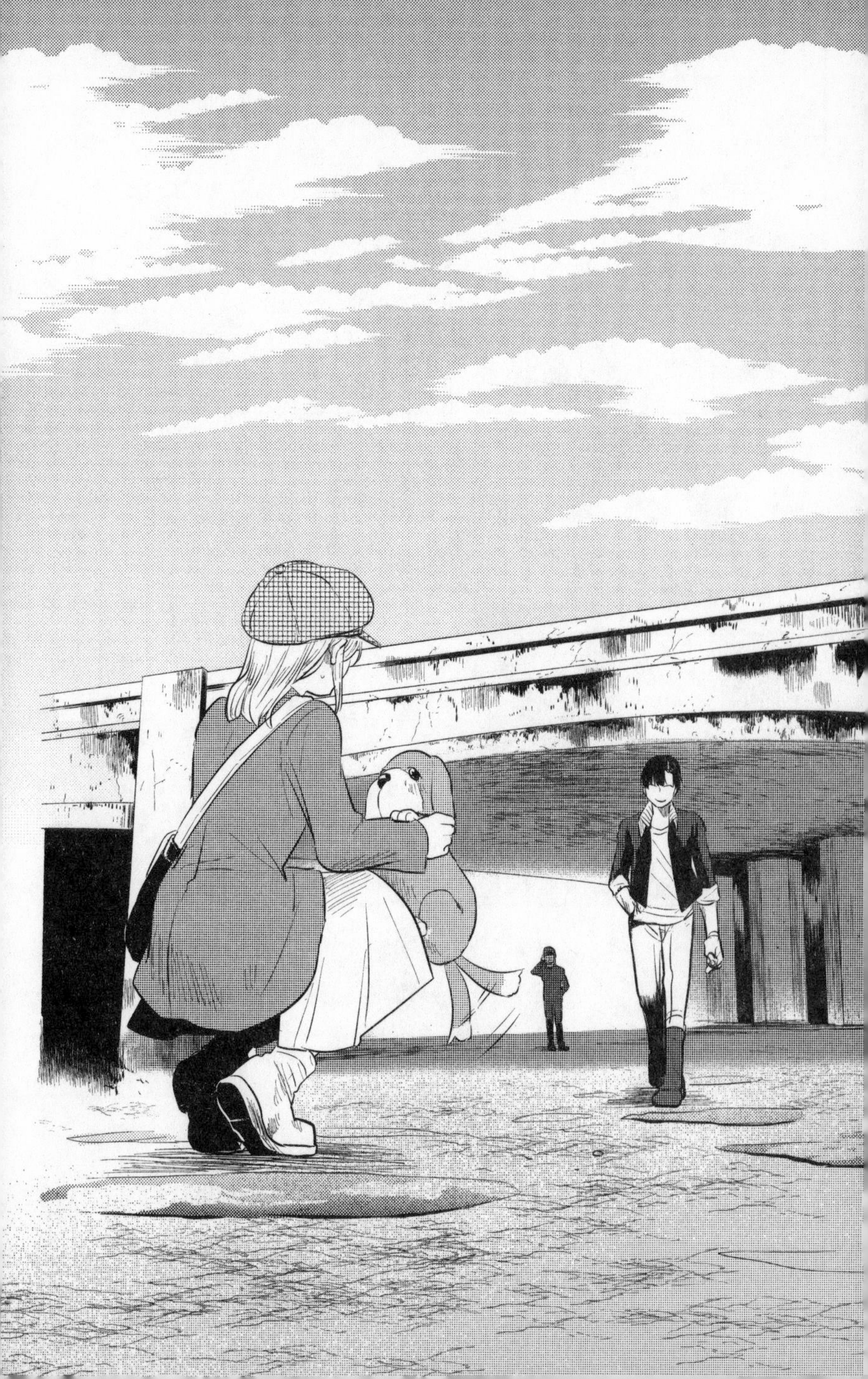

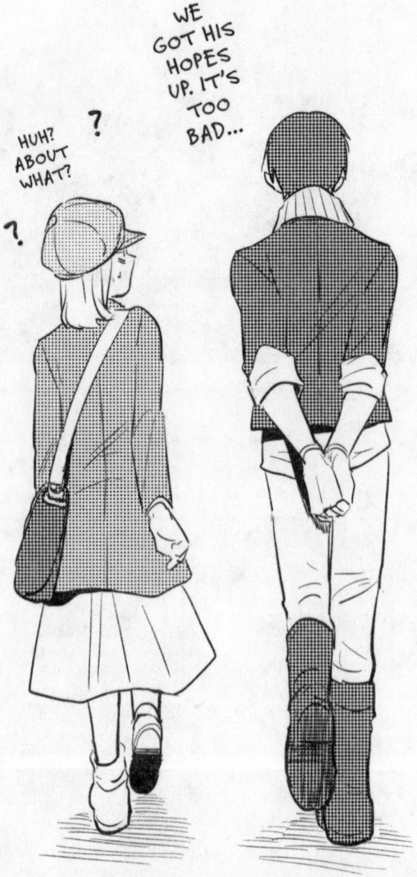
WE GOT HIS HOPES UP. IT'S TOO BAD...
HUH? ABOUT WHAT?

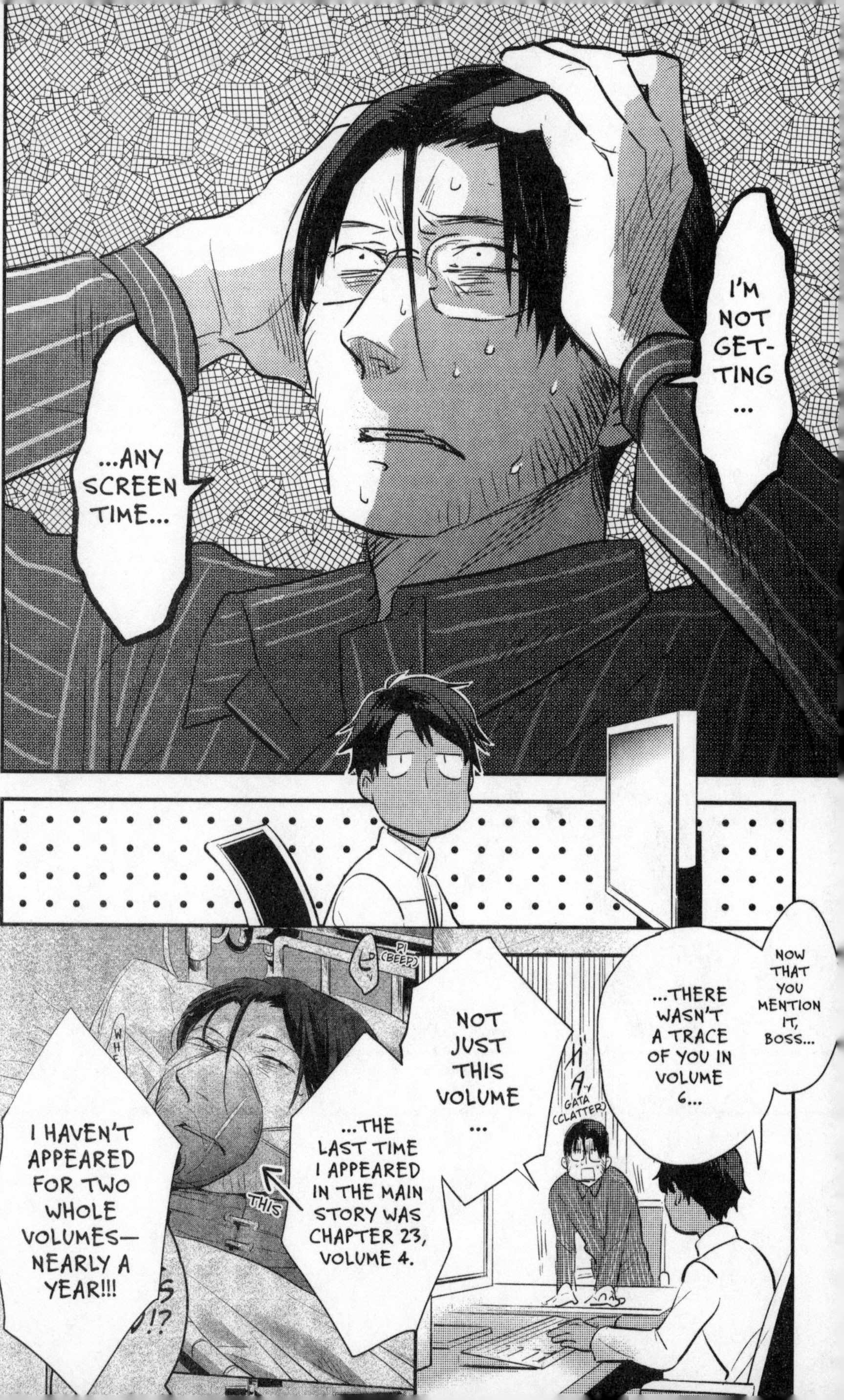
I'M NOT GET-TING...
...ANY SCREEN TIME...
NOW THAT YOU MENTION IT, BOSS...
...THERE WASN'T A TRACE OF YOU IN VOLUME 6...
GATA (CLATTER)
NOT JUST THIS VOLUME...
PI (BEEP)
...THE LAST TIME I APPEARED IN THE MAIN STORY WAS CHAPTER 23, VOLUME 4.
THIS
I HAVEN'T APPEARED FOR TWO WHOLE VOLUMES—NEARLY A YEAR!!!

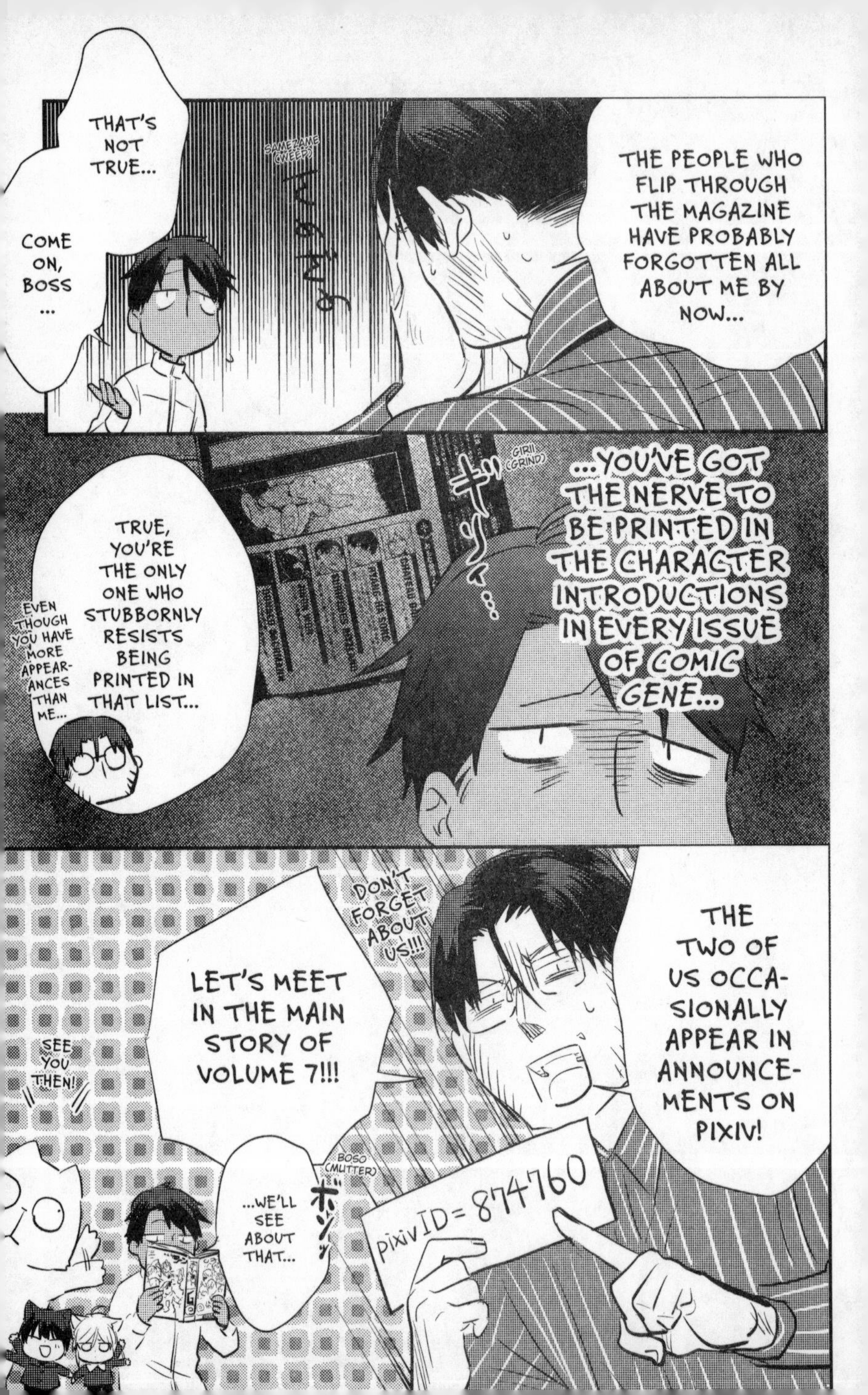
THE PEOPLE WHO FLIP THROUGH THE MAGAZINE HAVE PROBABLY FORGOTTEN ALL ABOUT ME BY NOW...
SAMEZAME (WEEP)
THAT'S NOT TRUE...
COME ON, BOSS...
...YOU'VE GOT THE NERVE TO BE PRINTED IN THE CHARACTER INTRODUCTIONS IN EVERY ISSUE OF COMIC GENE...
GIRII (GRIND)
TRUE, YOU'RE THE ONLY ONE WHO STUBBORNLY RESISTS BEING PRINTED IN THAT LIST...
EVEN THOUGH YOU HAVE MORE APPEARANCES THAN ME...
THE TWO OF US OCCASIONALLY APPEAR IN ANNOUNCEMENTS ON PIXIV!
DON'T FORGET ABOUT US!!!
LET'S MEET IN THE MAIN STORY OF VOLUME 7!!!
pixiv ID=874760
BOSO (MUTTER)
...WE'LL SEE ABOUT THAT...
SEE YOU THEN!

# AFTERWORD

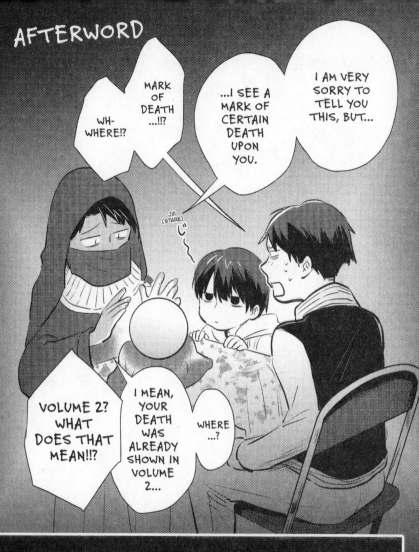

I AM VERY SORRY TO TELL YOU THIS, BUT...
...I SEE A MARK OF CERTAIN DEATH UPON YOU.
MARK OF DEATH ...!!?
WH- WHERE!?
JIII (STARE)
WHERE ...?
I MEAN, YOUR DEATH WAS ALREADY SHOWN IN VOLUME 2...
VOLUME 2? WHAT DOES THAT MEAN!!?


-ORIGO10-SAMA...FOR DONATING CHATEAU'S CHARACTER DESIGN.
-NONNO-SAMA...THE QUALITY OF YOUR V-KATSU AVATAR IMPROVED SO MUCH IT'S HILARIOUS.
-MY SISTER...MAKE ME SPAGHETTI.
-MY FRIENDS AND FAMILY, MY EDITOR, THE DESIGNER, ABSOLUTELY EVERYONE WHO WAS INVOLVED,

**AND EVERYONE WHO PICKED UP THIS BOOK.**
**THANK YOU SO MUCH!!**

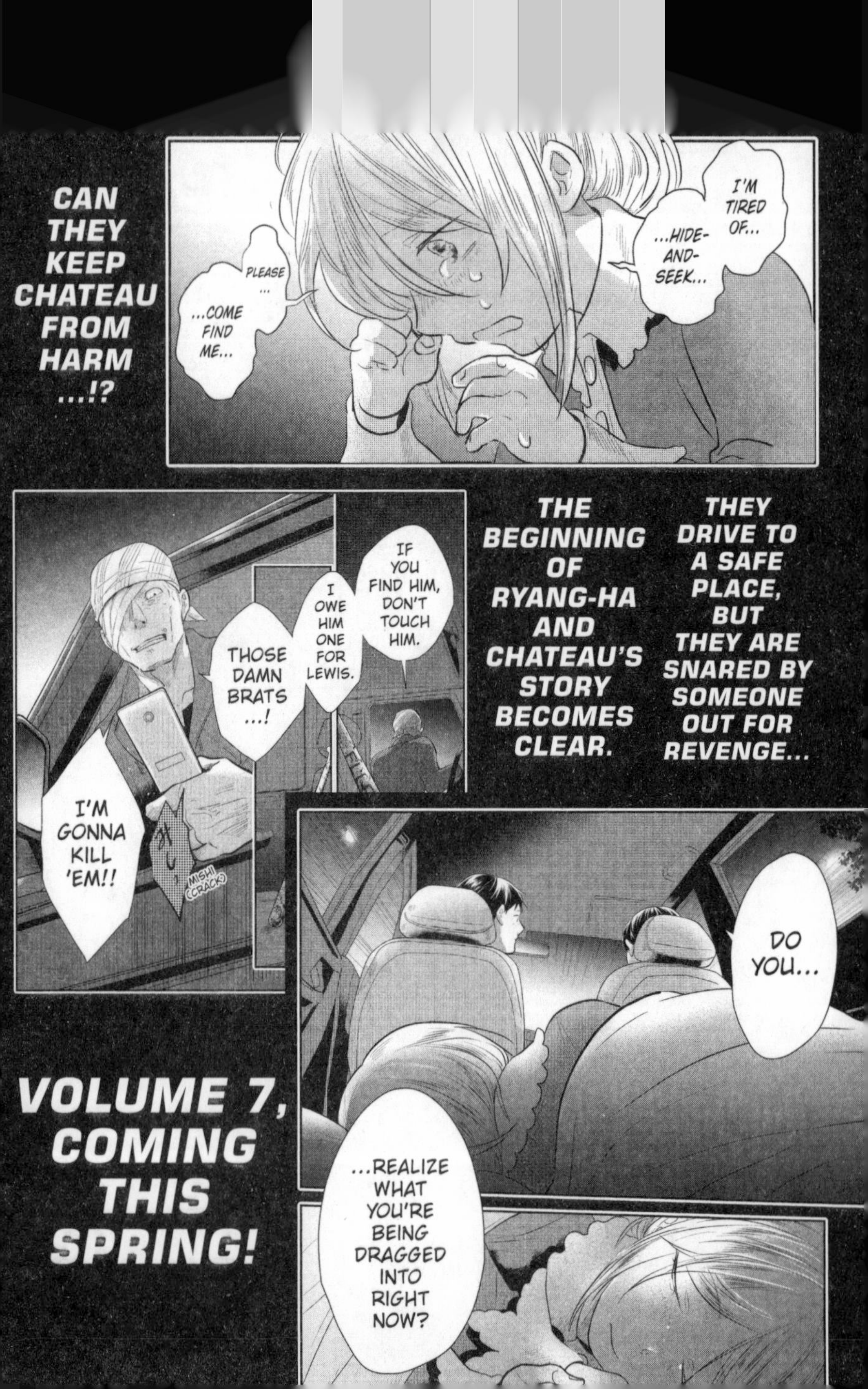
I'M TIRED OF...
...HIDE-AND-SEEK...
PLEASE... ...COME FIND ME...
CAN THEY KEEP CHATEAU FROM HARM ...!?
THEY DRIVE TO A SAFE PLACE, BUT THEY ARE SNARED BY SOMEONE OUT FOR REVENGE...
THE BEGINNING OF RYANG-HA AND CHATEAU'S STORY BECOMES CLEAR.
IF YOU FIND HIM, DON'T TOUCH HIM.
I OWE HIM ONE FOR LEWIS.
THOSE DAMN BRATS ...!
I'M GONNA KILL 'EM!!
MISHI (CRACK)
DO YOU...
...REALIZE WHAT YOU'RE BEING DRAGGED INTO RIGHT NOW?
VOLUME 7, COMING THIS SPRING!

# LOVE OF KILL 06

## Fe

Translation: Eleanor Ruth Summers          Lettering: Chiho Christie

KOROSHIAI Vol. 6
© Fe 2018
First published in Japan in 2018 by KADOKAWA CORPORATION, Tokyo.
English translation rights arranged with KADOKAWA CORPORATION, Tokyo, through Tuttle-Mori Agency, Inc., Tokyo.

English translation © 2022 by Yen Press, LLC

Yen Press
150 West 30th Street, 19th Floor
New York, NY 10001

Visit us at yenpress.com
facebook.com/yenpress
twitter.com/yenpress
yenpress.tumblr.com
instagram.com/yenpress

First Yen Press Edition: February 2022

Yen Press is an imprint of Yen Press, LLC.
The Yen Press name and logo are trademarks of Yen Press, LLC.

The publisher is not responsible for websites (or their content) that are not owned by the publisher.

Library of Congress Control Number: 2020951788

ISBNs: 978-1-9753-2549-7 (paperback)
        978-1-9753-2550-3 (ebook)

10 9 8 7 6 5 4 3 2 1

WOR

Printed in the United States of America